GRIERSON'S RAID

A Cavalry

Adventure

of the

Civil War

GRIERSON'S RAID

D. Alexander Brown

University of Illinois Press *Urbana, 1962*

CONTENTS

A NOTE ON SOURCES 1

> *First day — Friday, April 17*

A SOUTH BREEZE WAS BLOWING 5

> *Second day — Saturday, April 18*

THE SKIRMISHES BEGIN 21

> *Third day — Sunday, April 19*

BARTEAU IN PURSUIT 37

> *Fourth day — Monday, April 20*

GRIERSON'S GAMBIT 50

> *Fifth day — Tuesday, April 21*

THE BUTTERNUT GUERILLAS 61

> *Sixth day — Wednesday, April 22*

A MISSION FOR CAPTAIN FORBES 77

> *Seventh day — Thursday, April 23*

THE SCOUTS CAPTURE A BRIDGE 93

> *Eighth day — Friday, April 24*

ACTION AT NEWTON STATION 105

> *Ninth day — Saturday, April 25*

PINEY WOODS COUNTRY 119

> *Tenth day — Sunday, April 26*

"CAPTAIN FORBES PRESENTS HIS COMPLIMENTS" 135

> *Eleventh day — Monday, April 27*

ACROSS THE PEARL TO HAZLEHURST 145

> *Twelfth day — Tuesday, April 28*

COLONEL ADAMS SETS AN AMBUSH 160

> *Thirteenth day — Wednesday, April 29*

FOX AND HOUNDS 169

> *Fourteenth day — Thursday, April 30*

THE TRAP BEGINS TO CLOSE 180

> *Fifteenth day — Friday, May 1*

THE FIGHT AT WALL'S BRIDGE 189

> *Sixteenth day — Saturday, May 2*

THE LAST LONG MARCH 209

> *Seventeenth day — Sunday, May 3*

HEROES TO THE UNION 222

NOTES 243

INDEX 253

194046

A Note on Sources

This account is based upon five major sources: Benjamin Henry Grierson's manuscript autobiography and the Grierson Papers in the Illinois State Historical Library; his privately published *Record of Services Rendered the Government;* the Forbes family letters and journals of Stephen Alfred Forbes; Richard W. Surby's *Grierson Raids;* and the *Official Records of the War of the Rebellion.*

Grierson's lengthy autobiography apparently was in process of revision at the time of his death in 1911. Many sentences and paragraphs in the original manuscript were marked out and extended passages were penciled on the margins. Grierson devoted considerable space to the raid which made him famous, and although he relied heavily upon his official report for these chapters, he also included new material.

In addition he drew from his *Record of Services Rendered the Government,* a unique document with a fascinating history of its own. While Grierson was stationed at the Old Arsenal in St. Louis, some years after the Civil War, a close friend of Mrs. Grierson visited with them one summer and became interested in the general's adventurous background. The friend was Mrs. Ella L. Wolcott of Elmira, New York, and, using Grierson's private and official papers, she compiled a detailed chronological record of his military career. Subsequently, during a long tour of duty at Fort Concho, Texas, Grierson arranged to have this record printed on an army hand-press, which was in use only occasionally for publishing local orders. The type was hand set, and evidently no attempt was made to correct typographical errors. Distribution of the few copies printed was limited to the Grierson family, and it is undoubtedly one of the rarest items of Americana, the only library copies on record being in the Illinois State Historical Library.

The Forbes family letters and the journals of Stephen Forbes, collected and arranged chronologically by Ethel Forbes Scott, are rich sources of information on details of the raid, the cavalry dress and equipment, the weather, the food or lack of it, the countryside through which the raiders passed, the attitudes and emotions of the men before, during, and after the raid, all the various minutiae which help to bring history to life. Both Stephen Forbes and his older brother, Henry Forbes, were sensitive observers and recorders of events, persons, and everything that came into their ken, and many passages of their letters and journals, particularly Stephen's, are written with unusual eloquence and beauty. Stephen Forbes later became a naturalist and one of the great scientific writers of his time.

Richard Surby's *Grierson Raids* was first issued in 1865 as a section of a book which included two other narratives, *Hatch's Sixty-four Days March* and *Adventures of Chickasaw the Scout.* It was prepared from a diary kept by the author, who was a sergeant at the time. Surby also used the New York *Times* report of the raid to fill in details with which he was not familiar. Grierson read the manuscript and pronounced it "correct in every particular." Stephen Forbes in 1907 said the Surby account was marred by many typographical errors, especially in place and proper names, but was entirely reliable as to matters which came under the author's personal observation and usually so as to events occurring in his immediate neighborhood.

In 1883 Surby slightly revised his account for publication in the veteran's weekly, the *National Tribune,* and a small edition of this revision was then issued in book form by the *Tribune* under the title, *Two Great Raids,* a history of Morgan's raid being included in the same volume.

The War of the Rebellion: Official Records of the Union and Confederate Armies contains supporting documentation and is essential for tracing related military operations of the Confederate forces attempting to block Grierson's raid, and of General Grant's armies moving in conjunction with the raid.

Other useful sources consulted were Stephen Forbes's address before the Illinois State Historical Society at its eighth annual meeting, Springfield, Illinois, Jan. 4, 1907, and Henry H. Eby's *Observations of an Illinois Boy in Battle, Camp and Prison.* Eby borrowed some of his incidents from Wilbur Hinman's *Corporal Si Klegg,* the same source used by Stephen Crane for *The Red Badge of Courage.* But he also included some interesting original anecdotes about cavalry camp life in the West. Unfortunately — from this writer's viewpoint — Eby was on detached service at the time of the raid.

The following helped to complete the background and clarify some of the episodes in the story: *Reports of the Adjutant General of the State of Illinois,* 1861-66; *Journal of Mississippi History,* volumes 1-12; Springfield *Illinois State Journal,* 1863; T. H. Bowman, *Reminiscences of an ex-Confederate Soldier; or Forty Years on Crutches,* 1904; Albert G. Brackett, *History of the United States Cavalry,* 1865; E. Merton Coulter, *Confederate States of America,* 1950; Clement A. Evans, *Confederate Military History,* 1899; R. R. Hancock, *Hancock's Diary: or a History of the Second Tennessee Confederate Cavalry,* 1887; Adam R. Johnson, *Partisan Rangers of the Confederate States,* 1904; George H. Hepworth, *Whip, Hoe, and Sword; or the Gulf Department in '63,* 1864; Francis T. Miller, *Photographic History of the Civil War,* 1911; Lyman B. Pierce, *History of the Second Iowa Cavalry,* 1865; William Forse Scott, *Story of a Cavalry Regiment,* 1893; Fred Albert Shannon, *Organization and Administration of the Union Army, 1861-1865,* 1928; Emory Upton, *Military Policy of the United States,* 1912.

The drawings at chapter openings are adapted from etchings in *Life Studies of the Great Army* (1876), a portfolio by Edwin Forbes, who was not related to the two Forbes brothers in Grierson's brigade. Photographs have been made available through the courtesy of the Library of Congress, Louisiana State University Archives, Illinois State Historical Society, and Mrs. Ethel Forbes Scott.

The author wishes to express sincere appreciation to Harry E. Pratt, State Historian, Illinois State Historical Library, for his assistance in the search for documents relating to Grierson and the raid. Special thanks are also due Mrs. Marguerite J. Pease, Illinois Historical Survey, University of Illinois, and to Mrs. Ethel Forbes Scott for permission to use material from the Forbes family letters.

A SOUTH BREEZE WAS BLOWING

At dawn 1,700 cavalrymen were moving south out of the base camp at La Grange, Tennessee, the columns of twos coiling down into the shortleaf pine forests away from the town that had seen no fighting, yet was dying in the backwash of raids and counter-raids of two years of war.

The day was April 17, 1863: the Civil War at midpoint after its darkest winter. "The morning . . . was a beautiful one," wrote Sergeant Richard Surby, "with a gentle breeze from the south. The fruit trees were all in full bloom, the gardens were fragrant with the perfume of spring flowers, the birds sang gaily, all of which infused a feeling of admiration and gladness into the hearts of all true lovers of nature."[1]

On that morning, Quartermaster-Sergeant Surby had no certain idea as to where his regiment was riding. Like the other men he had heard the rumors, and in passing them on had enlarged upon them: "We are going on a big scout to Columbus, Mississippi, and play smash with the railroads."

First Day
Friday, April 17

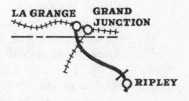

The rumors had been sweeping the base for a week, but the men had got their orders only yesterday: "Oats in the nosebags and five days rations in haversacks, the rations to last ten days. Double rations of salt. Forty rounds of ammunition."[2]

Columbus was about five days' march, the wise troopers had figured, a strong point in the Confederate defense from which General Daniel Ruggles occasionally dispatched annoying rebel raiders on the Union positions along the Memphis & Charleston Railroad. Columbus would be a good place to ride in for a strike, destroy supplies, burn a few railroad bridges and gallop back to La Grange. A ten-day holiday from camp drill. The reckoning was good enough. Even the regimental officers might have figured it that close. Perhaps no one except Grierson could have guessed that after ten days they would be ten days out from the headquarters base, deeper into the heart of the Confederacy than any Yankee cavalry had ever penetrated, and virtually surrounded by enemy troops.

Benjamin Henry Grierson, Colonel, Volunteers, was commanding the three cavalry regiments, the Sixth Illinois, the Seventh Illinois, the Second Iowa, and a detachment of Battery K from the First Illinois Artillery, six mounted two-pounder guns — all comprising the First Brigade, First Cavalry Division, Sixteenth Army Corps of Major-General Ulysses S. Grant's Department of the Tennessee. Grierson, like his officers and men, was an amateur soldier, his total experience of war packed into eighteen months of training, skirmishing, and some brief but sharp and bitter fighting.

Only a few days before this morning, he had been assigned the brigade command for a raid into the heart of the western Confederacy. His old regiment, the Sixth, was riding in advance as the brigade moved out past the white homesteads of La Grange, with their once elegant yards of rare and costly shrubbery torn and trampled, the fences gone, the doors ajar, and the houses tenantless, over the road that was, as Captain Henry Forbes wrote of it, "inches and inches deep with the finest and whitest of dust, past a cemetery, the palings torn apart and cast down, the marbles standing in mute reproach, the vines run riot over the ground."*[3]

---

* Captain Henry Forbes, commanding Company B, Seventh Illinois Volunteer Cavalry, described La Grange as follows: "It was a neat little

The horsemen, gay in the spring sunshine, passed little fields of scant, half-tilled cotton, and dry ditches filled with beds of white, rippled sand. They crossed Wolf River and moved unchallenged that morning down through the blue hills with their slopes of evergreen pines, across the line from Tennessee into Mississippi.

II

No written instructions were handed Grierson before he departed; he had received his orders verbally from General William Sooy Smith, commanding the La Grange base, orders which were quite specific in some points and extremely indefinite in others. General Smith told Grierson he would have discretionary power when he passed to the rear of the enemy's lines and lost communications with La Grange. "It would be his duty and privilege to use his own best judgment as to the course it would be safest and best to take."[4]

As casual as this may seem, the orders which set Grierson's brigade into motion had been a long time in the making. Their origin might be traced months back to a day in Washington when President Lincoln sat with Admiral David D. Porter before a map of the Confederacy and said: "See what a lot of land these fellows hold, of which Vicksburg is the key. Here is Red River, which will supply the Confederates with cattle and corn to feed their armies. There are the Arkansas and White Rivers which can supply cattle and hogs by the thousands. From Vicksburg these supplies can be distributed by rail all over the Confederacy. It means hog and hominy without limit, fresh troops from all the States of the far South, and a cotton country where they can raise the staple without interference. Let us get Vicksburg and all that country is ours. The war can never be brought to a close until that key is in our pocket."[5]

---

place of about a thousand people. The yards were beautifully improved, filled with evergreens and rare shrubberies. A fine College building crowned a gentle eminence to the east of the town and a Seminary for Ladies looked across to it from the north. All is vulgar desolation now. The College and its twin buildings are used for hospitals, and the churches are all appropriated to the same uses, with many of the private dwellings. The fences are all burned, the gardens trampled, the most elegant evergreens turned into hitching posts for Yankee horses, and all this in a town where there has been no strife of contending forces. It is a natural consequence of war." — FFL, Henry Forbes to Nettie Forbes, Jan. 24, 1863.

Admiral Porter then had been appointed commander of the Mississippi gunboat squadron, while General Grant came down from the north with a land army. They hammered away through 1862, but Vicksburg seemed impregnable. Bogged down in the muddy bottomlands west of the Confederacy's Gibraltar, Grant spent the winter laying plans for an 1863 campaign that would either win the war in the west or lose an army.

He believed that his only chance for taking Vicksburg was to move his army behind the city, on the east, but previous efforts to do this had failed because of the strength of the defending armies. But if he could create a diversion in eastern Mississippi to draw off potential reinforcements, if he could cut the rail line to Vicksburg to interrupt supplies and thus throw the Confederates off balance for a few days, he felt that it might be possible to move troops across the Mississippi River and in behind Vicksburg before the defenders could recover.

During 1862 Grierson's cavalry had more than once made a favorable impression upon General Grant, and on February 13 he sent a message from Lake Providence, Louisiana, to General Stephen A. Hurlbut, commanding the Sixteenth Army Corps, headquarters in Memphis: "It seems to me that Grierson, with about five hundred picked men, might succeed in making his way south, and cut the railroad east of Jackson, Miss. The undertaking would be a hazardous one, but it would pay well if carried out. I do not direct that this shall be done, but leave it for a volunteer enterprise."*6

Grierson's cavalry was busy during this time pursuing guerillas and partisan rangers in Tennessee, but Grant meanwhile continued to develop his plan for a diversionary cavalry raid to precede his land movement against Vicksburg. He sent another message to Hurlbut on March 9: "I look upon Grierson as being much better qualified to command this expedition than either Lee or Mizner. I do not dictate, however, who shall be sent. The date when the expedition should start will depend upon move-

---

* A letter from General Sherman, Dec. 9, 1862, substantiated Grant's confidence in Grierson. "Dear General: Colonel Grierson is about to start for Helena with your dispatches and I also toward Memphis. When he returns he will report to you in person. Colonel Grierson has been with me all summer and I have repeatedly written to you and spoken in his praise. He is the best cavalry officer I have yet had." — OR, ser. I, vol. 17, pt. 2, p. 396.

ments here. You will be informed of the exact time for them to start."[7]

The exact time was at dawn, April 17; the orders as given on April 10 by General Hurlbut to General William Sooy Smith at La Grange were to "strike out by way of Pontotoc, breaking off right and left, cutting both roads, destroying the wires, burning provisions, and doing all the mischief they can, while one regiment ranges straight down to Selma or Meridian, breaking the east and west road thoroughly, and swinging back through Alabama."[8]

Grierson was on furlough in Illinois that week, but Hurlbut telegraphed him to return to La Grange immediately.[9] On April 15 Hurlbut forwarded the final orders to General Smith: "If Grierson does not arrive in time, Hatch will take command. The details must be left discretionary."[10] General Smith was pleased with that last sentence. "Swinging back through Alabama" might not be so easy, with Nathan Bedford Forrest operating somewhere in the north of that state.

On the afternoon of the 16th, orders for the raid went out to the companies; they were to be ready to march at three o'clock the following morning. Grierson was still missing. He arrived on the midnight train from Memphis* with three hours to spare, but a conference with Sooy Smith delayed the brigade's departure until dawn.

III

Professional cavalrymen always maintained that two years were required to produce a seasoned trooper. The men of the First Brigade were approaching that point of perfection, along with some thousands of other Union cavalrymen of both the eastern and western theaters of the war. In these past two years the Union cavalry had played a sorry role, the butt of every infantryman's joke: "Nobody ever saw a dead cavalryman. If you want to have a good time, jine the cavalree!" The exploits of Confederate cavalrymen — Jeb Stuart and John Mosby in the east, the daring raids of Nathan Bedford Forrest and John Hunt

---

* "I have seen Gen'l. Hurlbut and I must leave here on the train at 1 o'clock and my command is ordered to leave La Grange tomorrow on the expedition I spoke to you about. . . . will be gone probably *three weeks* and perhaps longer." Benjamin Grierson to Alice Grierson, April [16] 1863. (Grierson Papers).

Morgan in the west — were known to every blue-bloused trooper. The northern newspapers and the New York picture weeklies had recorded the exploits of these southern *beau sabreurs* until they were in a sense heroes to the envious Yankees.

For want of a dashing leader among themselves, the Union cavalrymen in the west particularly admired Forrest, the eccentric rebel who never bothered to learn the simplest military commands, not even the manual of arms, but whose skillful cavalry maneuvers had upset a dozen well-laid battle plans, even those of so shrewd a general as Grant.

One reason given for the superiority of Confederate over Union cavalry was that in the South the lack of good highways had forced southerners to ride from boyhood, while in the north a generation of young men had been riding in wheeled vehicles. This may have been true in the east, but not in the west. Farm boys of Indiana, Illinois, and Iowa also were horsemen by necessity, but unlike many of their southern opponents, in civilian life they had borne the tedious burden of caring for the animals after plowing behind them all day. Young westerners who knew horses seemed to have little desire to assume the added responsibility of taking one of them to war. Many of them chose infantry service instead.

Certainly the social prestige attached to horsemen, the *beau sabreur* image so prevalent in the Confederacy, was unknown in the west. But even if the western Yankees did not regard cavaliers as aristocrats, before the war was a year old they were more than a little envious of the abilities of the "chivalric knights" who kept dashing up from the South to ride rings around them.[11]

Southern cavalry horses were also superior to northern horses, largely because southerners were fond of racing. Almost every southern town had its track, and the sport had developed a superior stock of blooded, fleet-footed animals. In the north, muscular and slow-moving draft horses were the preferred breeds, racing being almost unknown above the Mason and Dixon line.[12]

When the war began there were only seven mounted troops in the regular United States Army. General Winfield Scott, the aging commander, gave as his opinion early in 1861 that cavalry had been outmoded by modern warfare. Improvements in rifled cannon, he was convinced, would render the duties of the cavalry unimportant and secondary. War Department plans, influenced by Scott, limited the regular army's cavalry requirements for prosecuting the Civil War to six regular regiments. And when Lincoln made his call for volunteers, the states were advised to accept very few cavalrymen.

Federal War Department policies continued to operate against development of effective cavalry forces until General George B. McClellan took command, and even he had to arrange almost secretly with the state governors for the organization of a few companies of mounted troops. Such regiments were often misused, separated into mere squads and used for messenger service or as escort troops.

In its original secondary role, the Union cavalry naturally suffered from a deficiency of equipment, and for this reason many western regiments were inactive for several months following their organization. At Camp McClellan, near Davenport, Iowa, efforts were made to convert cavalry volunteers to infantry service, creating so much dissension that the governor of the state had to visit the camp and reassure the men. At the same time, Senator James Harlan of Iowa urged the War Department to authorize the raising of more cavalry regiments in the west. Harlan told the Secretary of War that in his opinion the best cavalry could be made of western men, who were accustomed to riding and the care of horses.[13]

Late in the summer of 1861, after reaching Camp Butler near Springfield, Captain Forbes of the Seventh Illinois said in one of his letters to his mother: "Our men have drawn their socks, two pairs each, very good material, two pairs of flannel drawers, the inevitable *red* shirt, and a blue fatigue coat. Tomorrow we expect to draw pants, blue shirts, boots and overcoats. We have not yet drawn our saddles, but shall reach them soon." He continued: "We have not drilled on horse yet, for the reason we have no saddles. We have daily foot drills, however, and shall soon be furnished in full."[14]

The captain's optimism about forthcoming equipment faded soon afterward, and if he and his men had not brought their own mounts to camp they would have had none for drilling. "Our horses stand it pretty well. A few of them take colds, but nothing serious. I ride the Babcock horse, and William McCausland rides the Weasel. My horse pleases me well and is learning to follow me like a dog."

11

Private Stephen Alfred Forbes, Company B, Seventh Illinois Cavalry. In later years Stephen said that this photograph, made soon after his enlistment, revealed his early lack of military bearing.

Captain Henry Clinton Forbes, Company B, Seventh Illinois Cavalry. The letters and diaries of Captain Forbes and his brother, Stephen, are an important source of information about Grierson's raid.

Colonel Benjamin Henry Grierson. General Sherman called his raid "the most brilliant expedition of the war."

He added somewhat proudly: "I have obtained one of the Cavalry saddles as a special favor in return for lending my horse to one of the officers, so I look quite war-like when mounted." The cavalry saddle was of course the McClellan, adopted through recommendations made by the general in 1860, a modification of the Mexican, or Texas tree. Some of the earlier models were covered with rawhide, and as one Union officer complained, when this covering split, the seat became very uncomfortable for the rider.

Weeks later Captain Forbes's young brother, Stephen, a private in the Seventh Illinois, was writing home on the same subject: "I expect you would laugh to see me in my uniform, especially the red shirt and close little cap, but we are clothed very comfortably, however, as we have immense overcoats which cover us from the tops of our heads nearly to our ankles and heavy boots that reach above our knees. Our saddles and arms we have not received."[15]

Fortunately, the saddle shortage was relieved before the regiment moved down to Bird's Point, Missouri, below Cairo, to act as land support for the mortarboat battles around Island Number Ten. However, as Stephen recorded in his diary, November 20, 1861, the men of the Seventh Illinois were "situated in an enemy's country with a prospect of a battle close at hand without arms enough to post guards, but we soon hope to receive all our arms for the entire regiment, as the colonel received a letter from Secretary Cameron stating that one thousand sabers and pistols were on the way to us from New York."[16]

Although pistols and sabers were issued sometime during the next three months, Captain Forbes reported in February, 1862, that carbines were still lacking. He added: "Perhaps you hear occasional rumors of the disbanding of the cavalry, etc. — it's the fashion you know. Well, as far as we are concerned, we expect to be retained while Illinois has a regiment of cavalry in the field. So don't expect us home until 'going to war on horseback' is at a greater discount than now." He appended a message to the younger members of the family:

Tell them I've got a hat with three black feathers in it and a gold eagle and cross sabers on it; that my boots come up over my knees and when I go out looking for a "Secesh" I buckle a saber around me with a big black belt, and another one with two big pistols in it that I can shoot eleven times and hit a man at 200 steps. Tell them I've got a great big stable with most a hundred horses in it, and as many men that live in little cloth houses, and eat bread and beef like everything, and when I want them to get on their horses and go and hunt "secesh" I tell the bugler to blow his bugle, and they all come out in a long row. Then I say "Attention!" and they all keep still, — then I say "Dress!" and they straighten out the row so it looks nice, — then I say "Draw saber!" and they pull their swords right out and put their hands at their right sides, — then I say "Fours right — March! Guide Left!" and away we go, sometimes walking, sometimes trotting, sometimes galloping like everything."

As the war lengthened, the saber as a weapon became a controversial subject among cavalrymen. When the Spencer repeating carbine was issued, some eastern regiments abandoned the saber altogether, and it was a common joke among the troopers that their sabers had lopped off more of their own horses' ears than enemy heads. One reason for its unpopularity in the east may have been that eastern regiments were first equipped with the long, straight Prussian-type saber, an awkward weapon indeed, while most of the western regiments received the newly manufactured light, curved American blade which could be attached to the end of a carbine to form a bayonet.[18]

At any rate, Captain Forbes and other western cavalrymen favored the saber, and it was used throughout the war by most western regiments. "My great dependence for cavalry is in the sabers," he said. "The carbines do good execution when the men can dismount and fire deliberately, as also the pistols, but for hand-to-hand work, it is the terror and thunder of the charge, the bristle and blows of the saberers that is mainly decisive."[19]

Cavalry pistols used during the Civil War included both the old powder and ball models and the new model army revolvers equipped for metallic self-exploding cartridges. In addition to pistols, one or two eastern regiments were armed with lances for a time, but these weapons were never used in the west, and the eastern lancers soon found them unsuited to the heavily wooded battlegrounds of Virginia. The outmoded lances were finally discarded in the east during the spring of 1863, about the time Colonel Grierson was starting his raid into Mississippi.

In March, 1862, the Seventh Illinois volunteers received their Sharp's carbines, breechloaders of single mechanism and easily carried, but requiring paper cartridges and percussion caps. They had to be recharged for each shot, and released an annoy-

Grierson's cavalrymen, posing with their mounts, were unaware that the photographer was a Confederate secret service agent, Andrew D. Lytle. What use the Confederates made of this picture is not known. Several photographs of the raiders were made by Lytle.

Union soldiers destroying railroad tracks in Confederate territory by heating the rails over burning ties, then bending them.

ing amount of smoke when fired. Later some squadrons were furnished Spencer carbines with rifled magazines, carrying six metallic cartridges in a tube in the stock. A seventh cartridge could be kept in position in the barrel. Some cavalrymen refused to carry the Spencer, however, after a few of the stocks exploded suddenly — the result of the pointed bullet of one cartridge striking too hard upon the cap of one lying before it in the tube.[20]

Private Stephen Forbes wrote on March 13 that he had "just been out target-shooting with my gay little Sharp's carbine which will shoot half a mile and kill a man." A few day later he felt that he was sufficiently equipped for battle and volunteered eagerly for a scouting expedition below Bird's Point: "Clapping my saddle upon my horse, buckling on my saber, and slinging my carbine, I put half a dozen hard crackers in my pocket and announced myself ready for the ride."

As weapons and equipment become more plentiful, the volunteer troopers made up for the long shortages by acquiring an excess of articles which they considered necessary for their comfort and convenience. No strict regulations applied to personal baggage, and horses were frequently laden to the breaking point with heavy tents, knapsacks packed with gifts from friends and families, and haversacks filled with rations. In addition to the saber and its four-foot metal scabbard, the unseasoned cavalryman usually carried on his person with his pistol and carbine a box of cartridges, a box of percussion caps, a tin canteen for water, and a tin coffee cup. Fastened to the saddle might be a saddlebag filled with extra clothing and toilet articles, a heavy leather halter, an iron picket pin with a long lariat for tethering the horse, usually two horseshoes with extra nails, a currycomb with horse brush, a set of gun tools and material for the care of arms, a rubber blanket or poncho, a pair of woolen blankets, and an extra blouse.

And as in almost every war, an armored bulletproof vest made its appearance, manufactured privately and sold by the artful sutlers who peddled trinkets and tobacco around the cavalry camps. "It was a vest of blue cloth, cut in military style, with two plates of steel, formed to fit the body and fastened between the cloth and the lining, so as to cover the front of the wearer from the neck to the waist. Samples of the plates were exhibited in the camps, with deep marks upon them where bullets had failed to penetrate."[21] This fraudulent device added another eight or ten pounds to the already overburdened mount.

"Fully equipped for the field, the green cavalryman was a fearful and wonderful object," said an Iowa veteran:

Mounted upon his charger, in the midst of all the paraphernalia and adornments of war, a moving arsenal and military depot, he must have struck surprise, if not terror, into the minds of his enemies. . . . When he was on foot he moved with a great clapping and clanking of his arms and accoutrements, and so constrained by the many bands crossing his body that any rapid motion was absurdly impossible. . . . When the rider was in the saddle, begirt with all his magazine, it was easy to imagine him protected from any ordinary assault. His properties rose before and behind him like fortifications, and those strung over his shoulders covered well his flanks. To the uninitiated it was a mystery how the rider got into the saddle; how he could rise to a sufficient height and how then descend upon the seat was the problem. The irreverent infantry said it was done with the aid of a derrick, or by first climbing to the top of a high fence or the fork of a tree.[22]

One or two campaigns and a few forced marches, however, quickly brought a change in the trooper's equipage. The men riding with Grierson's brigade in April, 1863, had long ago learned what was necessary for existence and what was not. Such excess baggage as armored vests, extra lariats, and picket-pins had been conveniently lost, and the standard pair of blankets had given way to a single one, with two men sleeping together. They had learned the fine art of packing a horse so lightly that the carbine was the heaviest part of the load.

Colonel Grierson's special equipment as leader of the raid, for example, consisted of an ordinary Colton's pocket map of the state of Mississippi and a small compass, both of which he carried inside his blouse with a jew's-harp that he probably used more often than either the map or the compass. Grierson also possessed a report made by a Mississippian loyal to the Union. No name was signed to the document but Grierson had received it in January, and among his military papers for that month is a mysterious receipt for fifty dollars paid to one Vernon Jonican. This report described routes by which a cavalry column might move through Mississippi, locations of well-stocked plantations, Confederate warehouses, the varying loyalties of the people in different sections of the state, the probable presence of guerillas, the geography of the country, and the distances between towns.[23]

IV

On the day Grierson led his men out of La Grange, the First Brigade was at less than half its strength, a normal condition for most Civil War units. The table of organization for a volunteer cavalry regiment listed twelve companies or troops consisting of a captain, two lieutenants, eight sergeants, eight corporals, two teamsters, two farriers or blacksmiths, two musicians or buglers, one saddler, one wagoner, and seventy-eight privates. Each regiment was headed by a colonel and staff of one lieutenant-colonel, three majors, a surgeon and assistant surgeon, one regimental adjutant, one regimental quartermaster, one regimental commissary, a chaplain, a sergeant-major, a quartermaster-sergeant, a commissary-sergeant, two hospital stewards, one saddler sergeant, one chief farrier.[24]

Grierson's brigade at full strength should have put around 3,600 men into the field, but this would have been unprecedented, and Grierson probably considered himself fortunate to have slightly less than half of his strength present for duty, or "1,700 strong" as he described them in his official report.

They marched down that first day through the Mississippi woods cover, at the standard cavalry rate of three miles an hour, resting for five or ten minutes on the hour.

The first day's march was almost uneventful. The Sixth Illinois took the western road, the Seventh Illinois and the Second Iowa moving down parallel on the east. In the afternoon the advance patrol of the Seventh encountered a young Mississippian in a butternut coat and jean trousers, driving an ox team. "He wore a very good looking hat," said Sergeant Surby, "which one of the boys took a fancy to and relieved him of, leaving the poor fellow looking rather sad."

When the Seventh's commanding officer, Colonel Edward Prince, came up shortly afterward he halted beside the wagon. The boy was sobbing. Colonel Prince asked him what had happened, and the boy sadly told the colonel of his confiscated hat. Shaking his head, Prince pulled out his wallet and gave the boy a two-dollar greenback. The young ox driver looked pleased, evidently considering the exchange a fair bargain.

At the end of a day's prescribed thirty-mile cavalry march, the three regiments joined to camp for the night, four miles northwest of Ripley, "on the plantation of Dr. Ellis." As they moved into the camp area they sighted their first Confederates, six men "scouring off across a distant field." A pursuit party dashed after them, captured three of the rebels, and brought them back for questioning by Grierson and his staff.

Commissary-sergeants ordered details to the Ellis Plantation's smokehouses and barns to ration out food and forage to the companies, and as darkness fell, cooking fires were lighted. The weather was still perfect, the springtime sounds and smells all around them. "The sky is hardly ever perfectly clear," Sergeant Stephen Forbes* wrote in one of his letters. "There is just haze enough to tone down the moonlight to the most beautiful dreaminess, to hide every distortion and beautify every grace of landscape. . . . Perhaps it seems a little strange that we should think anything about pleasant weather, we, who have come down here to kill our fellows and carry distress to families, to dislocate the country and destroy life by wholesale. For my part, I have always tried to keep myself human, to remember home and the places where the people have hearts, and charge all these which it is our fate and duty to do, to the account of a stern necessity."[25]

Only a few miles to the east of the brigade's first night encampment was the plantation of William C. Falkner. The "stern necessity" which moved young Sergeant Forbes had likewise impelled Colonel Falkner to leave his home undefended and to organize the First Mississippi Partisan Rangers, who on this day were guarding the northern approaches to Vicksburg. Falkner and his partisan rangers knew that Vicksburg must be held at all costs, but who among them could have suspected that the citadel's security was endangered by Yankee cavalry raiding so far east as Ripley?†

---

* Stephen Forbes became a first sergeant shortly before the beginning of the raid.

† Colonel William C. Falkner was the great-grandfather of the novelist, William Faulkner. His Civil War experiences and later adventures in railroad building along the Pontotoc Ridge traversed by Grierson's raiders appear in fictional guise in the Colonel Sartoris episodes of William Faulkner's Yoknapatawpha sagas.

THE SKIRMISHES BEGIN

While stars still glittered in the April sky, the reveille call was ringing across the plantation fields. Within a few moments the men were in motion, repetitive commands of company officers whipping across each other like echoes in the motionless morning air. Blankets were rolled in ponchos, horses were fed and saddled, and tiny breakfast fires glimmered.

Grierson's orders for the day put Colonel Edward Prince's Seventh Regiment in advance. Just before seven o'clock the regiment's flankers moved out and the videttes came in, chewing on hard bread and raw bacon, snatching a tin cup of coffee before falling in. The sun was well above the eastern hills when the march commands came reverberating down through the companies, and the column moved slowly out in twos on the narrow road toward Ripley, the squadrons at forty-pace intervals. Little spurts of dust were drifting back from the horses' hooves by the time the rear squadron had passed. Farther down, Colonel Reuben Loomis' Sixth Illinois, Captain Jason B. Smith's detachment

Second Day
Saturday, April 18

RIPLEY

NEW
ALBANY

of Battery K artillery, and Colonel Edward Hatch's Second Iowa were preparing to fall in behind.[1]

The brigade's long column moved slowly the first hour, the Seventh slipping cautiously into the town of Ripley at eight o'clock. Union cavalry was no novelty to the folk of this northern Mississippi town; the men of the Second Iowa had eaten cold Christmas dinners near here several weeks earlier.[2] The people now watched apathetically from windows and doorways. No Confederate soldiers were in evidence and no resistance was made by the inhabitants; indeed, the only men left in the town were either convalescent or were beyond military age. Of those who had gone away to war, some would be guarding the Vicksburg bastion, others would be with Falkner's partisan rangers or in one of the state troop encampments farther south.

The brigade rested for an hour in Ripley while Grierson and his staff conferred. They were now approaching the Confederate patrol areas, and it was Grierson's intention to create confusion as to his strength and objectives, to prevent if possible a massing of forces which might block his real mission. Colonel Hatch was therefore ordered to march his Second Iowa east of Ripley, as if intending a direct attack on the well-guarded Mobile & Ohio Railroad twenty miles away. After proceeding four miles, however, Hatch was to turn suddenly southward again and move rapidly along the road toward Molino, riding parallel with Grierson's main body.[3]

Shortly after the Iowans moved out, the Seventh marched south toward Orizaba and New Albany, with the Sixth covering the rear. The land was still hilly, the soil rocky, but there were more farms now, greening with wheat and corn which had replaced the staple cotton of past years. The farmhouses were small, with open "dog-trot" passageways running through their centers. Clustered around them were purple lilacs in full bloom, and full-leaved pear, peach and plum trees, their small green fruits already forming, their blossoms fading on the ground.

The mid-morning sun was hot and the sky was filling with white swollen clouds. As beautiful as they were, the weather-wise troopers regarded them warily.

Occasionally the order "Trot, March!" came down the column, not so much to expedite progress as to relieve both horses and men of the continual motion and fatigue of the same muscles.

The trots were short ones and the squad leaders were soon shouting, "Walk, March."

About four miles out of Ripley a patrol of eight Confederates appeared suddenly, firing upon the Seventh's advance party, but the cavalrymen in butternut uniforms were too far away to endanger their targets. The Yankee advance squadron moved off at a gallop, firing vainly in return. Suspecting an ambush, they halted and waited for Colonel Prince and the main body to come up. Grierson was back with the Sixth, and Prince decided to make a precautionary move. If patrols were operating in the neighborhood, he wondered if larger forces might not be below, probably on the Tallahatchie River twelve miles away. The river was fordable in places, if the fords were not too well defended, and there was a bridge at New Albany. He decided to send one battalion ahead on a forced march, avoiding the villages, with orders to take and hold the bridge.

The assignment went to Major John M. Graham's First Battalion.[4] The men rode off at a gallop, with all the precision of professional cavalrymen, and but for their exuberant grins and unmilitary cheers, the casual observer might never have suspected that only eighteen months earlier these men had left their midwestern farms, their schoolrooms, offices, or country stores, to take up for the first time the strange and unknown trade of soldiering.

II

Benjamin Henry Grierson, commanding these amateur soldiers, had learned what military science he knew from a cavalry drill manual. As a boy he had served a few weeks with an Ohio militia company, but this could scarcely be considered military training. "During muster days," he wrote in his unpublished autobiography, "the men worked systematically to get the officers drunk, and the maneuver usually wound up by marching to the tow path of the canal, where sooner or later they managed to charge upon and plunge the officers into the water to sober them."[5]

Wiry like most Scotch-Irishmen, Grierson was a gangling man, his swarthy, scar-marked face surrounded by rich black hair and a beard worn in the downspreading spade shape of the times. He was a musician with a profound distrust of horses, and he would have much preferred leading an orchestra instead of a brigade of wild-riding cavalrymen. At thirteen, when his family lived in

Youngstown, Ohio, after moving there from Pittsburgh where he was born, July 8, 1826, he had organized his first concert band. Before he left Ohio for Illinois in 1851 he was composing and arranging music for bands and orchestras. He liked to play old Scotch and Irish ballads on a flute or guitar, but when the music was a rousing march he preferred drums.

After completing the local school courses in Youngstown, he had wanted to go to college, and petitioned his congressman for a West Point scholarship. He won the appointment but his mother talked him out of accepting it by convincing him that he was born to be a musician.

Although life on the Illinois frontier in 1851 offered little opportunity for musicians, Grierson liked the rolling, wooded hills of Morgan County. He set himself up as a music teacher in the pleasant little village of Jacksonville, and began organizing amateur bands there and in neighboring towns. To demonstrate what he could do, he took his Jacksonville band to Springfield in the summer of 1852, and the *Illinois State Register* complimented the musicians as follows: "Grierson's Band of Jacksonville was unique in that the members played by the card instead of their own conception of what each particular piece of music ought to have been."[6]

One day in 1854 while he was teaching in Springfield, he encountered by chance his childhood sweetheart, Alice Kirk. He followed her back to Ohio, married her, and they returned to Jacksonville.

After a year of struggling to support a family on the meager income of a music teacher, Grierson decided to go into business with an old friend, John Wallihan. The partners established a general merchandise store in Meredosia, a town twenty miles west of Jacksonville on the Illinois River, which in those days of poor highways was the main artery of commerce from St. Louis up through the heart of the state.

By 1858 Grierson was an active partisan for Abraham Lincoln, composing several songs for his political campaigns. "Lincoln was at Meredosia during the [1858] campaign," Grierson said, "and stopped at my house the night after making a speech. After the speaking was over and Mr. Lincoln had retired, I went back to the building in which the meeting took place to assist in quieting a disturbance which might otherwise have arisen."

Meanwhile, Grierson's merchandise business failed to prosper. "We sold too much on credit," he said, "and were virtually left without a dollar." In the late autumn of 1860 he took his growing family back to Jacksonville, to try music once again as a means of livelihood. "I've often wondered since why I spent five years of my life in Meredosia."

A few months later the war came. Shortly after Lincoln issued his call for volunteers in April, 1861, Grierson accompanied a volunteer infantry company from Jacksonville to Cairo. His first military duty was to serve as an aide to General Benjamin Prentiss with the nominal rank of lieutenant. But he received no pay. For five months he lived on borrowed funds, awaiting a permanent assignment, only to be offered at last a major's rank in the only service he wished to avoid — the cavalry.

Ben Grierson's distrust of horses dated from an accident which occurred when he was eight years old. A supposedly friendly pony had kicked him in the face, splitting his forehead and mangling one cheek. For two months he was blinded, and he carried the scars to his grave. It is not surprising that he avoided all chances of going into the war burdened with cavalrymen and their skittish mounts. He countered the army's offer with a request to be transferred — anywhere to avoid cavalry service. But the commanding general of the Western Department, Henry W. Halleck — later general-in-chief of the Union Army — flatly refused Grierson's request for transfer. "General Halleck," Grierson said, "jocularly remarked that I looked active and wiry enough to make a good cavalryman."

And so in December, 1861, Major Benjamin H. Grierson reported for duty with the Sixth Illinois Cavalry Regiment encamped for the winter at Shawneetown, Illinois. He may have distrusted horses but he knew how to ride and drill, and when five captains under him complained that one of them should have had his rank, he offered to surrender it "to anyone for whom the officers and men might signify their preference." He won the election and a few months later also won the regimental command and the rank of colonel.

During a spring and summer of chasing guerillas in Tennessee and some hard riding and fighting under General William T. Sherman in northern Mississippi, the official dispatches began referring to the Sixth Illinois as *Grierson's Cavalry*.

III

Throughout the war the three regiments comprising Grierson's brigade had campaigned in approximately the same areas. The two Illinois regiments were both mustered in the late summer of 1861 at Camp Butler, where the men spent their first days lying under the trees, cracking nuts, eating wild grapes, pitching quoits, and sitting around campfires. While the regiments were being formed from the volunteer companies, they began drilling on foot and on horseback, and learned how to burnish their boots and saddles for dress parades.

The Second Iowa was organized at Camp McClellan in August, 1861, and after training at Benton Barracks, St. Louis, had moved into the Bird's Point skirmishes with the Illinois regiments and had also been active in the land operations leading to the capture of Island Number Ten. The Iowans quickly established themselves as saber experts by employing one Herr Graupner, a German fencing master, to teach them the art. Graupner charged the officers five dollars and the enlisted men two dollars and a half, guaranteeing that his graduates would win all saber duels over amateur swordsmen. While at Charleston, Missouri, the versatile Iowans also captured a printing press, and to while away the time published a newspaper called the *Charleston Independent*.[7]

The Seventh Illinois and the Second Iowa joined in the siege of Corinth and the battles around Iuka, while the Sixth was left behind to pursue guerillas in west Tennessee. All three had been separately active in Grant's central Mississippi campaigns which the Confederates had thwarted in the late autumn of 1862. When winter set in, the three regiments had come together at La Grange, but it was a winter of little rest for them. Colonel Robert V. Richardson's partisan rangers kept the Tennessee hills in a state of bloody turmoil — the Sixth lost almost an entire company to his band[8] — the same Colonel Richardson who would haunt them again before this raid was done, three hundred miles to the south.

These western Yankees oddly enough did not at first consider themselves to be Yankees at all. New Englanders and other eastern Unionists were Yankees; *they* were Westerners.* Re-

---

* Southwestern Confederates often called their enemies Westerners instead of Yankees. Referring to a rumor that his company might march

ferring to a Confederate stronghold under attack by eastern regiments, one of Grierson's raiders said: "It is a place which can be reduced by a little determined bravery, and the Western troops would make short work of it. But these Yanks! Ah! Ah!! They had so much rather not get shot. *So* much rather reserve themselves to eat pumpkin pies at future Thanksgivings than to abandon themselves to death and glory on the battlefield! I would give more today for the army of Illinois than that of entire New England. They will dare more, do more, go farther, strike deeper, and then not have got up half headway, nor considered themselves acting out of their ordinary modes."[9]

After eighteen months they could swagger a little, these countrymen turned soldiers. The letters and diaries[10] of Grierson's men reveal that in common with most of their comrades they had experienced the pains of severed home ties, the peculiar loneliness of young warriors, the dreams of glory, the disillusionment of reality, boredom, hunger, disease, and the suddenness of death.

They hated military routine: "There is no such a thought-killing life within the very narrow limits of my experience as this. For the mind is so entirely withdrawn from all its accustomed associations of thought and from all thought-provoking occupations, and the nature of the life we live is so well calculated to confine the thoughts within the channel of food and drink, that we lose all inclinations in that direction."

They suffered from dysentery, diarrhea, jaundice, cholera morbus, erysipelas, colds, sore throats, and measles, and they distrusted the camp hospitals:

"What ails you?"

"Why I have been to the camp hospital."

One of Captain Forbes's letters describes the situation: "I have courted the favor of a very kindly physician whom we frequently visit with cases, to the utter avoidance of the regular hospital which we detest in common as we would a lazar house. I will give an instance of their behaviour there. I wished to get a portion of salts for a man who had an erysipelas. I called at the hospital, making my request, and was peremptorily denied be-

north into Tennessee, a Mississippi captain wrote to his wife: "Our men will have to fight these Western men there and they are the best fighters they have."—Warren Magee to Martha Magee, April 19, 1863. *Journal of Mississippi History*, vol. 5 (1943), p. 210.

cause it was not precisely 8½ o'clock in the morning, and was deferred 24 hours. This not answering my purpose, I went on a Doctor hunt through the regiments, and succeeded at last in finding one in the 34th who was not only a M.D. but a gentleman, and procuring a special requisition from him upon the hospital stores, returned after two hours' hard work with the requisite dose. Faugh! There are so many men here whom a little official position spoils."

They elected their officers: "A change has been made in our company in regard to the officers, our captain having been promoted to the office of major and our first lieutenant elected to his place by the unanimous vote of nine hearty cheers . . . the next day our fourth sergeant, McCausland, was elected to the first lieutenancy after an animated contest. Today the only thing of any interest has been the circulation of any number of petitions for the office of fourth corporal. It was really amusing to see the eagerness with which they thrust their papers into the face of every man they met. So eager are some men for every little exaltation above their fellows."

They rough-housed in their camps: "One evening after retiring Westgate began tickling my face with a straw. He thought it a good time to have a little fun at my expense, as I had been out on picket duty the night previous and was very tired and sleepy. . . . I told him that I would put him out of the tent if he did not stop, and becoming impatient I jumped up and the scuffle commenced. After a few tumbles about the tent, Westgate struck one foot among the cooking utensils and finally stepped into the water bucket, which was full of water. . . . He was in trouble, his foot being forced into the bucket in such a position that it was a difficult matter to extricate it. . . . The feet being of the largest kind used for plowing corn in Illinois, and the utensil being only the regular size, pretty near a surgical operation was necessary."

They learned about company punishment: "Poor Hemmenway was drunk again for the second time since we came here and today he payed the penalty in stump-grubbing."

They received Christmas packages from home: "I can never forget the luxuries we received. They were just delicious. I received a box containing a roast turkey, a number of pies, cakes, and other things too numerous to mention."

But most of the time on the long marches, they "were very weary and hungry, having eaten nothing for twenty-four hours and marched 45 miles that day. Nor had we anything with which to appease the gnawings of hunger save a little coffee, which we hastily drank."

They learned how to sleep anytime and anywhere: "I made a bed of corn leaves in the corner of the fence out of the reach of my inquisitive companions, the hogs."

They learned what not to do, the hard way: "I then pulled off my fine cavalry boots and set them up near the fire, in order that they might dry out, and then retired. When I arose in the morning and took hold of my boots I found them brittle in some parts, having been scorched by the fire during the night. When putting them on they broke, so that they were ruined."

They hated the rain and cold: "I am sitting cooped up in my tent, looking out upon a prospect of black puddly ground and shivering horses, a grey dripping sky, and down the hillside, through the sombre pines, a valley of misty smoke."

And detested the mud: "The earth is supposed to have been in a plastic state at its creation, and I am inclined to think it will be again before long, from the looks of my boots. . . . We stamp the mud from our feet as we retire, sleep on the reeking ground, and get up into a nice little mud puddle about two feet in diameter. Next in the progress of events we breakfast off our box and go up on a mud-mixing tour up to the General's headquarters."

They wrote letters full of homesickness to their loved ones in the north: "I am down here in the dark pine groves, and the earth is brown, but you dwell in the white land, and the soft carpet of the snow is under your feet. I am old and brown with care, and the rain drips sullenly out of my sky, but you are in the beams of sunshine, and the year is young and bright around you. . . . I have not had a letter from home since the battle — and I have carried these freshest remembrances until they seem like perished roses, sweet but dead. . . . I send you a blossom of the 'wild purple magnolia,' indigenous to this climate."

They fraternized with the families of the enemy: "It is most enticingly pleasant to step into a neat, well-kept house tempting with books and bright eyes, and music with the tinkling of a guitar or a piano, but the distrust and suspicion with which all soldiers are regarded, and for which God knows they give more than cause enough, deprives a decent mind of all enjoyment or ease. This is what makes the hardship of soldiering."

They went to church with the conquered: "It is Sunday afternoon and I have been church going, listening to the old tunes grown strange through long disuse, hearing the Bible themes, the words of prayer resounding through the lift of an old time-worn church, and the clear, almost complaining voices of women mingling with the strong soldier chorus of the strangers in their sanctuary."

Most of them had read *Uncle Tom's Cabin,* and were disillusioned on seeing their first freed slaves: "Mrs. Stowe's Negroes are not here."

They lost their dreams of glory: "I recollect well how I used to imagine myself riding boldly over the hills and coming suddenly upon the enemy and blazing away at them with my revolver, when at least three men were to tumble down, of course, and then riding gaily back with a very picturesque stream of blood running down my left shoulder, never my right; when, after a few days of graceful bandaging, I would be all right and eager for another one, and have the honor of carrying rebel lead in my body to the grave. We have just discharged one man from the company for carrying a ball in his lung, for it would get to sinking down sometimes and make it rather hard work for him to breathe, and, would you believe it, he didn't act a bit more graceful nor enthusiastic than if he had had the asthma."

Although it would not have been difficult for a cavalryman to quit this war and go home, scarcely a deserter is listed on the rosters of the three regiments of Grierson's brigade. And when their volunteer services ended, a large percentage of them reenlisted as veterans. Those who were not killed or captured or did not die of disease remained with their regiments until they were mustered out late in 1865.

IV

While Major Graham's First Battalion was riding full speed for the Tallahatchie bridge at New Albany, Colonel Hatch and his Second Iowans, having completed their four-mile feint toward the Mobile & Ohio Railroad, were turning south toward Molino. Near Molino the Iowans' advance squadron was sighted by mounted scouts from Colonel J. F. Smith's First Mississippi Regiment of state troops, a home guard organization based at Chesterville, twelve miles south. Smith's regiment was made up mainly of farmers and townsmen of the area who for various reasons were considered exempt from conscription in the regular Confederate Army. Although the regiment's duty strength was around 350 men, only one company was in the field near Molino.

Unable to give the Iowans a battle with the small force at his command, Colonel Smith sent warning of the invasion back to Chesterville and proceeded to delay Hatch as best he could. These Confederates, of course, had no knowledge of Grierson's two other regiments moving south along the New Albany road only seven or eight miles to the west. And Hatch, uncertain of his opponents' strength, moved so cautiously that he marched only five miles below Molino during the afternoon, harassed continually by the skirmishing Confederates. He crossed the upper branches of the Tallahatchie late in the day, posted double videttes, and camped for the night. The sky was thickening and the weather smelled of rain.[11]

Major Graham's First Battalion of the Seventh Illinois, meanwhile, had ridden uninterrupted to within sight of the Tallahatchie bridge, where, as Colonel Prince had suspected, Confederate pickets were stationed. The guards opened fire on Graham's galloping lines. Surprised by the sudden appearance of blue uniforms, the pickets had no time to burn the bridge. Some of them began ripping up the loose planking, but the cavalry charge was moving too rapidly for them. The Confederates jumped on their horses and attempted a hasty flight, but Graham's onrush swept up four prisoners.

Ordering his men to dismount, the major prepared for a defensive battle which never came. He set some of his men to replacing the torn flooring for the use of the main column, but the main column never came that way, either. Colonel Grierson decided to use the ford three miles upstream, halting briefly for watering and feeding.[12]

It was late afternoon by the time the rear guard left New Albany, "a small place composed of a few dry-goods stores, whose stock needed replenishing; also some fine residences; altogether a pleasantly situated country town."[13] The march was slowed deliberately for Colonel Hatch's benefit, but no word

came from him. As they moved southeastward along the Pontotoc road, the sky ahead of them towered with thunderheads
quivering with tiny flashes of lightning. The two days of good
cavalry weather were coming to an end.

Five miles below New Albany they halted for the night along
a small stream "on the plantation of Mr. Sloan," a few miles
short of the standard day's thirty miles. Rain clouds were thickening with the coming of darkness, and Grierson ordered his men
to prepare for the rough weather immediately ahead. As soon as
their horses were unsaddled and picketed, some of the troopers
began erecting little shelters of fence rails and ponchos. Others
collected dry brush for beds. They used their saddles for pillows,
rolling up in blankets, and as Sergeant Stephen Forbes described
it, lay with their faces "under the ponchos, listening to the pat-
ter of soft rain overhead." The unlucky ones were assigned to
vidette duty.

In his *Record of Services,* printed privately for his family,
Grierson gave a detailed account — which reads like a comic
opera — of his experiences that evening with the plantation
owner, Sloan. "As usual," Grierson said, "we demanded the keys
of smokehouses and barns, food for men and horses. Mr. Sloan
wanted in a small way to resist where resistance was of course
impossible; would not give up his keys until the locks were
broken. When he saw his stores issued out, he was completely
beside himself; alternately was going to cut my throat, and
desirous of having his own throat cut." Grierson tried to calm
the emotional planter and had almost succeeded when Sloan
discovered a squad of cavalrymen driving up his horses and mules
which he had believed were safely hidden in the woods. "He
fairly foamed," said Grierson, "and for the fiftieth time demanded that we take him out and cut his throat and be done
with it."

Grierson loved acting; he had written and acted in several
comic operas while teaching music at Jacksonville. He now turned
and winked at his orderly, a huge, athletic, and heavily bearded
man. "Mr. Sloan is very desirous of having his throat cut," he
said solemnly. "Take him out in the field and *cut his throat, and
be done with it.*" The orderly, falling into the spirit of the play,
immediately responded by taking out his large hunting knife
with one hand and seizing Mr. Sloan's collar with the other.

"Now began a hubbub. Mrs. Sloan — who all along had been more self-possessed than her husband . . . began to scream in chorus with the servants." She begged Colonel Grierson to pay no attention to what her husband said, and far down the long hall through which the orderly was walking him, Sloan's voice came roaring back in a hasty plea for his life. The scene ended quietly with Grierson promising to leave some tired horses in exchange for Sloan's fresh stock.[14]

Major Graham's four prisoners, the only profitable return from his dashing capture of the Tallahatchie bridge, proved to be talkative and informative. Two of them were from a state troop regiment, an unofficial unit headed by one Captain Weatherall and composed of a group of men who appeared to be unwilling to serve in the regular Confederate Army, but were hell-for-leather to chase any Yankees who might appear in their home counties. The other two were regulars from Lieutenant-Colonel Clark R. Barteau's Second Tennessee Cavalry. From these prisoners Grierson learned that Major Alexander Chalmers and a detachment of the Eighteenth Mississippi Cavalry were camped at King's Bridge, a few miles to the northwest, that a small horse herd was hidden in some bottomlands a few miles to the east, and that Colonel Barteau was probably less than twenty miles away with four or five hundred regulars and about the same number of state troops at his disposal.[15]

V

Lieutenant-Colonel Clark Russell Barteau, commanding the Confederate's Second Tennessee Cavalry, was a man harassed both by his Union enemies and his Confederate friends. Following the disasters of Shiloh and Corinth in 1862, he and his Tennesseans had withdrawn to northeast Mississippi to heal their wounds, reorganize, re-outfit, and become a part of Brigadier-General Daniel Ruggles' First Military District, headquarters at Columbus. Revenge was naturally a strong motivating force among the men of his regiment, and they had spent the winter raiding northward, with headquarters base at Okolona. They had also kept the Mobile & Ohio tracks protected between Okolona and Verona.[16]

Before winter ended, however, the regiment was "miserably

armed and deficient in numbers, with not even ammunition sufficient for a skirmish." The men had also suffered a severe epidemic of measles. The plight of Barteau's stubborn cavalrymen won the sympathy of General Ruggles, and early in March, 1863, he begged General John C. Pemberton, commanding the Department of Mississippi, to supply the Tennesseans with "good serviceable arms, and 50 cartridges per man."[17] Pemberton grudgingly relinquished some of his precious Vicksburg material, and with the coming of spring more Tennesseans filtered south through the Yankee lines to increase Barteau's duty strength.

Scarcely two weeks before Grierson's brigade rode south out of La Grange, Colonel Barteau's abilities as a cavalry commander were recognized in an order giving him command of all Confederate mounted troops in the northern portion of General Ruggles' district.[18] It was Barteau's responsibility, therefore, to intercept and turn back any Union raid moving south into eastern Mississippi.

Barteau was well aware that his position was an unenviable one, for he was caught among three forces — the contending Union Army, the contentious Mississippi state authority represented by Governor John Pettus and Major-General Samuel Gholson, and the regular Confederate military authority represented by General Pemberton.

Although Mississippi had contributed as large a share of soldiers to the Confederacy as any southern state, most of them had marched away to Virginia in the early months of the war. As soon as the first Union armies began invading the state from the north, and others began coming up the river from captured New Orleans, Mississippians lost all enthusiasm for military service outside their state borders. They could see no logic in traveling to Virginia or even to middle Tennessee to fight Yankees when there were plenty of Yankees to fight right on the front lawns of their best plantations.[19]

When President Jefferson Davis removed Mississippi's hero, Earl Van Dorn, from command of the Department of Mississippi in October, 1862, and sent John C. Pemberton to direct the defense of Vicksburg, the state's leaders were deeply offended. They may have lost confidence in Van Dorn's abilities as a military commander, but they had wanted General Joseph Johnston instead of Pemberton. And although they knew that

Pemberton had given up his life's career in the United States Army to join the Confederacy, he was regarded with suspicion. Pemberton might be an ardent believer in states' rights, but he was also a Pennsylvania Yankee, little better than a "galvanized Confederate."*[20]

By the spring of 1863, the Confederacy's tightening conscription laws were garnering but few soldiers in Mississippi. To insure that Mississippians would remain to fight Yankees in Mississippi, the state legislature authorized Governor Pettus to raise state troops, independent of the Confederate Army.

And so during the early spring, Major-General Gholson, whose home was in northeastern Mississippi, set out with the backing of the governor to muster three regiments of cavalry for state service. He soon had Pemberton's command in an uproar. General James R. Chalmers, directing the defenses below Memphis, complained with some bitterness that Gholson was ordering sorely needed partisan rangers out of his western district into the eastern district, among them Weatherall's cavalry and J. F. Smith's cavalry.[21] As most of the men in these organizations lived in northeastern Mississippi, General Gholson had little trouble persuading them to return to patrol their home counties. If it was right and proper to fight for one's state before one's country — they may have reasoned — then perhaps it was right to fight for one's county before one's state.

After his proselyting activities among Chalmers' western troops, General Gholson remained in the northeast area to complete the organization of the three proposed state regiments. Colonel Barteau, therefore, while nominally in authority, was in the awkward position of directing a body of troops with two commanding officers who might very well issue orders independently of one another. Barteau's immediate commander, General Ruggles, decided the problem was insoluble and told Barteau that when state troops were in the field, out of courtesy to General Gholson and "to preserve concert of action," he should yield obeisance temporarily to Gholson as commander.[22]

This, then, was the predicament confronting Colonel Barteau late in the afternoon of April 18, when scouts came in to his

---

* A "galvanized Confederate" was a captured Union soldier who for his freedom agreed to fight for the cause of the Confederacy. There were also "galvanized Yankees" fighting for the North.

base near Verona with news of Grierson's cavalry at the New Albany bridge. He guessed the Yankees might be heading for the state troop camps at Chesterville, to break them up before General Gholson could complete training and organization of his regiments. Barteau immediately ordered his Tennesseans to be ready to march for Chesterville before dawn. Even so patient a man as Barteau must certainly have cursed the rain, the Yankees, and the hopeless disorder of his command.

BARTEAU IN PURSUIT

Colonel Grierson's swiftly moving brigade of cavalry riding southward into eastern Mississippi was not the only diversionary force being used by General Grant in the springtime preparations for what he hoped would be the final assault on Vicksburg. By the time Grierson's raiders reached New Albany on the 18th, four other movements were well under way. From Memphis, three infantry regiments, a battery of artillery, and two hundred cavalrymen were marching south toward General James Chalmers' stronghold at Panola. From La Grange, General William Sooy Smith was moving 1,500 infantrymen by rail to Coldwater, with orders to engage Chalmers' flank along the lower Tallahatchie. From Corinth, 5,000 infantrymen were marching east along the Tennessee River toward Tuscumbia. And from far up in Tennessee, Colonel Abel Streight was bringing a mounted brigade down for a raid into eastern Alabama.[1]

With these five long-planned and well-synchronized movements, Grant and his generals hoped not only to distract the

NEW ALBANY

PONTOTOC

Confederates' attention from activities around Vicksburg but also to force them to withdraw some reserve troops from the Vicksburg-Jackson defense area. Grant was counting on the two cavalry raids to break the lines of transport for enemy troops and material, leaving the Confederates' commanding general, John C. Pemberton, temporarily isolated from the remainder of the South.

It was evident from the orders issued by Grant during the winter that he considered Grierson's raid as the main thrust, the feint with the punch. From his disastrous past experiences in Chalmers' well-defended area below Memphis, the general must have known that the small forces he was sending there could do little more than keep the Confederates tied down. General Sooy Smith's flanking expedition served only as a smokescreen to the right of Grierson's cavalry. The expedition from Corinth was designed as a similar diversion on the left of Grierson's drive. As for Streight's raid into Alabama, it was calculated to keep General Bedford Forrest's fast-riding rebels occupied far to the east, and might also do some damage to the railroads supplying Vicksburg with troops and ammunition. Streight's raiders, however, were rated second in priority to Grierson's men, being mounted mainly on mules and cast-off horses.

Grierson's cavalrymen had drawn the best horses available — captured Mississippi blood stock and animals collected by the remount station in St. Louis. During the fall and winter, representatives of the quartermaster had searched throughout the western half of the Union, posting notices on the streets of every town and in the local newspapers requisitioning horses "to be not less than fifteen hands high, between five and nine years of age, of dark colors, well broken to the saddle, compactly built, and free from all defects. No mares will be received."[2]

But even the best of mounts can be slowed by perverse weather, and when Colonel Grierson awoke early on Sunday morning, April 19, the sun was not shining as he had hoped. Instead, rain was still falling heavily from an unpleasant gray sky. The clay roads would be sticky, making fast movement impossible.

During breakfast with his staff, Grierson quickly fitted his strategy to the weather. He was fairly confident that no strong Confederate forces were yet massed on either his left or right, and he decided to put his men into a series of diverse movements designed to confuse the enemy as to his real intentions. "I sent a detachment eastward to communicate with Colonel Hatch," he said in his report, "and make a demonstration toward Chesterville, where a regiment of cavalry was organizing. I also sent an expedition to New Albany, and another northwest toward King's Bridge, to attack and destroy a portion of a regiment of cavalry organizing there under Major [Alexander H.] Chalmers. I thus sought to create the impression that the object of our advance was to break up these parties."[3]

The three detachments sent out by Grierson were drawn from the Seventh Illinois. Colonel Prince selected Captain George W. Trafton, commanding G Company, to lead the raid back into New Albany, and shortly after six o'clock the men were riding north. Trafton also had a second company under his command, but the records do not give its identity.

As they moved slowly back over the five miles into New Albany, a driving rain pelted into their faces, soaked around the collar openings of the ponchos, gradually saturating their blouses and shirts. The hooves of their floundering horses splattered them with daubs of adhesive, orange-colored mud.

During the night a small force of Mississippi state troops had collected in New Albany, and when they sighted Trafton's two companies more than a hundred rebels moved out to give battle. Some of the Confederates were unmounted. Trafton charged, his men firing and then drawing sabers, driving the state troops back through the town and inflicting several casualties.

On this particular Sunday, Grierson's men remained for only a short time in New Albany, but they visited the town again some months later (during another campaign) when their activities were graphically chronicled by Elizabeth Jane Beach, wife of New Albany's only physician, Dr. Asahel Beach.

To young Mrs. Beach, Grierson's Yankees were in no sense romantic cavaliers; they were deadly and recurrent molesters of her home and security, as she explained in a letter to her parents in Georgia:

I have the same old tale to write, the Yankees have been here again. They camped here on the Tallahatchie. We heard they were coming before they got here, so the men all put out, of course, with their stock.

My house, garden, & orchard, were thronged with them all the time, toating off corn & fodder, chickens, vegetables, cooking utensils, and every thing they could find, searching my house over & over. I had a great many nice young chickens, just large enough to fry, they caught them all. I have now *five* old hens, that is my amount of chickens. They took *every thing* they could *find* that we had to eat. Things that I could not hide, such as chickens, vegetables, shoats and milk, but I had every thing else hid, even to my salt & lard, and they did not happen to find it. I believe I have told you where my hiding place is, over the piazza, the planks are sawed out and placed in again, so that it can't be discovered by looking at it.[4]

By the end of the first day of the Yankee encampment in New Albany, Elizabeth Beach was in a mood of high indignation. She decided to visit Benjamin Grierson, who had set up headquarters in the town house of James Hill.

I talked with Grierson about half an hour. He treated me very politely, but I don't think he has much feeling. You ought to have seen how grand him and his staff looked. There were five of them, him and his adjutant, sergeon and two others. They were sitting in Mrs. Hill's passage *dressed into fits,* with three or four bottles of champaign and boxes of segars setting around them.

Grierson asked Mrs. Beach several questions about her husband. She told him that he was a physician and had gone away in order to save his horse, that he had already lost four horses to the Yankees and could not afford to lose another one.

"Has he a fine horse now?" asked Grierson.

"Yes," replied Mrs. Beach. "He could not practice medicine on a sorry horse, and good horses are scarce in this country now. He got him a good one and went off to keep you Yankees from getting him."

"Oh," said Grierson, "he had as well stayed at home. We would not bother him nor his horse either."

"I know better than that," the doctor's wife retorted. "He has been taken once, and his horse every time."

The interview was concluded when Mrs. Beach asked Grierson to place a guard at her house.

I told him that his men were searching all over my house and tearing up every thing. Told him that they had already got all I had to eat, that I only asked protection that night for myself and children. He said certainly he would send me a guard, and if I would treat him right he would protect me until they left. So he sent one of his body guard, and we rested quietly that night. I treated him very kindly, made him a good pallet in the passage and we were not bothered with any other Yankees that night.

But not long after the guard left, more of Grierson's soldiers, in a looting mood, visited the Beach home. *"All day* working like ants, all over the house up stairs and down, in every hole and corner, searching & peeping everywhere." They finally found Elizabeth Beach's secret hiding place:

One *rascal* went up in the corner and in stooping to put his hand under the floor, put it against the planks, and they slipped a little, he pulled them off, and says, by george, boys here is the place, they just ripped the planks off and in they went. One says run down and guard the door, don't let another fellow come up here, we'll divide the things amongst us. I had in there, meat, flour, sugar, coffee, molasses, lard & salt, all of Asa's good clothes, Sarah's, mine and the childrens. We all had new shoes in there that we had not worn, in a pillow case. They pulled them all out and looked at them. I stood over them and as they would pull out the shoes & clothes, I would grab them and tell them that they could not have them, but everytime they came to anything of Asa's they *would* take it. Took his over coat, a pair of new blue jeans pants, three pair of summer pants, all his drawers except the ones he had on, one shirt, a new silk handkerchief. So you know he is very near without clothes.

Before the Yankees departed New Albany they "took *every solitary* thing I had, except one jar of lard and my salt. There was not even a grain of corn on the place to make hominy after they were gone. They treated Mr. Hill in the same manner, took and killed nearly every thing he had. Every one of his negroes went with them, there is not a negro on his place large nor small."[5]

Looting of civilian property was a problem confronting the officers of both armies in the Civil War. Troops raiding into enemy country were usually under orders to destroy everything which might be used by the opposing army, and the line between war materiel and civilian property grew more and more indistinct as the war lengthened. Because the Confederacy was, for the most part, the invaded area, Southern citizens were the principal sufferers, being forced in effect to support two armies.

In the first year of the conflict, the Union military leaders were strict in enforcing regulations against plundering privately owned property. They felt that they might win over a portion of the rebels to the Union cause if property rights were carefully respected. On one occasion, during the early Tennessee campaigns, while Company C of the Seventh Illinois was serving as an escort troop for General Grant, the general discovered that some of the men had killed and dressed a hog belonging to a rebel farmer. He halted the column and rode out of ranks immediately.

"Where did you procure that hog?"

"Foraged it, sir."

"Men, don't you know that kind of work is strictly against orders?"

Private Henry Eby, who witnessed the incident, reported that Grant lectured the men severely, as a father would talk to his erring sons, and then ordered a sergeant to put them under guard and report them to headquarters.

"I often felt grieved for people in the South," Eby continued, "when their stock, grain and fences were appropriated for the use of the army. . . . I can remember when orders were given to the soldiers allowing them to take only the top rail off a fence for fuel, but each rail in turn became a top rail and in a few minutes the whole fence would disappear."[6]

Sergeant Stephen Forbes also expressed his disapproval of the wholesale looting done by some of his comrades:

The column halted for a few moments in front of the dwelling of a poor widow said by all her neighbors to be loyal to our cause, and immediately her yard and house were filled by a crowd of thieves (I cannot call them soldiers, for shame) who instantly appropriated everything they could carry. Some attacked her poultry, chasing the chickens and geese through her very house, and stones and clubs flew in all directions. Others butchered her hogs and splitting them in two, buckled them on their saddles, still warm and dripping with blood. Others took fence rails and burst in the doors of her smokehouse and granary, and in a few moments every morsel of sustenance which a hard year's work had brought her had disappeared as if before a pack of ravening wolves. The poor lone woman wrung her hands and cried in an agony of despair and terror, and prayed to God to help her, while her children sobbed and screamed in a perfect frenzy of fear.

A soldier in rear of me said: "I don't hardly like to see the boys go down on poor folks that way."

"Damn them," said I, so full of indignant rage that everything looked white. "I wish that every one of the wretches might be hung in chains and burned to death."[7]

On another occasion, young Forbes was more philosophical:

This is the most disagreeable part of a soldier's duty, for taking the all of a defenceless citizen when the women cry and the men turn pale, appropriating the last horse of a poor old woman, and driving off a man's team from before his plow, certainly seems to be tolerably small work for a soldier, but then what is all war but one monstrous evil by the use of which we hope to overcome a much greater, and so long as it tends to subdue the rebellion I suppose that the means are justified by the end.[8]

II

While Captain Trafton's expedition was dispersing the rebels gathered in New Albany, two other companies moved off to the northwest toward King's Bridge in search of Weatherall's and Chalmers' regiments. Under a grove of dripping trees they found the enemy camp, several tents and lean-to's deserted in the rain, the damp bedding left unrolled on the ground. The Mississippians had fled, evidently before dawn; the charred cooking fires of the previous night were rain-soaked.

The Yankees set fire to everything that would burn and scouts took up the trail of the scattering enemy. They captured four rear-guard rebels, but otherwise the chase through the muddy bottomlands along the Tallahatchie was a fruitless one. Colonel Prince had ordered them to rejoin the main command by ten o'clock, and they were forced to turn back to the Pontotoc road.

At the same time, Grierson's third detachment — also two companies — proceeded eastward under orders to communicate with Colonel Hatch's Iowans and instruct him to make a demonstration toward Chesterville, the Mississippi state troops rendezvous point. This expedition was also ordered to search out a horse herd, reported by one of the prisoners as being hidden in a thicket a few miles from the road. They moved off under a cover of woods, the drenched trees dousing them with sudden showers of collected raindrops.

As the Confederates were believed to be in strength somewhere between the Pontotoc road and the Mobile & Ohio Railroad, the expedition to the east moved cautiously. Scouts were kept well forward at long rifle range to draw the fire of any ambuscade. Wherever the terrain made it advisable, extra flankers were thrown out, riding at rifle range from the sides of the column and abreast of it, to keep the column at security with a margin of time to form a front in any direction before an attack could be precipitated upon it. When any suspicious noise was heard in the thick brush along the way, a platoon would be dismounted and sent forward in a line abreast, the men fifty feet or more apart.[9]

They found only a few horses but they did reach Colonel Hatch's advance guard, and the orders from Grierson to demonstrate toward Chesterville were passed on to the commander. The two companies then swung about hastily, riding back to rejoin the main command at Sloan's Plantation. They were the last of the three expeditions to return to camp, and by the time they struck the Pontotoc road, the rain had stopped.

Meanwhile, the Sixth Illinois, after a leisurely Sunday morning breakfast and prayer service, had moved out toward Pontotoc, Grierson riding with his old regiment. The six companies of the Seventh, which had also remained in camp, were waiting with mounts saddled, and as soon as the three diversionary parties reported in, Colonel Prince ordered the regiment to move south after Grierson.

The Pontotoc road, churned by the hooves of the Sixth Illinois, was now a shallow quagmire dotted with pools of yellow water. The horses occasionally slipped and stumbled in the tenacious, ankle-deep mud. Nor did the sun come forth to dry the surface; low rolling clouds swept across the sky, spraying a fine mist over the column.

It was almost mid-afternoon before the regiment halted for feeding and watering along a thick greensward near an old farmhouse. There was no sign of life about the place, and after a few minutes an unofficial searching party entered the building. The men found a keg of powder, several revolvers, and a few old United States Army muskets concealed in one of the storerooms. Because it was standard procedure to burn any building in which weapons or ammunition were found, someone set a blaze going without waiting for orders.

As soon as he saw the smoke and flames, Colonel Prince sent a fire-fighting party into action, but the house and most of its contents quickly burned to the ground. "The officers made every effort to find the guilty party," said Sergeant Surby, "but it occurred mysteriously, no one knew anything about it."[10]

Shortly after four o'clock in the afternoon, the Sixth Illinois, moving three or four miles in advance of the Seventh, began approaching Pontotoc, a county seat with a population above three thousand. Grierson expected to meet serious resistance here, and he sent the advance troops dashing toward the town to draw out the defenders' strength. A small band of armed citizens and some of Captain Weatherall's state troops fired a few volleys into the advance, but upon seeing the main column approaching, all except one man fled in a scattered retreat. This rebel proved to be more foolhardy than brave, firing persistently on the invaders. Some accounts give his name as Beers, others as Reno; whatever his name, he died in vain. Grierson's raiders quickly occupied Pontotoc, surrounding the new brick courthouse and searching the more resplendent residences. They found Captain Weatherall's temporary headquarters, capturing several prisoners and a wagon load of ammunition. The ammunition and all other military equipment in the headquarters building were destroyed.

As soon as the Seventh Illinois arrived (at a gallop, after Colonel Prince heard the firing) the Sixth Regiment assembled in marching order and moved off to the south to find a suitable campsite for the night. Shortly after they left, a searching party from the Seventh discovered a hidden Confederate Army salt depot in an old mill. Because salt was extremely scarce in the South, almost as valuable as ammunition, Major John Graham and three companies of his First Battalion were ordered to remain behind the main column and destroy the precious store, estimated in the official report as between four and five hundred bushels.*

Six miles below Pontotoc the three regiments came together again as the afternoon darkened into twilight. They camped along Chiwapa Creek on Daggett's and Weatherall's Plantations, the latter owned by a brother of the state troop leader who had so recently fled his headquarters in the town. Colonel Hatch brought his Second Iowa down from Poplar Springs after making his feint toward Chesterville. The Iowans had been harassed for most of the past eighteen hours by 200 or more state troops who had initiated their fighting by charging past the Yankee pickets around midnight, and had kept up desultory skirmishes through most of the day's march.

But that night as he laid plans for an early morning boots-and-saddles call, Colonel Grierson could count the day as a lucky Sunday. Casualties were minor, he had not lost a man, and since Friday he had thrust seventy miles into enemy territory.

III

While Benjamin Grierson was growing to manhood in Youngstown, Ohio, Clark Barteau was completing his last classes in a

---

* Only a few weeks before this incident, a Mississippi soldier stationed below Vicksburg was writing to his wife, who wanted to slaughter her hogs but had no salt left to preserve the meat: "If there was any chance to get salt here I would try and send you some, but there is none here." — Warren Magee to Martha Magee, December 4, 1862. *Journal of Mississippi History,* vol. 5, 1943, p. 207.

rural school less than a hundred miles away in a farming section near Cleveland. In 1851, the same year that Grierson moved to Illinois, young Barteau entered Ohio Wesleyan University. Four years later Clark Barteau was in Hartsville, Tennessee, earning his living as principal of a boys' academy.

On this rainy Sunday of April, 1863, as he led his Second Tennessee Regiment out of Verona north in single file along the railroad, Colonel Barteau may have reflected on the fate that had brought him there, that had brought him responsibility for the lives of the men riding silent behind him, that had brought him accountability for the fortunes of this dark corner of the Confederacy for which he felt no tie but that of the refugee for a somewhat specious sanctuary.

Now nearing his thirtieth birthday, Barteau had lived only six years of his life in the South when Fort Sumter fell. In those same years while Grierson was establishing his mercantile business on the Illinois River, Barteau was editing and publishing the Hartsville (Tennessee) *Plaindealer*, committing himself in its columns to states' rights and attacking the abolitionist crusade as being based on falsehoods and fanaticism. He quit his schoolteaching and began reading law. He married a Tennessean. By 1861 the Ohio Yankee was beyond compromise. He would fight for the South.

As he rode north, following the road that slanted toward a dark green line of hills to the west, time hanging as dreary as the weather, Barteau surely thought of his wife and the child as he had last seen them more than a year gone now, of the hour he had stolen from the fleeing Seventh Tennessee Cavalry Battalion (and he then only a private in the ranks) to stop by his home for a final farewell. She had been braver than he, probably less aware than he of the full meaning of the fall of Fort Donelson. And he remembered her there in the doorway, her breath steaming in the frosty February air, the child in her arms as he turned and waved for the last time, spurring his horse away in a gallop down the frozen road.[11]

Then had come Shiloh and it was doubly bitter in remembrance, his own brother fighting for the Union there, and the South had lost, and lost again at Corinth, the Seventh Battalion shattered in death, the living scattered through northern Alabama and Mississippi. When the men joined again at last near Fulton in Mississippi, only four skeleton companies could be assembled from the Seventh. They found three companies left of the Tennessee First Cavalry, and the seven companies (scarcely four hundred men) camped together in June. Most of the officers were dead, wounded, missing, or discredited.

Clark Barteau was more surprised than gratified when the Tennesseans elected him — a man from the ranks — to command their newly formed Second Cavalry Regiment. He was amused when his staff tried to scrounge up three more companies so that he could qualify for a full colonelcy. His title scarcely mattered; accomplishing what was necessary to return home to Tennessee was his main objective.

Undoubtedly he was pleased this morning that Captain Moses McKnight had brought Company C back from the Alabama conscripting tour in time for this skirmish. McKnight's company was above strength, one hundred and fifteen men, almost half of them fresh from the "plow-handles, workshops and counting rooms of Middle Tennessee,"[12] well mounted on horses stolen from the Yankees.

Before ten o'clock the Tennesseans were climbing directly into the hills guarding Chesterville, bivouacking three miles from the state troops' camp. When Barteau rode up through the Chesterville pickets he found the men organized for action, although they were obviously poorly trained and armed. "Shotgun cavalry," the Yankees had named them in derision.

Barteau was relieved to learn that General Gholson was absent, thus eliminating the delicate problem of seniority of command. Two commanding officers were present, Major W. M. Inge of the Twelfth Battalion of Mississippi State Troops, and Captain T. W. Ham, leader of an independent company. They reported wild rumors of 6,000 invading Yankees, rumors which Barteau discounted. He judged from the reports of the Yankees' rapid approach that Colonel J. F. Smith's First Mississippi cavalrymen were serving only as harassing skirmishers.[13]

Convinced now that his assumption of an attack upon the Chesterville troop rendezvous had been correct, Barteau prepared to dig in for battle. Early in the afternoon Colonel Smith's cavalry came dashing in from the northeast with news that the Second Iowa Regiment was only five miles away. This of course was Hatch's demonstration, as ordered by Grierson, and it served to keep Barteau's Second Tennessee Regiment and all the state troops waiting until after nightfall for an enemy which never appeared. Hatch had swung about and moved on to Pontotoc to join Grierson.

It was ten o'clock Sunday night before the first of Weatherall's men reached Chesterville with the news that the Yankees had raided Pontotoc. Barteau was surprised and disappointed; he had been outmaneuvered. He suspected now that the Yankees might be driving for the Mobile & Ohio Railroad which he had been defending all winter; possibly they might attack Okolona or Aberdeen where Confederate Army stores were vulnerable. Would the enemy continue southward and then turn toward the railroad? Or would they swing east immediately from Pontotoc, heading toward Verona and Aberdeen? To Barteau the latter move seemed more probable.

After conferring with Colonel Smith, Major Inge, and Captain Ham, he assembled all available mounted troops, a total strength equal to one of Grierson's three regiments. The column moved out to the south at midnight under a starless and oppressive sky.

IV

About the same time, almost 200 miles to the southwest in his Jackson headquarters, Confederate General John C. Pemberton was reading the last of the day's numerous messages which with each passing hour had brought more ominous intelligences from all points of the compass. Responsible for the defense of Mississippi and the key point of Vicksburg, General Pemberton was dividing his attention among a number of problems: movements of Grant's forces across the river; operations of enemy gunboats along the river; slowness of Confederate rail transportation; shortage of artillery ammunition; lack of co-operation from the governor of Mississippi; and the need for more troops, particularly good cavalry, since General Forrest had been transferred to General Joseph E. Johnston's command in Tennessee.

On April 10 Pemberton had telegraphed Richmond headquarters that he needed more cavalry in northern Mississippi, especially in the northeast where a large amount of the Vicksburg army's food and other supplies originated. But Richmond had not responded.

And now ten days later, seventy-two hours after Grierson's brigade had left La Grange, Pemberton received the first news of the concerted enemy movements driving south from several points along the Tennessee border. He was worried by the heavy force of Union cavalry reported coming down the eastern edge of Mississippi.

Pemberton knew he was in trouble, and he immediately called for help from the nearest quarter. He dispatched a telegram to General Johnston, asking for a cavalry raid from Johnston's department against the Yankee forces on the Tallahatchie. "The enemy," he concluded, "are endeavoring to compel a diversion of my troops to Northern Mississippi."[14] And such a diversion, Pemberton knew, could prove fatal to the defense of Vicksburg, the key that Lincoln wanted in his pocket.

GRIERSON'S GAMBIT

Fourth Day
Monday, April 20

PONTOTOC

HOUSTON

From midnight Sunday until the dawn of Monday, Lieutenant-Colonel Clark Barteau's mixed regiment marched southeastward to Garman's Mills. At 8:30 in the morning the advance troop was astride the Pontotoc-Okolona turnpike, eight miles north of Okolona, in the midst of endless fields of young corn. Two years ago only cotton plants would have been growing here, but since the beginning of the war the rich valleys along the Mississippi-Alabama border had been transformed quickly into grain fields.

Colonel Barteau rode forward, dismounted, and read the imprints in the road's receptive surface. No cavalry troops had passed since the rain.

As were his comrades and his foes, Barteau was involved in a series of deadly games played by many players who moved by certain rules of warfare mixed with the romantic trappings of medieval chivalry. For example, Barteau's Second Tennessee Cavalry this morning was without the services of one of its best non-commissioned officers, Sergeant Richard Hancock, who would later write the regiment's history. Sergeant Hancock was not ill, nor wounded, nor on leave, nor a captive. He was a paroled prisoner, having been captured while on a scout to the north during the winter. He had sworn to his enemy that he would engage in no further fighting until an exchange had been arranged for a Union soldier of equal rank who had also been captured.*

For the time being Sergeant Hancock was a free man, free to go where he pleased, to do anything he wanted except participate in the war. His opponents knew that Sergeant Hancock would no more violate his parole than one of King Arthur's knights would have broken a vow. "I went back to camp several times while I was a paroled prisoner," the sergeant recorded in his diary. "However, I spent most of the time among my relatives in Alabama."

And here was Barteau, needing every good man he could muster in his attempt to thwart the enemy. His companies were depleted of non-commissioned officers while Sergeant Hancock, lonesome for his comrades, was perhaps loafing around the headquarters camp at Verona with his parole in his pocket. But by the rules of the game Sergeant Hancock was out of the fighting for another month: "Being notified May 22nd that I was exchanged, I started to camp the 23rd."[1] Both the sergeant and his colonel would doubtless have preferred death to the dishonor of re-entering the action before that proper day.

Barteau could not have speculated deeply upon the ironies of the contest in which he was involved, being too close to the scenes and the actions. But irony was there in his own history. It was there in the person of Grant whose wife was a slaveholder when the war began, while he was now fighting to end slavery. And in the record of Sherman who hated war, and had tried to stop his Southern friends from war by detailing its horrors, red-

---

* Under the parole and prisoner exchange cartel between the Union and Confederate governments, it was agreed that prisoners would be exchanged man for man and rank for rank, officers to be exchanged for an equivalent of soldiers, a general being worth sixty enlisted men, a colonel fifteen men, a lieutenant four men, a sergeant two men, etc. Any excess of prisoners were to be paroled and sent home not to engage in further military activities until exchanged. "Surplus prisoners not exchanged shall not be permitted to take up arms again, nor to serve as military police or constabulary force in any fort, garrison, or field work held by either of the respective parties, nor as guards of prisoners, depots or stores, nor to discharge any duty usually performed by soldiers, until exchanged under the provisions of this cartel." — OR, ser. II, vol. 4, p. 267.

bearded Sherman who was head of a Louisiana military school and often boasted that he had more friends in the South than in the North, who wept when Louisiana seceded. Sherman, the warhater, now before Vicksburg preparing to make his name the epitome of the war and the scourge of the South.

And Pemberton, the Pennsylvania rebel who held the fate of the southwestern Confederacy in his hands, a Northerner fighting for a Southern principle. And Yankee General Hurlbut, Grierson's commander, a Carolinian with family ties in the heart of the Confederacy. And Tennessee-born Farragut, bringing his gunboats up the Mississippi to help Grant deal the death blow, Farragut whose home was in Virginia. And Josiah Gorgas, another Pennsylvanian, but now Confederate ordnance chief, who scarcely slept these days for keeping munitions and weapons flowing toward Vicksburg.

The irony was there in the suspense between actions as reported by Captain Henry Forbes of the Seventh Illinois: "I received thirteen paroled cavalry the other day at the hands of Lt. Col. Kelly of the rebel cavalry who came to our lines with them. The boys all said they were treated with distinguished kindness, and really they parted, when the Col. rode away with his escort, with many good wishes shouted out, as if they were brothers and not enemies."[2]

It was there in the respect the invaders held for the women of their opponents, the proud Southern women who took no part in the fighting but who, like heroines of their favorite novelist, Sir Walter Scott, figuratively sat in pennanted pavilions beside the jousting fields urging their men to battle without quarter.

I have been very busy for the past two or three weeks [wrote Miss Cordelia Scales of Oakland Plantation] preparing for some tableaux and charades which came off yester week. We had a great deal of fun & everyone seemed to enjoy it so much. It was some of my own getting up. I will tell you some scenes we had. I opened the exercises by singing "The Volunteer" on the guitar. A Volunteer was standing by me dressed in all his regimentals. He was an officer. Some one said he lost his heart that night & I wont say who to. I know mine is gone. The song is a new one sent by a gentleman friend of mine from New Orleans. . . .

I wish you could see me now with my hair parted on the side with my black velvet zouave on & pistol by my side & riding my fine colt, Beula. I know you would take me for a Guerilla. I never ride or walk now without my pistol. Quite warlike, you see. . . .

I met with an old schoolmate of Dabney's [her brother] from Anapolis, his name was Meriman. I liked him as well as I could a Yankee; & surprising to say he was a gentleman. I remarked to him one night that it seemed to be the policy of the Yankee government to send one or two gentlemen with every regiment to let it be known that there were some gentlemen in the north, and Col. Gilmore was present & he seemed to take it all to himself & commence to thank me for considering him one, when I turned to him & said you need not think that I consider that you fill the bill Col., that remains to be seen hereafter. You ought to have seen how blank he looked; all the officers laughed at him so much. They had a large flag waving in our grove & you could not see anything but blue coats & tents. The Col. made the band come up & play Dixie for me. . . .

The next day Captain Flynn came up; he asked me if I knew what he came for. I told him no; he then said it was to beg a great favor of me & he hoped I would be so kind as to grant it, that he wanted me to sing "My Maryland" for him. At first I thanked him & told him I did not play for Federal officers but Pa said I must that Capt. Flynn had kept us from starving & had been so kind to us so I consented. He was so much pleased with it that he got me to write the words off for him. I put a little Confederate flag at the top of it & wrote under it "no northern hand shall rule this land." He sent it on North to his wife. I wish you could have seen the parting between Capt. Flynn & myself, the Major & him & a good many officers came up to tell me goodbye & the Major was saying he was going to reduce the South to starvation and then send us north. I said to him I had rather starve to death in the South than be a beggar in the North, Major. Capt. Flynn jumped up, caught me by the hand & said "Miss Scales, You are a whole-souled Rebel & I admire you so much for it. I do wish I could stay here and protect you while our army is retreating. I'd fight for you, God knows I would." That sounds strange for a Yankee, don't it?

The next we had were the "Grierson Thieves." . . .[3]

II

Barteau had made his move, but he wondered now, standing there on the Pontotoc-Okolona road studying the markings in the damp earth, if he had checked his opponent. On his long night ride he had crossed three roads; there was another one on his left leading directly south to Houston. And the Yankees might move on any of the four.

He summoned the state troops commanders and they conferred briefly. The four companies assembled in tighter formation on the wide turnpike and then began marching towards Pontotoc. Scouts were thrown far out in front to warn of any enemy cavalry coming down from the north. The time was approximately noon when the column stopped for feeding and watering at a road junction where a small bridge crossed a creek, five miles below Pontotoc, Barteau unaware that Grierson's camp of the previous night was only three miles to the west of the Houston road.

Sometime during the nooning, his advance scouts galloped in from Pontotoc with the startling information that the enemy had moved west from the town early that morning, taking the road to Oxford!

Puzzled by this piece of information, Barteau immediately ordered his men to horse and rode briskly into Pontotoc. He suspected that his opponent had opened the day's match with a gambit.

III

Between two and three o'clock in the morning of April 20, while Barteau's regiment was moving down to the Okolona road, Grierson's buglers were waking the Union brigade. In the depressing darkness the Yankees cursed the buglers and rolled out of their damp blankets. They stumbled about in the blackness, drunk with sleep, kicking at the dying campfires, seeking for dry pieces of wood. Within a few minutes the campsite along Chiwapa Creek was choked with smoke from a hundred wavering fires.

Horses were saddled, blankets rolled, coffee was boiling in the pots and tin cans. Companies were assembled for morning reports. The commands echoed along the creek: Prepare for inspection! Prepare for inspection!

Right — Dress! Front! After almost two years it was as automatic as breathing, each trooper standing to the left of his horse, face rigid to the front, chest on a line with the horse's mouth, reins held with the right hand six inches from the horse's mouth, nails downward, body erect.

As officers and sergeants moved through the formations, the proffered carbines were given only brief glances. Most of the company commanders already knew which men they would order to fall out: a trooper who had been complaining of chills and fever, another who had suffered from dysentery all during yesterday, a wretched recruit who had chafed the inside of his crotch as raw and red as fire. As soon as the men in the ranks saw which of their comrades were falling out, they guessed the purpose of the inspection. Sick, cripples, and prisoners going back to base camp!

"I gave orders to the regimental commanders," Grierson wrote in his autobiography, "to cause a close inspection of regiments to be made with a view of selecting therefrom all men and horses any way disabled or not fit for further hard marching, in order that they might be sent back to their camp at La Grange, thus freeing the command of any encumbrance or what might become such in our onward movements."[4]

From each company two or three men were ordered to step out of ranks; two or three horses laming or showing incipient saddle sores were led to one side. "When the least effective portion of the command was sent back," said Grierson, "I inspected every man and horse in person."[5] With precision, these "least effective" men and mounts were assembled beside the road, the total assemblage numbering more than a hundred troopers from the three regiments. Platoons and squadrons were formed quickly. The dozen or so rebel prisoners were brought up and placed in position in the lengthening column. "The Quinine Brigade" some one named it, and the name caught on immediately.

Colonel Grierson, meanwhile, was finishing a letter to Brigadier-General William Sooy Smith, La Grange, Tennessee:

HEADQUARTERS FIRST CAVALRY BRIGADE
Five Miles south of Pontotoc, April 14, 1863.*

GENERAL: At 3 a.m. I send an expedition, composed of the less effective portion of the command, to return by the most direct route to La Grange. Major Love, selected to take command, will hand you this. They pass through Pontotoc in the night, marching by fours, obliterating our tracks, and producing the impression that we have all returned. I have ascertained that the bridges on the Mississippi Central Railroad, over the Yockeney, at Water Valley, have never been repaired, and I thought the forces could be used to better advantage than by sending a regiment to Oxford, as they would be obliged to return to New Albany to recross the Tallahatchee. I have ordered a single scout, however, to go from Pontotoc toward Oxford, strike the railroad, and destroy the wires.

I start at 4 o'clock in the morning, and on the night of the 20th shall be 50 miles below here. Everything looks exceedingly favorable. Rest assured that I shall spare no exertion to make the expedition as effective as possible. I may possibly find an opportunity to communicate with you again in four or five days, but do not wonder if you should not hear from me in thirty days.

---

* Although this letter is dated April 14 in the OR, it actually was written on April 20, 1863.

We have yet encountered no force except the unorganized cavalry scattered through the country. We have succeeded in killing 4 or 5, and wounding and capturing a number. The prisoners return with this expedition.

Respectfully, your obedient servant,

B. H. GRIERSON,

Colonel, Commanding Cavalry Brigade[6]

Grierson had summoned his staff, and one may imagine that they stood around a campfire near the plantation house, drying the dampness from their wool uniforms. Major Hiram Love of the Second Iowa was there, already aware of his assignment; Lieutenant Daniel Wilt of Company L, Seventh Illinois, who was to be Love's second in command; and Captain Jason B. Smith, who was not assigned to make the return journey but had been summoned to receive special orders concerning one of the two-pounder steel Woodruff guns.

As Grierson gave Major Love his orders, he attempted to impress upon him that the weak detachment's chances of getting through to La Grange in the face of the gathering enemy were long chances indeed. He handed the young officer two folded papers, one the message to General Smith, the other a short note to be mailed to his wife.

There was only a hint of a dismal gray dawn when Major Love and his detachment of 175 men, their small body of prisoners, and a string of captured horses and mules, filed out of the encampment. One of Captain Jason Smith's two-pounder cannon, with its complement of a corporal and five men, rolled down to join the procession. Above the rattle of coffee tins and harness chains the commands came hoarsely through the dripping trees: Fours, right! March! Halt! Forward, March!

The Quinine Brigade swung away beyond the wooded camp in columns of fours as ordered by Grierson, to leave behind them imprinted on the road a false story of a reversing regiment.*

Before another hour had passed, the Second Iowa, assigned to take the advance on this day, had filed out of camp and was in marching order on the clay-packed road that pointed straight south to Houston. The Sixth and Seventh Illinois followed after

---

* "The sending them by night through Pontotoc was a good ruse," Grierson said afterwards. "Making all the 'spread' they could, the people of Pontotoc believed and reported the whole column returned." — *Record of Services, 1863,* pp. 102-103.

them, and as soon as the horses were warmed up, the column began moving at a more rapid than usual rate. Trot commands were frequent throughout the morning, and the late noon stop for watering on Sakatouchee Creek was cut short.

As the brigade drove southward the sky remained heavy, mist blowing in the riders' faces. The men were hunched over their saddles, eyes half-closed against the wind and wetness. They were scarcely aware of the almost continuous stretches of young corn and wheat, unbroken except by rail fences separating the fields.

By mid-afternoon a small advance patrol of the Second Iowa was in Houston, dashing about the streets and creating a clatter designed to divert the surprised citizens while the main column slipped around the town. "I had discovered that we had left the main road," said Sergeant Surby, "and was making a new one through a wheat field of some extent; it was about six inches in height and of a beautiful green, which was a change from the mud."[7]

The wheat field itself was a change from the unvarying succession of cotton crops, the commodity upon which the Confederacy was based economically, the culture and harvesting of which had become ritualized until fixed into the fabric of slavery. But necessity brings swift changes, and now in the second growing season of the war, young wheat was standing where neither the land nor the planters had known it before. Soldiers on short rations around Vicksburg were passing a rumor around during this very month, a rumor that a large force of them would soon march north "to get as much of Tennessee as we can in order to raise more wheat and corn."

As soon as the column was beyond Houston, the three regiments turned into the road again. Grierson was hopeful that his detour would leave the more observant informers there uncertain for a time as to whether a company, a regiment, two regiments, or a brigade had passed to the south.

The road now turned southeastward, men and horses weary of the melancholy weather, the long uneventful day, the tedious hours in the saddle. Grierson kept them moving until early twilight began to close in. On the plantation of Dr. Benjamin Kilgore, just outside the village of Clear Springs, they halted for the night, each regiment seeking high dry ground for its campsite. They were twelve miles below Houston, forty miles from the morning's starting point.

IV

At corps headquarters in Memphis, General Stephen A. Hurlbut, who had issued the order setting Grierson's cavalry in motion, was after four days still very much in the dark as to the fate or accomplishments of the brigade. Hurlbut, the Southerner turned Yankee, was never at a loss, however, for conjectural opinions on the activities of the various roving units of his Sixteenth Army Corps. He dispatched frequent telegraphic messages to General Grant at Milliken's Bend and to Major-General Henry W. Halleck who was commanding the entire Union Army from Washington. Communications were never good at best in the Western theater of war, and as Memphis was then some distance from the action, perhaps Hurlbut was forced to depend upon his imagination if he was to send any messages at all.

The day after Grierson left La Grange, Hurlbut had informed General Halleck with some positiveness that the brigade would cut the Mississippi Central Railroad at Oxford, the Mobile & Ohio Railroad near Tupelo, and the Vicksburg railroad* at Chunkey River, and would then return north through Alabama.†

On this day, Hurlbut, having no news from Grierson, decided nevertheless to forward two bits of conjecture to General Grant: "My cavalry from La Grange have before this destroyed the railroad below and near Tupelo, and in the confusion may get fairly started across Alabama before they are known." As a matter of fact, throughout their four-day march none of Grierson's men had come within ten miles of the Mobile & Ohio, or Tupelo. Hurlbut's second conjecture, however, would prove to be more accurate: "Grierson will cut the railroad, if he lives, at or

---

* "Vicksburg railroad is used as an identifying phrase, not as the name of the road. In 1863 the line was known as the Vicksburg & Jackson Railroad as far east as Jackson, and as the Southern Railroad beyond that point. The name has varied through the years.

† Hurlbut had no official reason for communicating directly with the general-in-chief. Such reports properly should have been routed through Grant's headquarters, but since Grant was isolated far down the river, Hurlbut took it upon himself to keep General Halleck informed directly of activities involving the Sixteenth Army Corps.

near Chunkey Bridge, about Wednesday night or Thursday." And then he closed his message factually and to the point: "No news here of any moment. Your obedient servant, S. A. Hurlbut."[8]

V

At the same time, General Pemberton, the Yankee turned Southerner, was also in the dark as to the exact movements of Colonel Grierson's raiders. From his headquarters in Jackson, Pemberton began issuing the first of a series of orders concerning Grierson, orders which would occupy much of his thoughts during the next two weeks, a critical fortnight for the western Confederacy, a time when the commanding general should have been free to concentrate upon blocking Grant's Mississippi River crossing and strengthening the defenses of Vicksburg:

BRIGADIER-GENERAL RUGGLES, COLUMBUS:

I hear from several sources, but not your headquarters, that enemy is approaching Pontotoc. This is a mere raid, but should not be unmolested by you.   J. C. PEMBERTON.[9]

Ruggles by no means had been idle, but he was sufficiently impressed by the scolding tone of his commander's message to begin issuing reports. He explained that he had just returned to Columbus from a hurried inspection trip to Verona and Chesterville. He informed Pemberton that the Yankees had reached Pontotoc on the previous evening, but he offered no guesses as to where they might be now.

As soon as Ruggles had learned that the Second Tennessee was in pursuit of the invaders, he had dispatched the Second Alabama Cavalry under Lieutenant-Colonel James Cunningham to Okolona for the support of Barteau in the event the enemy turned toward Columbus. In his first telegraphic report back to Ruggles, Colonel Cunningham estimated the Yankees' strength at 6,000. "I have just learned from our scouts," Cunningham added, "that the enemy passed down the road leading to Houston to-day and will probably reach that place to-night. Colonel Barteau is in their rear, in pursuit of them."[10]

Ruggles immediately forwarded this message verbatim to Pemberton's headquarters. Having had considerable experience with scouts and knowing their propensities for exaggerating enemy numbers, Ruggles revised the figure in a telegram of his own to 3,000 federal soldiers.

Later in the day Ruggles received a dispatch from Captain F. Ingate, a quartermaster stationed at Okolona, also forwarding it to Pemberton: "Reliable scout reports enemy about 2,000 strong, with five mounted howitzers, on Houston road . . . Negroes report hearing them say they were going to the Southern road [the Vicksburg railroad] or Grenada."[11]

Other intelligence reports received during the day from the vicinity of Pontotoc led Ruggles to accept the estimates of 2,000 enemy cavalrymen and four field guns as a fairly accurate one, and he so informed Pemberton in his final message of the day.

Pemberton was now well apprised of the strength of the thrust into northeastern Mississippi, but he could no longer be certain whether it was a "mere raid," and, if so, what mission the raiders were attempting to perform, or whether his scattered Confederate forces in that area could intercept and turn back the swift-moving Yankee cavalrymen.

He did not know that by the day's end Lieutenant-Colonel Barteau's men had marched sixty-eight miles from their midnight starting point at Chesterville.

Barteau had lost valuable time at Pontotoc while he was making certain that the force which had marched west toward Oxford at dawn could have been no more than two companies. His suspicions that the movement was a ruse devised by his opponent to draw him off pursuit of the main body were confirmed by a reconnaissance party which followed the enemy tracks two miles west of Pontotoc. At that point it was discovered that the Yankees had turned north up a secondary road to New Albany, heading back for their Tennessee base.

Dismissing any temptation to follow this warm trail, Barteau immediately ordered pursuit of the main enemy force down the Houston road. Grierson, however, was now ten hours ahead of Barteau, and by day's end the Confederates and their horses, punished by almost twenty-four hours of continuous marching, were forced to halt a mile and a half north of Houston. They camped in battle formation, not knowing that they were thirteen miles from the Yankees below the town, and even if the two wearied forces had been close enough to battle each other on that dreary Monday evening, neither could have offered the other much of a fight.

THE BUTTERNUT GUERILLAS

Had Colonel Grierson's train from Memphis to La Grange arrived three hours later on the night of April 16, Colonel Edward Hatch, commanding the Second Iowa Cavalry Regiment, would have been commander of the entire brigade which was now raiding deep into Mississippi. This narrow twist of fate, plus the fact that he was the only officer in the brigade whose record showed any kind of military training, might have irked a less disciplined soldier than the ambitious thirty-two-year-old lumber merchant of Muscatine, Iowa.

Edward Hatch was one of the few genuine Yankees among these Westerners, having been born and brought up in Maine. After attending a Vermont military school for three years he went to sea, but soon found that the life of a sailor held no appeal for him. To earn a living he joined his father in a lumbering business in Pennsylvania. Early in 1854 young Hatch journeyed to the western plains, lived with the Indians for a while, engaged in logging operations along the Black River in Wisconsin. The following

year he moved his family to Muscatine, Iowa, continuing as a lumberman.

In the spring of 1861 his business interests brought him to Washington, D.C., and he was there the day war was declared. When rumors of an immediate invasion of the capital began flying through the city, he joined an impromptu company of soldiers who volunteered to guard the White House and other government buildings. As soon as regular soldiers arrived and the panic died away, he hurried back to Iowa with a lieutenant's commission in his pocket and became active in helping raise the Second Iowa Cavalry, eventually winning command of the regiment.[1]

Late into the night of April 20, 1863, Edward Hatch was conferring with his brigade commander, Colonel Grierson, in the plantation house of Dr. Benjamin Kilgore near the village of Clear Springs, Mississippi. From the official reports of Hatch and Grierson and from the account of Sergeant Lyman B. Pierce of the Second Iowa Regiment, it is possible to reconstruct something of what was discussed late on that Tuesday evening.

With Grierson and Hatch were Colonel Edward Prince, the ambitious commander of the Seventh Illinois, and Colonel Reuben Loomis, who had succeeded to Grierson's old command, the Sixth Illinois. Also present were First-Major Mathew H. Starr, Lieutenant-Colonel William Blackburn, and Lieutenant Samuel L. Woodward, the brigade adjutant and close friend of Grierson.

The subjects being discussed were ones which each of them probably had thought about more than once on the day now behind them: the fact that they were entering enemy territory which no other Union troops had ever invaded, and the certainty that aroused Confederate forces in formidable numbers were gathering on all sides of them.

Grierson was of the opinion that another decoy party should be thrown off — to the east this time — a party strong enough to draw off forces which General Ruggles would be sending in pursuit from the Confederates' base at Columbus. He wondered if a regiment armed with one of Captain Smith's two-pounder guns might not be able to overcome the Confederate cavalry and then make a dash for the Mobile & Ohio to burn a few bridges. He believed that it might even be possible to make a quick raid on Columbus if General Ruggles was sufficiently alarmed by now to send out the greater part of his cavalry, leaving his base open.

The main objective of the brigade, Grierson reminded his officers, was to cut the Vicksburg railroad which was still more than a hundred miles to their south, a railroad which was vital to General Pemberton's defense of the key Mississippi River fort. The principal mission of the decoy party, he added, would be to disengage the main command from the enemy pressing behind it, leaving the column free to move rapidly southward. But if the decoy party could also damage the enemy before returning to La Grange, that would be an added feather in their caps.

His staff was in general agreement that the brigade would have to throw off at least one of its three regiments if it hoped to impede the enemy as well as damage him.

But which regiment was it to be? Loomis' Sixth Illinois? Prince's Seventh Illinois? Or Hatch's Second Iowa?

It is easy to imagine Grierson during these moments of suspense, seated at a table smoking a cigar, his Colton's pocket map of the state of Mississippi spread out before him. One of his photographs of 1863 shows him sitting hunched forward, his chin resting in his long-fingered, musician's hands.

According to an observant cavalryman who served with Edward Hatch, the Iowa colonel's full blue eyes would "shine like meteors" when he was under excitement.[2] Hatch's eyes must have shone now as he saw Grierson looking at him. He and the other regimental commanders knew then that Grierson's choice was to be the Second Iowa.

In his autobiography Grierson said the reason he selected Hatch for this disengaging operation was that "his horses, on account of the hard and constant work they had been performing, were not in my judgment as suitable as those of the Seventh Illinois Cavalry, nor were the officers and men so well known to me at that time as those of the Seventh Illinois which was from my own state."[3]

Grierson's orders to Hatch were "to proceed to the Mobile and Ohio Railroad in the vicinity of West Point, and destroy the road and wires; thence move south, destroying the railroad and all public property as far south, if possible, as Macon; thence across the railroad, making a circuit northward; if practicable, take Columbus and destroy all Government works in that place, and again strike the railroad south of Okolona, and, destroying it, return to La Grange by the most practicable route."[4]

He added that he would like to have the Iowa regiment follow the main column along part of its route to Starkville, to cover the Sixth and Seventh's tracks by a reverse movement such as Major Love had made that morning. He explained that he planned to spread his forces out, cutting across country on back trails as an added measure of concealment while Hatch was deliberately attracting the attention of the pursuing enemy. Grierson also stated that he would like to attach Assistant-Surgeon Erastus D. Yule of the Second Iowa to the Seventh Illinois, as the latter regiment lacked a surgeon and was dependent upon the services of a veterinarian.

During that late night meeting, Grierson talked with Lieutenant-Colonel Blackburn, bringing up a subject which had been discussed between them on the march during the day — the need for better scouting now that they were entering unknown territory. Blackburn was enthusiastic. He had found a good man to lead the scouts, the quartermaster-sergeant of the Seventh Illinois, a former private in Blackburn's old company. Richard Surby was his name, one of the older men, around thirty years of age. He had been a railroad worker, had traveled extensively, knew the South, and could do a fair imitation of the Southern drawl.

Grierson indicated he would leave the organization of the scouts in Blackburn's hands; he wanted them out front tomorrow for the march to Starkville. Both officers agreed the scouts should discard their regulation uniforms and wear some sort of Confederate costumes, irregular pieced-out uniforms such as the shotgun guerillas usually wore. It would be dangerous if the men were caught and identified as Union soldiers; they would probably be shot as spies. Grierson wanted that fact impressed upon the scouts, and insisted that each man in the group should enter voluntarily upon the hazardous duty.[5]

Sometime during the conference, Hatch requested permission to move his regiment out of camp at three o'clock the following morning. Grierson either did not hear the request or forgot about it. The brigade had been bugled out before three o'clock on the last morning; men and horses had showed signs of it all afternoon. Grierson had in mind a start soon after dawn, with the men well rested for the hard-riding, exhausting day ahead of them. Hatch was thinking of the dangers which his men must meet alone. Perhaps it was body and bone weariness that led to the misunderstanding between Hatch and Grierson as to the time of the next morning's march. At any rate, before he retired for the night Colonel Hatch advised his regimental officers of the morrow's plans, reminding them that reveille should be sounded at three o'clock in the morning. But no similar orders appear to have been given the two Illinois regiments.

II

As was his custom, Colonel Hatch visited the Iowa camp before taking breakfast, finding the men huddled around the few surviving fires, warming their coffee and bacon and vainly attempting to dry their soggy uniforms. He bade his assistant surgeon, Erastus Yule, farewell. (On Grierson's order, Yule was transferring to duty with the Seventh Illinois, but like Hatch, the surgeon was not destined to see the end of this raid.)

Because of the misunderstanding over time of departure, Hatch waited almost three hours before the buglers finally got the Illinois regiments from under their poncho covers. The leisureliness in the Illinois camps annoyed Hatch. He could not march until the Illinois men marched. "For some reason unknown to me," he later recorded in his report, "the column did not move until 7 A.M."[6] This delay, as Hatch was to discover before the day was ended, would make it impossible for him to execute Grierson's orders.

Not long after the column passed through the sleeping village of Clear Springs, Hatch halted his regiment and ordered Company E to move a short distance along the trail taken by Grierson. He sent with this patrol the mounted two-pounder gun which had been assigned to his regiment.

Sergeant Lyman B. Pierce, the Second Iowa's regimental color bearer, has described the thoroughness of Hatch's attempts to conceal from the enemy all evidences of Grierson's departure for Starkville. "This patrol," he said, "returned in columns of fours, thus obliterating all the outward bound tracks. The cannon was turned in the road in four different places, thus making their tracks correspond with the four pieces of artillery which Grierson had with the expedition. The object of this was to deceive the rebels, who were following us, into the belief that the entire column had taken the Columbus road."[7]

III

Thirteen miles to the north, Colonel Barteau's Confederate cavalrymen were moving also, a strong advance guard well out in front, the men alert for the enemy whose signs of passage were still plain on the washed road.

Most of the men of the Second Tennessee wore Union issue ponchos,* taken individually in raids against the Yankees during the past year. They were proud of these captured ponchos, guarding them jealously when not in use, although the Union Army already considered them outmoded and was beginning to issue rubber blankets as improved replacements.

The Mississippi state troops accompanying Barteau's Tennesseans had yet to experience either a raid or a battle, and therefore possessed no captured ponchos. Some of these men, however, had wrapped their shoulders with pieces of oilcloth. ("Please send me an oilcloth to sleep upon and throw around me when it rains," a Mississippi soldier wrote to his family in 1862.[8]) Because the poncho did not keep a steady rain from leaking around the wearer's collar and saturating his blouse, and was not waterproof as a ground cover, the state troopers lucky enough to possess the undignified strips of oilcloth were probably as dry or drier than the proud wearers of the ponchos.

Weather and ponchos and oilcloths were all forgotten shortly before eleven o'clock that morning, when the Confederate column rode into Dr. Kilgore's Plantation and heard from the Negroes, still poking around in the debris of Grierson's campsite, that the enemy rear guard had marched out scarcely two hours earlier.

Barteau immediately sent his advance patrol out on the gallop, the main column following at a trot. Half an hour later the advance sighted about twenty Yankees, Hatch's rear guard, and charged them with such suddenness that the Iowans fled, scattering across country in the direction of the Starkville road. As soon as Barteau came up to this point (it was the place where Hatch

---

* The poncho which had been adopted by the United States Army after the war with Mexico, the country of its origin, was merely a piece of enameled or oiled cotton cloth about five by four feet. It was worn over the shoulders like a serape by means of a slit in the middle through which the head was thrust. The rubber blanket which was superseding the poncho was made of muslin or light cotton cloth coated on one side with rubber. It was larger, lighter, more flexible, and had no slit in the middle to admit dampness from the ground, and could be used as a tent.

had covered Grierson's tracks) he dismounted and studied the hoof markings.

On the previous day Barteau had not been misled by the stratagem of Major Love's reverse tracking. However, the movements of Love's "Quinine Brigade" had at no time offered any threat to the Mobile & Ohio Railroad which the Second Tennessee, after months of patrolling, had come to consider the primary transportation artery of the Confederacy. But this morning as Barteau and his officers studied the numerous hoofprints of Hatch's regiment, and particularly the four reversing wheel marks of the two-pounder cannon, they were quickly convinced that the main column of the Yankee raid had finally turned toward their valued railroad.

Had Barteau not been thinking solely of the Mobile & Ohio and of the security of Columbus beyond it, had he taken time to search more thoroughly a few hundred yards to the south and west, he would have found the tracks of twice as many horses, scattered by single platoons, with the curves of the iron shoe markings turned toward another railroad, one much more vital to the Confederates' cause. But it never entered Barteau's mind that any Yankee cavalry force would dare to ride the hundred perilous miles south to that other railroad — the idea was a fantastic one — and the few tracks which he and his men did see heading away to the south he dismissed as belonging to the rear guard which his advance party had scattered as his column had come up to them.[*]

Once he had made up his mind, Barteau did not hesitate. He set his column moving rapidly in pursuit of Hatch down the eight miles of muddy road to Palo Alto, convinced that at last he had the main column of the tricky Federals trapped for good and all.

Shortly after twelve o'clock the rain slackened, and Barteau was probably wondering if he should halt his column for a midday bivouac. But suddenly, as they approached the wooded ridge before Palo Alto, a carbine cracked somewhere ahead.

"Trot, march! Gallop, march!"

As his horse lunged over the top of a rise in the road, Barteau

---

[*] Grierson described this deception in his *Record of Services:* "It had lately rained, and the freshest tracks pointing *backwards,* led the enemy when they examined the trail three hours afterward, to believe that the whole command had marched eastward from Clear Springs toward Columbus." — RS, p. 103.

saw them, the dark column of the enemy, moving slowly into a
lane a mile away, their picket troop straggling behind in a yet
unformed rear guard company.

"To the charge!" The bugle was going and the flying horses'
hooves were splattering mud as the Tennesseans spread out in
ragged platoon lines, the animals faltering and slithering on the
gummy earth. In a matter of minutes they swept around the rear
guard, the squadron of Iowans staring at their captors in stunned
surprise as they were forced to dismount and drop their arms.

As he galloped forward, Barteau studied the landscape, a fal-
low field, beyond it a church, a neck of woods, and the long lane
into which the surprised Yankee column was moving, a lane
bordered on one side by a high rail fence thickly webbed with
brush and young white-trunked oaks, on the other by a hedgerow.
Barteau immediately saw the lane as a trap in which to box the
Yankees. Already they were dismounting and firing on the first
wave of the Confederate charge. He ordered the men bugled back
("Rally by fours!") and called up his officers. He sent Major
George Morton with four companies of the Second Tennessee in
a swinging dash around the lane to its far end, with orders to hold
while the remaining Confederates attacked the enemy rear.

Major Morton performed his task perfectly, but the Confederates could not get at the Yankees in their thick cover, and the
Yankees would not come out of the lane to fight. After skirmishing for almost two hours, Barteau finally decided to try different
tactics, as he later reported: "I placed Smith's regiment and
Ham's four companies immediately in his [Hatch's] front, dismounted, and, protected by the church, a small number of trees,
and the brow of a slight eminence. I gave instructions that should
the enemy advance on them to reserve their fire until he should
arrive close enough to make it destructive and deadly, and to
hold the position until a charge should be made fully in his rear;
that I would move the Second Tennessee and Major Inge's battalion around to his rear and make the charge as soon as
possible."[9]

Barteau may have forgotten that few of the state troops had
been under fire before. He may have underestimated the frighten-
ing effects of the two-pounder cannon which Colonel Hatch had
moved into firing position within the hedged lane. At any rate,
before Barteau's charge was well under way the Yankees burst

out upon Smith's and Ham's troops, who "retreated in the utmost disorder, although everything was done which could have been by these two officers to make them stand."[10]

Sergeant George Hager of Barteau's Company B said later that the attack on Hatch's Iowa cavalry "would have been complete and we would have captured his whole command, had not a battalion of Mississippi state troops which had joined us on the march given way in disorder on one side as we charged on the other. We had him forced between two hedges with only one outlet, but as it was we gave him a lively chase."[11]

At the moment that Colonel Hatch opened up with the two-pounder cannon, Lieutenant-Colonel James Cunningham was leading his Second Alabama Cavalry slowly northwest from West Point, less than ten miles from Palo Alto. Cunningham had just received a scout's report from Sparta, informing him that Yankee cavalry was raiding in that vicinity, and when he heard the cannonading he erroneously assumed that the battle sounds came from Sparta instead of Palo Alto. As Sparta was a half day's march from his position, he decided to stop for a noon bivouac.

Thus the confusion which Grierson had hoped to create by throwing off Hatch's Second Iowans to the east was working to the Union raiders' advantage. Cunningham's informer had seen Grierson's men near Sparta and the Alabama officer had no way of knowing that Hatch's regiment was closer at hand. If, instead of halting for noon feeding, the Second Alabama cavalrymen had galloped forward to Palo Alto with their three pieces of artillery to reinforce Barteau's men, Colonel Edward Hatch's predicament would have been grave indeed.[12]

IV

A view of the Palo Alto fight from the Union side is necessary to complete the story, and a Southern newspaper furnishes an interesting sidelight on the mood of Hatch's Iowans immediately before they were attacked. "At one house," reported the Richmond (Virginia) *Examiner*, "a portion stopped and called for milk. This was handed them in fine cut-glass goblets, which, after they drank the milk, they dashed to pieces on the ground."[13]

Whether or not this long-range report was accurate in detail, there is no doubt that by high noon of Tuesday, April 21, most of the men of the Second Iowa were in a fit mood to smash cut-glass goblets. They resented being cut loose from the exhilarating mission of the main column; they were still grumbling over being roused out of their wet blankets into a wetter darkness at three o'clock in the morning. Their breakfasts had been scanty, their coffee cold, and then they had sat their mounts until dawn waiting for the sluggish Illinois regiments to start marching.

Colonel Hatch, sensing their deepening moroseness, ordered the midday halt earlier than he had originally intended. The column had covered less than ten miles, but he guessed that a few pots of coffee set to boiling while the horses were being watered would help to speed the afternoon's march.

Some of his mounts were also showing the effects of strain, and as soon as the regiment halted near a neck of woods, he ordered a detail of twenty-five men sent out into a forest on the flank to search for concealed horses.

The brief but unhurried halt, the slackening rain, and the hot coffee improved the men's spirits, and by the time Company E rode in some of them were laughing and joking. Company E, which had marched behind Grierson to cover his tracks, had been acting as rear guard, and its arrival was a signal for the other companies to prepare to move out.

Most of the men were already in their saddles, the advance companies turning back upon the road into the hedged lane, when Colonel Hatch heard in the distance a sudden rush of running horses and the crack of a carbine. He whirled his horse about, shouting an order to keep the column moving into the lane, and watched the first wave of the Confederate charge spinning out from the road, the lines jagged from the bad footing. Lowering his reins, he rode quickly into the lane, which he saw as excellent cover for his troops rather than a trap as his enemy Barteau was seeing it.

"Prepare to fight — on foot!"

Company H was on picket [said Sergeant Lyman B. Pierce]. They gallantly repulsed the first charge made by the rebels, and aided by Company E held the enemy in check until Hatch could form a line, which he did in the edge of timber, where his men, being covered by the trees, could command with their rifles the open field in their front, across which the enemy must advance. Our little cannon was placed in a favorable position, and did good service, notwithstanding the rebels had made their brags at a house at the edge of the field that they wanted but three minutes in which to capture it.

The rebels formed beyond rifle range, and came down on a charge. Our boys kept the cover of the trees until they were within short range, when they opened upon them such a murderous fire from their trusty revolving rifles that they were not only repulsed, but stampeded and scattered all over the wood.* The rebels acknowledged a loss of twenty-five in this skirmish, and citizens said their loss was much heavier. Owing to the completeness of our cover not a drop of Yankee blood was shed.[14]

As the Yankees surged out from the hedged lane, the Confederate guards assigned to the Iowans captured in the first charge also fled with the Mississippi state troops, leaving their captives free. Hatch pushed the state troops back for three miles, and "from that time until dark it was a constant skirmish."[15]

At nightfall the positions of the contending forces were reversed from what they had been at the time of attack. Barteau's Tennesseans were now between the Yankees and the Mobile & Ohio Railroad, digging in for the night, certain that they had at least won a minor victory by blocking a force which they believed to be the main column of Yankee raiders. When morning came, and with it reinforcements, they would send the invaders flying.

Colonel Hatch, however, had no intention of remaining where he was until morning. By that time scouts might bring the rebels news of Grierson's column driving southward. "Believing it was important to divert the enemy's cavalry from Colonel Grierson," he later reported, "I moved slowly northward, fighting by the rear, crossing the Houlka River, and drawing their forces immediately in my rear."[16]

V

Meanwhile Grierson was moving rapidly toward Starkville. Near the village of Montpelier, he halted briefly. "While seated on my horse," he said afterward in his autobiography, "I hastily wrote with pencil a few lines to Mrs. Grierson; the note was entrusted to a scout whom I had selected to send west to the Central Railroad to cut the telegraph lines and to proceed thence by the most practicable route to La Grange, where he arrived in

* Hatch's First and Second Battalions were armed with Colt's Revolving rifles, and he had trained these men like infantrymen. As Sergeant Pierce said, they figured "less in dashing exploits, but did more hard fighting." The Third Battalion armed with sabers and carbines did most of the charging for the regiment.

due time after performing the duty assigned him, mailed my letter and reported our whereabouts to General Smith."[17]

The Illinois regiments marched steadily southward, the men in the ranks silent and thoughtful under the dismal rain. They had grown accustomed to having the Iowans marching on their flank or in column with them, and the knowledge that the brigade had lost a third of its strength left them for the first few hours with a strange feeling of vulnerability. Those who had been certain ever since leaving La Grange that the fifth day would bring them to Columbus for a raid knew now that they were on a different and undoubtedly more dangerous mission.

"Various were the opinions expressed by the men as to our destination," observed Sergeant Surby.

But as the morning wore on and the two regiments formed a solid column on the Starkville road, the men became occupied with the difficulties of fording numerous swollen streams. Before the stop for noon feeding, "they felt equal to any task and, notwithstanding the heavy rain that was falling, they were cheerful and enlivened the march with songs and jokes," Surby said.

Probably the most cheerful of them all was Lieutenant-Colonel William Blackburn, who under the worst adversities which can befall a cavalryman always maintained an ebullient front. And today, full of romantic plans for his scouts, he disregarded the wretched weather and kept his beautifully maned mount galloping up and down the road in front of the column.

Had William Blackburn lived longer than the twenty-six more days which fate allotted to him, he might very well have become the "Jeb" Stuart of the Union Army, for there was an insouciant, extravagant quality in his character matching that of the brilliant Virginian. To Blackburn, the war was a merry frolic. He loved long hard rides and dashing charges, and if any member of Grierson's raiders deserved to wear a plume in his hat, Blackburn was the man.

He was a handsome, ruddy-cheeked officer, taller and larger than most men, so that his uniform always appeared to be stretched tight across his body. One of the few surviving manu-

---

* Grierson's note to his wife was as follows: "April 21, 1863, from Clear Springs, 12 m. So. or E. of S. of Houston. All well April 21st. Tuesday 6 o'clock a.m. — Montpelier, 7 o'clock. 16 mi. from Houston, about 18 miles to Starkville. All O. K."

scripts in the files of the Seventh Illinois which carries Blackburn's bold signature is indicative of his character: "Found the 'rebs' thick from Salem to Wolf, but in small squads and as wild as ducks; distributed the force in all directions, and had plenty of chases, a good many shots, and a few captures."[18]

While he was commanding Company A, Blackburn had been attracted to a kindred spirit in his ranks, Sergeant Richard Surby. Surby was a Canadian, a hardy outdoorsman, who had left home at fifteen and made his way up and down North America, working several years for the Great Western and New York Central Railroads. In April, 1861, he was living in Edgar County, Illinois, and when the call for volunteers came he decided to join up with a cavalry company which Blackburn (then a livestock dealer) was organizing at Paris. Before they left Camp Butler, Surby had won the rank of second duty sergeant.

Richard Surby was, in his own words, "possessed of a venturesome disposition," and it is possible that a conversation he had with Blackburn led to the organization of the scouts. In his account of the raid, he claimed credit for the plan. "Colonel Blackburn," he added, "had full permission to organize and control the scouts; it was not long before I was ordered to report to him, and was somewhat surprised when he requested me to act as scout, and take command of a squad of men. This suited me, and without hesitation I accepted the position with thanks, fully resolved not to abuse the confidence reposed in me. I received orders to take six or eight men, proceed at once on the advance and procure citizens dress, saddles, shot guns and everything necessary for our disguise. It did not take long to do this, and by noon reported myself and men ready for duty."[19]

Surby gave no details of how he procured the "Secesh" apparel; undoubtedly he and his squad confiscated the articles from farmhouses along the road to Starkville. Almost any Southern home had some parts of the Confederate war dress, which never throughout the war was uniform in cut or color. As one of John Hunt Morgan's rebel raiders said, their clothing was uniform only in its variety. Until October, 1862, Confederate soldiers had provided their own clothing in exchange for commutation, a necessary arrangement because of a lack of clothing factories in the South and one which naturally created a variegated dress. Gray was official and traditional, but more often than not the color was butternut brown, the clothing being dyed either in copperas solution or walnut hulls. Confederate soldiers often sent Union blue blouses, trousers, and overcoats home from the battle-fields to have the color changed, and many a southern wife or sister had learned to make copperas dye by soaking old iron in a cask of water impregnated with salt and vinegar.

Partisan rangers, state troops, and guerillas wore an even more individualistic dress, and as the scouts hoped to pass for these irregular Confederates, the necessary disguises were fairly easy to come by. Gray slouch hats, gray shirts, butternut jeans — anything except blue would suffice.

Blackburn and Surby selected all the scouts from the Seventh Illinois, probably because they knew most of them personally. They were William Buffington, Arthur Wood, and Isaac Robinson from Company B; George Steadman from Company C; Charles Weedon and Licurgus Kelly from Company E; Samuel Nelson from Company G; and Uriah Fowler from Company H. Each man was armed with two pistols, some of them taken from Confederates already captured along the path of the raid. Four Sharp's carbines and four shotguns and a sporting rifle were divided among them, and four scouts carried sabers.

"Riding up through the nooning bivouac of the Sixth Illinois, we excited some little curiosity," Sergeant Surby recorded, "and sold the boys completely. They thought we were prisoners and bored us with a thousand questions. After this we went by the name of 'The Butternut Guerillas.' "[20]

As soon as they could eat a hasty lunch and meet for brief instructions from Colonel Blackburn, the scouts gave their bundled blue uniforms and their army carbines over to the care of friends in their companies, and rode out in front of the column again. Blackburn's orders to Surby were to keep a quarter of a mile to two miles in advance, to obtain all possible information about the roads, many of which were not shown on Grierson's small map.

The scouts were to report back regularly what they could learn of the roads' destinations, distances and conditions, the number

---

* "Butternuts" had become a nickname for rebel soldiers because of the color of their uniforms. In this very year of 1863 sympathizers for the Confederacy in the North began wearing butternut emblems to indicate their preference for the Southern cause. — *Illinois State Journal*, May 8, 1863.

of streams and whether bridged or fordable, and before noon and nightfall of each day they were to search out favorable camping sites near forage and water. When talking with farmers and hunters along the way, they were to pose as members of Tennessee Confederate units.

To protect himself and his scouts from their own comrades, Sergeant Surby devised a system of simple signals and passwords which would identify them as the Butternut Guerillas, and he carefully explained these to the different advance squadrons whenever there was a change of march order.

In the middle of the afternoon of this first day of scouting, Surby was riding unobtrusively into Starkville, finding it deserted in the rain. He reported back to Colonel Blackburn that there was no evidence of enemy soldiers in or around the town, and by four o'clock the sodden column was marching in at a trot.

Few Starkville citizens had seen Yankee soldiers before this day, and although rumors of their coming had reached the town, the people were obviously surprised to see so many cavalrymen in blue.

None of the participants in the raid seems to have left any detailed accounts of the brief halt in Starkville. Grierson merely reported that they captured a mail and a quantity of Government property, which they destroyed.

The Columbus (Mississippi) *Republic* was more explicit:

At Starkville they robbed the inhabitants of horses, mules, negroes, jewelry and money; went into the stores and threw their contents (principally tobacco) into the street or gave it to the negroes; caught the mail boy and took the mail, robbed the postoffice, but handed back a letter from a soldier to his wife, containing $50.00, and ordered the postmaster to give it to her. Doctor Montgomery was taken prisoner and kept in camp all night, six miles from town, and allowed to return home next morning, after relieving him of his watch and other valuables. Hale & Murdock's hat wagon, loaded with wool hats, passing through at the time was captured. They gave the hats to the negroes and took the mules. Starkville can boast of better head covering for its negroes than any other town in the state.[21]

Sergeant Surby had gone ahead with the scouts, and a mile or two down the Louisville road they captured two Confederate soldiers, one a lieutenant on leave from Vicksburg. The lieutenant, according to Surby, "was seated in a fine buggy with a beautiful span of iron gray horses attached; the horses Colonel Grierson assigned to the battery."

The land lay lower now; streams were more numerous and all were overflowing their banks. For more than a mile the column floundered through a swamp, the horses belly deep in mud, a forlorn-looking column, with the water pouring from the men's hat brims and running down their ponchos.

As darkness came on, they had to swim the horses across a rushing stream. Five miles below Starkville, Grierson ordered a halt near one of the swollen branches of Talking Warrior Creek. In the midst of a violent rainstorm, men and horses huddled together under the low-hanging trees.

A MISSION FOR CAPTAIN FORBES

"The most reliable intelligence we receive," said Henry Forbes, "is through Negro slaves."[1]

From Negroes who had attached themselves to the brigade at Starkville, Grierson learned of the location of a large tannery and leather factory, and as he surveyed the soggy condition of his camping site by lantern light, he decided that he might as well put a battalion to work on that factory. Most of the horses, he knew, required a few hours' rest; the men needed rest, too, but they would be miserable bivouacked in the rain and this miasmic swamp in which it was impossible to build fires to smoke away the mosquitoes. He believed that all except the weariest of his troopers would as soon be having some excitement as lying there in the dark letting the insects bite into them.

Grierson chose Major John Graham's First Battalion of the Seventh Illinois to make the five-mile march to the tannery. Within a few minutes, Graham's battalion was saddling up to start a nightmare ride through almost total darkness,

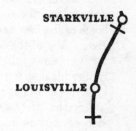

swimming bayous, wading swamps, and dodging overhanging tree limbs. They found the tannery exactly where the Negroes said it would be, a pine-board building recently enlarged by the Confederate government. A lantern was burning in one of the unglazed windows.

Major Graham's men quietly surrounded the factory. One platoon dismounted and rushed the section lighted by the lantern. A startled Confederate quartermaster, and a group of workmen checking supplies for shipment to the quartermaster's headquarters at Port Hudson, surrendered without resistance.

Graham made a quick inspection of the tannery and was surprised at the quantity of boots, shoes, saddles, and bridles already packed and marked for shipment to Vicksburg. He ordered his men to fire the building, and as soon as it was in full blaze they turned back to rejoin the brigade, taking the rebel quartermaster with them.[2]

At dawn the Sixth Illinois began moving out to ride advance for the day, the men considerably cheered to find the skies clearing. The night had indeed been a miserable one of mud, mosquitoes, and the continual throbbing of deep-throated bullfrogs. Some of the men had slept on fence rails, as described by Private Henry Eby of the Seventh: "Three or four rails were used under me with some rubbish on top of them. My saddle for a pillow, rubber blanket for a cover, and hat over my face. This rail bed kept my body out of the water."

Grierson, too, was relieved to see that the rain had finally stopped, but he knew that progress over the route to Louisville would be slow and tortuous because of the flooding. He also knew that by now the Confederate command would be learning of his passage through Starkville and would recognize Hatch's movement toward West Point as only a part of the main Union column. The rebel telegraph lines would be busy this morning with orders and counterorders setting Confederate troops in motion to stop the invaders.

And where would the rebels expect him to strike? Grierson studied his pocket map and found the place he wanted the rebels to *believe* he was driving for; it was the town of Macon on the Mobile & Ohio Railroad, thirty miles to the southeast. Grierson reasoned that if he could convince the enemy that Macon was his objective, he would be free for at least another day to drive on unhampered into the heart of Mississippi.

While the Seventh Regiment was following the Sixth out of the bivouac area, Grierson conferred with Colonel Prince, and then made his decision. He would send one company on a quick dash toward Macon, with orders to create as much attention as possible there, cutting the telegraph lines and destroying a railroad bridge if possible. He wanted a good company strongly loyal to a good captain.

The company chosen was B Company; the commander, Captain Henry Forbes.*

II

Captain Henry Clinton Forbes was a sensitive, well-read farming man who usually carried a copy of Emerson's *Conduct of Life* in his saddlebag, a man subject to shifting moods of elation and despair, and who regarded the war as a great personal tragedy. He disliked military life intensely but had a high sense of duty and a sincere belief in the precepts of his times.

In 1861, after the harvests were gathered on the farms along the tier of Illinois counties adjoining Wisconsin, the young men had begun volunteering, and on a September day Henry Forbes and his younger brother Stephen went over to Cedarville to enlist in a cavalry company. The members of this company called themselves the "Winnesheaks," and taking their own horses and some of their dogs, drifted down to Camp Butler for training. Henry Forbes, being older than most of the others, was elected captain, and the Winnesheaks became Company B of the Seventh Illinois.

Captain Forbes, who had been acting the role of father in his fatherless family, continued the same role at Camp Butler. When his boys failed to get their pay on time he lent them money; when tobacco and gloves were not issued he purchased enough for the company on his own credit, trusting the boys until pay

---

* The New York *Times* (May 18, 1863) account of this incident states that Grierson first decided to send two scouts to Macon, and that Private Post of the Second Iowa and Private Parker of the Sixth Illinois volunteered, then "backed out at last from the perilous undertaking." Neither Surby nor the Forbes accounts mention any such plan, or the reluctant volunteers. Furthermore, the Second Iowa was no longer with Grierson when the column came opposite Macon, and no Private Post is listed on that regiment's rosters.

day. When cold weather came suddenly in October and there were no blankets available, he took leave, went home, and collected blankets from all over his county. He shipped sixteen boxes of bedding down to Springfield.

After more than a year and a half, Company B had lost its share of men from disease and wounds and other men had come to take their places, but they were still the Winnesheaks at heart, one big male family with Captain Henry Forbes the paternal leader — stern, just, and kindly — his boys ready to follow him through hellfire with the fierce loyalty of a blood clan.

Now on this morning of April 22, Captain Forbes saw cantering towards him alongside the column his commander, Colonel Edward Prince. Prince turned his horse about, riding easily beside the captain, and without preliminaries began explaining the necessity for another feint toward the Mobile & Ohio. The delusion must be maintained, the colonel explained, that the Mobile & Ohio was the main object of attack. The brigade was still ninety miles from its real objective, the Vicksburg railroad, sole artery of supplies for the Confederate armies at Jackson and Vicksburg.

To mask the real purpose of the raid, would Captain Forbes undertake with his company to approach Macon, break the railroad, and cut the telegraph wires? Afterwards it was possible, though only faintly possible, that Captain Forbes might be able to rejoin the Seventh Regiment.

"What course will the brigade take after destroying the Vicksburg railroad?" asked Captain Forbes.

Colonel Prince assured the captain that he could give him no positive information as to the course the brigade would take. It seemed highly probable they would swing eastward into Alabama, retreating northward to the Federal lines. This element of uncertainty, he admitted, naturally increased the dangers challenging the commander of the detached company.

Prince offered a few suggestions, and after he had finished speaking, Forbes evidently asked permission to have three of his men return to Company B from special duties with Sergeant Surby's Butternut Guerillas. He wanted William Buffington, Isaac Robinson, and Arthur Wood. Prince agreed to release the scouts and Forbes sent a man up column to recall them.

Before turning to gallop forward to the head of his regiment,

Prince added as an afterthought: "If too strong a Confederate force should be at Macon, the Captain should try and cross the Noxubee and move toward Decatur in Newton County, by the shortest route."[3] Colonel Grierson, he explained, expected to pass through Decatur sometime during the next forty-eight hours.

At the first break in the heavy woods cover, Captain Forbes ordered his lead squadron off the road. He was thinking of the half dozen or more partly disabled men and mounts in Company B. He would detach them to another company. He was thinking of his younger brother, Stephen, nineteen years old — Stephen to whom he had been a father since the boy was ten — of the bitter irony of Stephen's being caught in this wild mission on his first field duty after seven months' absence, four in rebel prisons, three in that Rhode Island hospital where Henry had gone all the long way from Illinois to see him. (The difficulties of obtaining the furlough had seemed insurmountable, but he had been bound to see if the boy was all right.) Stephen was a quiet one, but Henry had heard him say he would prefer death to being captured again.[4]

The last platoon of Company B turned off the muddy road, the horses pressing flank to flank as Lieutenant William McCausland and the sergeants struggled vainly to form presentably dressed lines in the boggy swamp.

Captain Forbes sat stiffly on his horse, facing the forty men. He explained briefly what was expected of Company B. He was confident that Company B could accomplish the task. If any man felt physically unable to gallop march by day and by night without rest, he might voluntarily withdraw from the expedition without prejudice on his record. If any man suspected that his mount could not perform the same task, he should report now.

Four or five men reported failing horses, but in the end it was Forbes who rode stiffly down the line, his mount splashing water at every step, and ordered several men detached. There is no record that he spoke to his brother, Stephen, who would have been sitting at attention, his elbows held out, his cavalry hat set rakishly, his solemn boy's face probably flecked with tiny dried dots of gray mud, his eyes staring off into space like a proper trooper at attention.

They marched all day, thirty-five men of Company B and Captain Henry Forbes, trotting and galloping much of the way, straight into the eastern sun until they were near the Confederate's picket line along the Mobile & Ohio. Somewhere below Artesia Depot, after they had moved swiftly out of the bottomlands and approached the hilly higher ground where the railroad ran, they turned south toward Macon.

Young Stephen Forbes, riding near the head of the little column, was the only one of the company who had looked upon this particular stretch of enemy country before this day. When he realized they were traveling near Artesia Depot, he must have remembered that name with dark dread.

Almost a year ago the thing had begun, somewhere around Corinth, a June day, the sun brighter than now. He had ridden right into the midst of them in the woods, the Confederates calling: "Hey, Yank!"

"What do you want?"

"Want you, Yank."

They had taken him to a place called Baldwyn where he had talked back to their colonel, Colonel Wirt Adams, a Mississippian. Adams had roared at him, a hot-blooded rebel he was.

And then because Stephen was a message bearer they had taken him to General Bragg's headquarters near Blackland, with Old Bragg sitting there on the porch of a house with two or three of his officers, just like in a picture.* They didn't get a thing out of him, and neither did Beauregard's men. They must have thought he knew something important, taking him right up to Beauregard's headquarters. He had seen Beauregard close up, the military moustache that gave him a foreign air, his hair nearly white. Old Beauregard had looked sick to death that day.

He remembered Artesia Depot. The rebels had shuttled him and the other prisoners down there from Columbus. The guards had been decent enough fellows. It had been hotter than an oven in the freight cars under that broiling Mississippi sun, and the guards had known it would be a long time before the main line train came down the Mobile & Ohio to hook them on for the long ride to prison.

---

* Stephen Forbes's full description of General Braxton Bragg: "He is a tall, slim man, rather awkward in his appearance, has dark eyes not quite black, wears a short black goatee and grey hair, has a face rather impatient and irate in expression, a little inclined to be contemptuous, and conveys a general impression of a man who would require a great deal more of others than of himself."—FFL, Stephen Forbes's prison journal, June, 1862.

He had written some of it down later, on the twelve sheets of paper he had paid a dollar for when he was in a Mobile prison that had once been an old slave house. "We were marched around to the shady side of the Artesia depot," Stephen wrote, "where with the guards ranged in front of us, we speedily became the special objects of curiosity to almost the entire population of the hamlet."

A home guard armed with a double-barreled shotgun wanted to kill them then and there. "Kill the Yankees, damn 'em, they every one of 'em ought to be hung! I be damn if I don't burn two or three Yankees yet before this war is over."

The Confederate captain in charge of the prisoners forbade any more talking.

They slept upon the depot platform all night, waiting for a train which finally arrived at eight o'clock the next morning when they resumed their journey in the freight car. They ran until night, the train rarely moving faster than eight or ten miles an hour, "through a varied country, sometimes extremely rich, bearing corn four or five feet high, and sometimes covered with pines. Bare and hilly regions were followed by wet and swampy tracts, intersected by slow almost stagnant streams of inky-looking water which crept lazily through the masses of tangled underwood."[5]

Stephen Forbes did not describe his emotions on his second venture into this same enemy country, almost a year after his capture, but he must have been pleased to be galloping so rapidly and so free, putting Artesia Depot farther behind him. Once during the afternoon the company moved in closer to the railroad than they intended. They heard the shrill, querulous little whistle, and then off through the trees saw black pine-wood smoke curling from the bellied stack as the engine racked along, its cars swaying madly over the uneven tracking.

Stephen remembered a ride on such a train; they had been transferring him from one prison to another, carrying the two books he'd bought in Mobile, the Holy Bible and Crosby's *Grammar of the Greek Language;* he remembered how they had let him go into town to buy the books, a guard following him with a shotgun, and the people staring at him on the street.

He remembered the ride in the open flat car covered with canvas over a wooden frame: *We were attached directly behind the engine and the road was rough and wild, and we started out at a tearing rate with the wind blowing strong in our faces. We sat as tight as we could well be packed, swaying to and fro with the motion of our shrieking, smoking engine, and with red countenances and watery eyes . . . making wry faces at the shower of cinders and floods of steam, while the ragged pine trees and rough hillocks flew by us with a rush as we plunged through deep cuts, rattled over bridges, and flew along through dark forests.*[6]

While the train whistled past, Captain Forbes halted the column among the pines, the men holding their horses as motionless as possible until it disappeared with a gray-black streamer of smoke fading away across the sky.

They rode steadily southward then, halting only occasionally to unbit and water their mounts. "As we marched toward Macon," Captain Forbes recorded, "we found ourselves in the midst of the left-hand crest of the panic-stricken overflow from the main march. As our march cut through this course diagonally, near evening we got outside it and approached Macon, and we were all alert to know whether or not the town was garrisoned. We fed and supped, threw out a little picket to the front, and, turning a fence across the road to obstruct riders, awaited developments."[7]

They did not have long to wait. The company had halted on the Augustus Plantation less than three miles from Macon; about nine o'clock a young Confederate scout, John Bryson, came out from town riding a regular patrol. Concealed along the road, the Yankee pickets took him in easily and brought him immediately to Captain Forbes.

Forbes treated Bryson like one of his boys, gave him coffee and tobacco, and asked a few casual questions. "Much diplomacy was finally rewarded," the captain said, "with a statement that a train loaded with infantry and a battery of artillery was expected any moment in Macon."

Unknown to Captain Forbes, earlier in the evening a Macon citizen named Dinsmore had heard rumors from some of the town Negroes that a Union force was at the Augustus Plantation. As news of Grierson's raid on Starkville had reached the Macon area during the day, Dinsmore was inclined to believe the rumors.

He rode out toward the camp, tied his horse in the woods, walked to the slave quarters and asked the Negroes if the Yankees were there. The frightened slaves said they were there, all right, in the plantation house eating supper. Dinsmore hurried back to Macon, hoping to gather a force of armed citizens to attack the raiders, but as the Macon *Beacon* declared in its next issue: "Not ten men could be raised about Macon to attack them. At 3:00 o'clock in the morning 2,000 of our troops came up from Meridian, but they were either not informed of the presence of the Federal company or did not choose to disturb the repose of our quondam friends." The *Beacon* did not explain, however, that rumors current in Macon the night of April 22 set the number of Yankees outside the town at 5,000 troops, and that it was some time afterwards before the truth was known.

Captain Forbes said that his scouts heard "a great whistling of engines" that night, and he suspected they heralded the arrival of Confederate troops reported by the rebel scout, John Bryson. "We thought it best," he added, "to consider Macon too large a prize to be captured by thirty-six men. Had we revealed our numbers by venturing among the enemy, they would have swallowed us up as a half mouthful, but as it was, they treated our Company with the most distinguished respect. Meanwhile we accomplished what we were sent for; we kept all eyes on the Mobile & Ohio Railroad."

III

During the morning of April 22, Captain Forbes's Company B and Colonel Grierson's main column were moving in directions almost opposite, Forbes marching eastward while Grierson was swinging westward along the Whitefield road to avoid the direct but impassable trail which cut across six flooding creeks, headwaters of the Noxubee.

Even this extended route was extremely difficult in the low, swampy bottoms. According to Grierson, they marched "for miles belly-deep in water, so that no road was discernible."[8]

Surby's Butternut Guerillas, operating without William Buffington, Isaac Robinson, and Arthur Wood, who had gone with Captain Forbes to Macon, found no difficulty in persuading the inhabitants of this insulated back country that they were Confederate soldiers. Indeed, many of the people accepted the mud-camouflaged main column as a rebel troop. Isolated by the floods, they had heard nothing of a Yankee raid. Once when the column passed a schoolhouse, the teacher called recess and the children raced out to the roadside, cheering the muddy horsemen for loyal Confederates.*

The scouts, growing more expert in their assigned duties, gained the favor of the countrymen and easily located several droves of mules and horses, including some of the finest Mississippi racing stock. Surby would leave one scout to inform Colonel Blackburn, and when the column came up Blackburn would send a squad out into the woods to find the animals. They would sometimes bring in as many as twenty-five horses and mules at a time. Broken-down mounts could now be cut loose from the column, and the herd of led horses was rapidly improved in quality.

Late in the morning Surby and three of his men were passing a large plantation house.

My attention was suddenly attracted by a motion made at one of the windows. I gave the order to halt; no sooner done than the front door flew open and three lovely looking females dressed in white appeared at the opening, their faces beaming with smiles, and in a voice soft and sweet invited us to dismount and come in. . . . Various were the questions asked about the "Yanks" all of which we could answer satisfactorily; they informed us their father and brothers were in the Confederate Army.

One of the boys complained of being hungry; no sooner said than one of the ladies ran into the house, and soon returned with two black servants following, loaded down with eatables; we had to accept half a ham, that would make a hungry man laugh; biscuits, sweet cakes, fried sausage, and peach pie, all in abundance were pressed upon us, while one of the young ladies plucked some roses and presenting one to each bade us adieu, with many blessings and much success in our "holy cause"; on my way back I met a company of the Sixth Illinois, and cautioned them to still deceive the "ladies," and I presume it was some time ere they learned how bad they had been sold.[9]

Later, when they approached another plantation house, Surby and his men walked right into a pair of rebel soldiers home on furlough. In their Secesh clothing the scouts were immediately accepted as comrades by the two Confederates, who invited them

---

* "They flocked to the roadside, hurrahing for Beauregard, Van Dorn, and the Confederacy. One little girl thought she recognized one of the men, and running up asked where John was, and if her uncle was along." — Grierson's *Record of Services*, 1863.

into the house. When Surby announced that some Yankees were coming, the two rebels excitedly called to their Negro servants to saddle horses for flight.

Having told them that we would accompany them some distance [Surby wrote], the demijohn was brought out, glasses placed upon the table, and a cordial invitation given to help ourselves to some "old rye," which invitation a soldier never refuses. . . . We started out, the young men armed with shotguns, eight negroes following with fourteen mules and six fine horses. It was about one and a half miles to the road, upon which the column was advancing, and in the direction that we were going; when about half way I had a curiosity to examine their guns, which they seemed proud to exhibit; making a motion to one of my men he followed suit, thus we had them disarmed.[10]

The Confederates joined in the laughter that followed. It was a good joke, they had been careless, but they were old soldiers, they didn't fool easily. "We soon came in sight of the column," Surby continued, "when our Confederate friends 'smelt a rat,' and with downcast countenances became uncommunicative. Shortly after this we passed through Whitefield, a small place of little importance."

Southward to Louisville the road was little more than a crooking trail through gloomy cypress trees, flooded in one place for six miles, the water standing motionless, oily black, and forbidding.

Captain Jason Smith was having trouble with his four field pieces. To keep his ammunition dry he ordered it removed from the caissons and packed on horses. One of the gun carriages collapsed; the crew dismantled it, lashed the 140-pound gun barrel to a mule's back, and slogged on.

Just before reaching Louisville, the scouts made their prize haul of the day, a mail courier with official Confederate dispatches and a registered parcel of Confederate money. Lieutenant-Colonel Blackburn proudly turned them over to Colonel Grierson; and as some of the letters were in French, Blackburn brought up his French sergeant-major, Augustus Leseure, to serve as translator. The dispatches, Sergeant Surby reported, "contained some valuable information."

As the bedraggled column approached Louisville, Grierson halted the brigade briefly, sending Major Mathew Starr with a battalion of the Sixth Regiment on a dash into the town to set up pickets while the brigade moved through. When Starr galloped into the neat little village he was surprised to find no one on the streets. He kept his men moving rapidly until they were all dismounted and strategically protected by cover.

Louisville, being on a high road, had received warning from the east of a possible Yankee raid. Almost every house was closed, some windows were boarded up. Louisville had never been invaded before and the people feared the Yankees as the conquered always fear the unknown conquerors.

The brigade moved through a silent town, deserted and still as death, and in the darkness that had come suddenly there was an eerie quality more disturbing to the Union men than the presence of the unseen Southerners hidden behind locked doors and windows. As soon as the Sixth passed through, Major John Graham's First Battalion of the Seventh replaced Starr's pickets.

"Major Graham will remain until the column has been gone an hour," Grierson ordered. He did not like the looks of the town, the electric feeling of fear and hatred in the air. "Let no one leave with information of the direction we have taken, drive out any stragglers from our troops, preserve order, quiet the fears of these people."[11]

Grierson gave a second order to Captain John Lynch, commanding Company E of the Sixth Regiment. Lynch and one of his corporals were to disguise themselves as rebel citizens and proceed eastward toward Macon on a reconnoitering expedition. If possible they were to cut the telegraph line along the Mobile & Ohio Railroad. Grierson could not be certain whether Captain Forbes's company had succeeded in reaching the railroad. As he explained, he wanted everything done that could possibly be done "to prevent information of our presence from flying along the railroad to Jackson and other points."[12]

If Grierson expected to find easier marching after passing through Louisville he was bitterly disappointed. "A great splashing of mud . . . deep and wide gullies frequently yawned by our sides, black and mysterious in the night as bottomless abysses. . . ."

Four miles south of the town they began a long march through another swamp. On each side of the road, dark trees towered against the sky. "The water everywhere," said the New York *Times* account, "was three to four feet deep, with every few hundred yards a mire-hole in which frequently for a few moments man and horse were lost to view. The Seventh Illinois being in the rear found these holes almost impassable, from the action of the large body of cavalry which had preceded them, and they were compelled to leave drowned some twenty noble animals whose strength was not equal to such an emergency. The men so dismounted removed their saddles, placed them on some other led beast, and pushed onward cheerfully."[13]

At last, after marching ten miles from Louisville in the darkness, they found dry ground around Estes Plantation. The time was after midnight; with scarcely a halt they had covered at least fifty wearying and circuitous miles. And now their prize, the end of action, the Vicksburg railroad, lay only forty miles to the south.

IV

Colonel Edward Hatch, moving northward after his escape from Lieutenant-Colonel Clark Barteau's cavalrymen at Palo Alto, celebrated his thirty-second birthday on April 22 by raiding Okolona, which had been left undefended by the Confederates pursuing vainly in his rear. The Second Iowa had marched all night, avoiding main roads most of the way.

Sergeant Lyman Pierce later wrote:

We soon entered a large swamp through which we traveled by an obscure path, guided by a negro until we struck the river. . . . Here Hatch found some flood-wood lodged against a fallen tree; with this he constructed a rude foot-bridge, and we unsaddled our horses and each trooper carried his saddle across the bridge on his back. The bank on the side from which the horses must enter was about six feet above the stream and very nearly perpendicular. Three or four troopers would seize each horse and throw him into the stream, when they would, by the aid of long poles, compel him to swim to the opposite bank, where two men stood hip deep in water to aid him up the bank. In this way the entire command was crossed in safety, between the hours of 10 o'clock P.M., and 3 o'clock A.M., of as dark a night as I ever experienced. Large bonfires were built on each bank to expel the darkness. The cannon was taken to pieces and hauled across by means of a rope. As soon as the column was all over, we saddled up and moved out. . . .

We moved towards Okolona, where the rebels had eight pieces of artillery, but so completely had Hatch fooled them as to the objective point of his march, that the enemy, . . . had been all despatched to various points to oppose us, and now that we were rapidly nearing Okolona, they were obliged to run their cannon South [on railroad flat cars] for safety.

We charged into the town just before sunset, where we burned thirty barracks filled with Confederate British stamped cotton. This done we moved five miles out of town and camped for the night on a wealthy plantation, which afforded everything we needed both for animals and men.[14]

V

Lieutenant-Colonel Clark Barteau had not yet abandoned hope of defeating or capturing Colonel Hatch's Second Iowans, who had so skillfully evaded his trap in the lane near Palo Alto. But the sun was up on the morning of April 22 long before Lieutenant-Colonel Smith, Major Inge, and Captain Ham had reassembled their scattered state troops. And then about the time Barteau was preparing to give the march orders, Lieutenant-Colonel James Cunningham and his Second Alabama Cavalry came trotting up the road from West Point.

To further delay action, the old recurring question of command authority now arose. Cunningham, believing that he outranked Barteau, expressed a desire to assume command of the pursuit. Barteau stubbornly declined to yield, claiming that General Ruggles had assigned him field responsibility for all Confederate cavalry in northeast Mississippi. In a report to headquarters he later censured Cunningham for not remaining at Okolona to defend the Confederate Army stores and barracks, as well as for his tardiness in coming up from West Point.

After some wrangling, the column finally moved out along Hatch's trail to Buena Vista. Here Barteau divided his forces. He sent the state troops northwest along the swamp-circling road to Okolona, on a long chance they might come around upon the enemy's front. Then taking the seasoned Second Tennessee and Second Alabama Regiments, he attempted to overtake Hatch by following him across the Sakatouchee and its flooded swampland toward Okolona.

But Barteau was not so fortunate as Hatch. His guide became lost in the darkness and the two regiments floundered in the mud for hours. When they finally struck high ground, about eight miles from Okolona, the men and mounts were completely exhausted. Barteau called a halt until morning. He may have guessed that he was already too late to save Okolona.[15]

VI

During the forty-eight hours after Grierson's brigade was positively located at Pontotoc, with its strength fairly accurately estimated at 2,000 troops, the Jackson headquarters of the Confederate commander, General John C. Pemberton, received several contradictory official reports and numerous unofficial panicky rumors of the Yankee cavalry raid.

Already annoyed by the failure of General Ruggles' cavalry to halt the raid, Pemberton was now becoming genuinely alarmed by the widespread reports of civilian panic south of Pontotoc. He was particularly concerned over the security of Confederate stores and ammunition which he was depending upon to sustain a long summer campaign against Grant's army.

On April 22 he received two unwelcome messages, one informing him that the enemy had reached Starkville, the other from Ruggles reporting Barteau's fight with the enemy at Palo Alto. Ruggles ended his telegram with a question: "Can you send troops from Grenada to effect a diversion?"[16]

Pemberton dared not spare troops from Grenada, the strongpoint of Vicksburg's northern defense ring, but he remembered that General Abraham Buford's infantry brigade, en route from Alabama to reinforce Vicksburg, was bivouacked somewhere near Meridian. Pemberton also recalled that he had attached to his Jackson headquarters a hard-bitten North Carolinian, Major-General William W. Loring, who had lost most of his troops by transfer to the Vicksburg district. He decided to send Loring to Meridian, with orders to take command of all troops in that area and to take action against the dangerous Union cavalry raid, part of which apparently had eluded Ruggles' forces.*

Pemberton telegraphed Buford at Meridian, informing him that Loring was en route to take command. "If the enemy is advancing," he added, "move without wagons, by rail, within striking distance of him."[17]

---

* General William W. Loring had won some fame early in the war by attempting to seize New Mexico for the Confederacy. Engaged in fighting the Apaches there in 1860, he had accumulated quantities of military supplies in the various forts, had built up a staff of pro-Southern officers and troops. Unionists, however, discovered his plans, and he was forced to resign his commission in the United States Army and leave the department before he was able to act.

Later in the day Pemberton received reports of a heavy force of enemy troops approaching Macon. (This was Captain Forbes and his thirty-five men of Company B.) Pemberton immediately decided, as Grierson had hoped he would, that the Starkville raiders had turned toward Macon. Having no reply from Buford, Pemberton sent a second urgent telegram, addressed to Commanding Officer of Troops, Meridian:

Proceed with all troops now at Meridian up Mobile & Ohio Railroad to such point as you may meet with enemy, and cooperate with General Ruggles. General Loring will be in command of all the troops. Exercise great discretion, and gain all information as you advance. On reaching Macon, ascertain the state of affairs in that vicinity.[18]

These orders, of course, set in motion during the night of April 22 the Confederate troops which kept Captain Forbes from venturing into Macon.

Pemberton then informed General Ruggles that reinforcements en route to Vicksburg were being diverted to co-operate with him, and that General Loring would be in command of all troops of the expedition. The harassed commanding general concluded his day's occupation with the Grierson raid by sending a telegram to General Joseph E. Johnston in Tennessee, a call for help similar to the one he had sent three days earlier: "Heavy raids are making from Tennessee deep into the State. . . . Cavalry indispensable to meet these raids. . . . Could you not make a demonstration with a cavalry force in their rear?"[19]

But nowhere in all the day's official messages of the Confederate command does there appear to be any intimation of what Grierson's real objective was, any comprehension of the grave danger facing Vicksburg's vital rail line. In fact, Pemberton's disposition of the Meridian troops actually weakened the defense of the Vicksburg railroad, favoring the much less important Mobile & Ohio road. Perhaps because of the very audacity of the action, neither Pemberton nor any of his field officers could admit the possibility on Wednesday April 22 that two regiments of Union cavalry were then only a long day's march from Vicksburg's lifeline.

THE SCOUTS CAPTURE A BRIDGE

Boots and saddles was sounding for the men of the Sixth and Seventh Illinois Cavalry Regiments, camped around Estes Plantation. The lucky ones had gotten four hours of sleep. Weather-conscious after the past few days, they examined the thin clouds stretched like gauze across a pale morning sky. Then, while waiting for coffee to boil, they scraped dried mud with their knives from boots and uniforms.

Captain Jason Smith was attempting to put his collapsed two-pounder gun back into operation. Stripping one of the plantation's buggies of its frame and wheels, he mounted the gun on this substitute carriage, fastening it down with blocks and leather straps. A crowd gathered to watch, exchanging jibes with the batterymen.

By the time Colonel Grierson ordered the Seventh to lead out, Smith's men had a horse hitched between the buggy shafts. An odd-looking weapon, the captain allowed, but he judged it would stand up under a few charges.

Seventh Day
Thursday, April 23

LOUISVILLE

PHILADELPHIA

Colonel Grierson had been studying his map again. If the weather held good, the brigade should be entering the Pearl River valley by mid-morning, should reach the flooded stream before noon. Grierson was worried about the bridge, estimating from the size of the river and its tributaries that a crossing under flood might be impossible. If news of the raid had swept ahead of them, the bridge certainly would be heavily guarded, might already have been destroyed. And should the Pearl River crossing be blocked, even for a few hours, the delay would give the Confederates time to assemble troops along the Vicksburg railroad and might prove disastrous to his mission.

He ordered Lieutenant-Colonel Blackburn to send the scouts forward on the double with instructions to use extra caution in approaching the bridge. If the bridge was unguarded they were to secure it immediately. But if it was heavily guarded, that information should be brought back at once to the main column.

The Butternut Guerillas galloped away over a narrow road running through thinly settled country. As they neared Pearl River the trail dropped into thickly wooded bottoms, and Sergeant Surby slowed the pace. About two miles from the bridge, Surby took a short lead over his seven scouts. A few moments later as he rounded a curve, he saw an old man approaching on a mule. The two riders watched each other closely as they approached, both halting simultaneously opposite. A few yards to the rear the Butternut Guerillas held up, spreading out across the road.

"We passed the time of day and entered into conversation," Surby wrote afterwards. "The old man informed me that a picket was stationed at the bridge, composed of citizens, numbering five in all, his son being one of the party; all were armed with shotguns. They had torn up several planks from the center of the bridge, and had placed combustibles on it ready to ignite at our approach."

Surby then asked the old man his name and place of residence, and when they were given, the sergeant drew paper and pencil from inside his shirt and wrote down the information. This frightened the old man; he began to babble: "Gentlemen, gentlemen, you are not what you seem to be, you certainly are Yankees, for we got news in Philadelphia last night that you all were coming this way."

94

Resolved to frighten the old man into an unconditional surrender of the bridge, Surby replied quickly: "It lies in your power to save your buildings from the torch, to save your own life, and probably that of your son, by saving the bridge."

Trembling with fear, the old man said that he was confident of saving the bridge but could not promise the surrender of his friends. "The bridge is the important point," Surby told him. He ordered the man to return to the pickets and advise them to surrender and accept paroles; if they damaged the bridge, the old man's house and barns would be destroyed.

The Butternut Guerillas rode forward with their captive to within three hundred yards of the bridge, descending into low bottomland considerably flooded. Through a screen of brush they could see the bridge, a long, narrow structure set high on a solid trestlework, with guard rails running along the sides. The long rails were broken in several places, and the muddy waters of the Pearl boiled furiously around the supports, tugging at the river debris collecting against them. It was obvious that no horseman could safely ford that crossing. The bridge must be captured.

Remaining in concealment, Surby sent the old man ahead to bargain with the Confederate pickets. "I impatiently followed the figure of the old man with my eye," Surby wrote in his account. "When within a dozen yards of the bridge, he halted, and commenced telling his errand; but ere he was hardly half through, I could perceive some signs of uneasiness on the side of his listeners; they all at once jumped upon their horses and away they went. We then advanced to the bridge, replaced the planks, found two shotguns, that they had left in their flight, and leaving one man to wait for the column and turn the old man over to the Colonel, I proceeded with the rest to Philadelphia."[1]

Surby suspected that the rebel pickets might return with reinforcements, but if such was their plan they were too late in acting. As the scouts moved out of the Pearl River bottoms, however, they quickly met signs of the recent passage of the five pickets. The scattered farmhouses appeared closed and deserted; occasionally they would see a man hurrying off, mounted or on foot, across a distant field.

Because the fleeing rebels had alarmed the countryside, Surby decided to abandon all pretense of being Confederates. The bridge guards certainly would have described them as Yankees in disguise, and he told his men to fire on any armed citizens. But most of the countrymen were keeping a safe distance from the road; there was little opportunity to exchange fire.

The squad moved at a slow walk so as not to push too far in front of the column. The land leveled now almost to a rolling plain, pine-studded, the soil reddening, the sandy road drying rapidly to a fine dust under the bright, not sun.

The closer they came to Philadelphia the more evidence there was of possible resistance ahead. Instead of single farmers riding hurriedly away, three or four would be seen together, out of range, the sun glinting on their weapons.

"Within about three hundred yards of town," said Surby, "they were discovered drawn up in a line across the road, upon which we were approaching. I immediately sent a man back, requesting the commanding officer of the advance guard to send me ten men. I waited long enough to see they were coming, and turning to my men ordered them to charge, and as we neared them amid a cloud of dust, we commenced to discharge our revolvers at them, which had the desired effect of stampeding them; they fired but a few shots, and in a few minutes we had full possession of the town; resulting in the capture of six prisoners, nine horses and equipments."[2]

In a few minutes the column arrived on the gallop, quickly encircling the town. Colonel Grierson dismounted to interview the prisoners. One of them was the county judge, "a very worthy man," and from him Grierson learned that the Philadelphians had heard early that morning of the brigade's approach, and were organizing a party to burn the Pearl River bridge at the very moment when later news came that the Yankees had already crossed. The judge declared that he had attempted armed resistance because he feared for his life and property.

To calm the few townspeople who still dared to show themselves in the street, Grierson made an extemporaneous speech, explaining that his cavalrymen "were not there to interfere with private citizens or to destroy their property or to insult or molest their families, that we were after the soldiers and property of the rebel government."[3]

The speech was brief with no applause, but it was apparent that the fear and tension were eased. Before leaving Philadelphia, Grierson summoned Colonel Prince, giving him orders to remain with the rear-guard battalion and swear the citizens to a period of silence concerning the Union cavalry movements. As the column moved out, Prince in a good-natured manner asked the Philadelphians to line up in the town's main street. "The last I saw of them," Sergeant Surby commented, "they were standing in line with arms extended perpendicular, and Colonel Prince was swearing them not to give any information for a certain length of time."⁴

Shortly after three o'clock in the afternoon, as the column moved south toward Decatur, two horsemen in Secesh disguises overtook the rear guard, waving their carbines and shouting a greeting. They were Captain John Lynch and Corporal Jonathan Bullard of Company E, returning from Macon. Almost twenty-four hours had passed since Grierson had sent them east from Louisville to cut the telegraph lines along the Mobile & Ohio. Lashing their spent horses, they raced speedily up the side of the column to report to the colonel.⁵

Captain Lynch had failed to reach the telegraph wires. After riding all night from Louisville, he and Corporal Bullard had come within half a mile of Macon at eight o'clock on the morning of the 23rd. In their rebel clothing they had expected no trouble, but suddenly a Confederate picket appeared on the road, halting them and demanding identification.

"I've been sent out from Enterprise," replied Captain Lynch, "to ascertain the whereabouts of the Yankees."

"You need not go any further," said the picket. "They are now within two miles of here."⁶

Lynch knew then that Forbes was in the vicinity. He asked how many Confederate soldiers were defending Macon, and was told there were two regiments of cavalry, one of infantry, and two pieces of artillery. Considering it inadvisable to approach the railroad telegraph lines while so large an enemy force was on the alert, the captain told the picket he had left a couple of men at a plantation a mile to the rear, and would have to ride back for them. He and the corporal swung their horses about, riding away at a slow canter until they were out of sight of the picket; then they galloped until Macon was some distance behind. After a seventy-four-mile circuit beginning at Louisville, they had finally rejoined the column.

Grierson congratulated Lynch, even though he had failed to cut the telegraph lines.* The news that Captain Forbes had reached Macon, drawing strong Confederate forces to that point, was good news for the brigade, but Grierson doubted more than ever now that he would ever see the men of Company B again.

Around five o'clock in the afternoon, Blackburn's scouts sent back information that a well-stocked plantation was just ahead. Grierson decided to hold up for a few hours to rest and feed the horses before beginning the final drive to the Vicksburg railroad, only twenty-five miles away.

II

At the moment Captain Lynch was confronted by the Confederate picket half a mile west of Macon, Captain Forbes and his thirty-five men were marching quietly away from their camp north of the town. Following back trails and using woods cover where possible, they detoured westward and then turned south, somewhere crossing the same road used by Captain Lynch.

During the morning they captured a lone Confederate artilleryman who talked freely and seemed rather pleased when Captain Forbes informed him that he would be paroled as a prisoner. Forbes asked him if he were a volunteer. The man replied that he had volunteered to escape conscription, adding that he was opposed to the war.

When the captain asked if he could guide the company to the Mobile & Ohio bridge over the Noxubee immediately below Macon, the rebel said that he would do so. Forbes was determined to attempt one strike against the railroad before abandoning his mission completely. He sent the captive out with his scouts, warning him that any false move would mean his death.

Around noon the scouts informed Captain Forbes that they had sighted the Noxubee bridge and that it was heavily guarded. Forbes went up to have a look. The Confederates had anticipated his visit; his little company was outnumbered by a well-armed bridge guard.

Reluctantly he gave the order to countermarch. "We were now entitled to overtake the brigade, if we could," Forbes wrote, "and stretched our march for Philadelphia which we knew they must pass on their way to Newton Station."[7]

---

* "All honor to the gallant captain, whose intrepid coolness and daring characterize him on every occasion." — Grierson's official report of the raid, O.R., ser. I, vol. 24, pt. 1, p. 528.

When the company reached the main road running west, he ordered his men into a long gallop. By day's end they were out of the flat woods country into the sandy-lands, coming down off a green wooded ridge into Gholson, family home of Confederate General Gholson, commander of the Mississippi state troops. (General Gholson was on this day hurrying north to take command of his troops who, with Colonel Barteau, were still pursuing Colonel Hatch's Second Iowa Regiment.)

Company B paid General Gholson the compliment of halting and feeding near his home village, then continued the march toward Philadelphia. Not a man objected to this night march; they sang merrily as they rode along under the stars.

Sergeant Stephen Forbes had a little song of his own, which he had heard the Negroes singing along the Mississippi:

> Oh, in the old and happy days
> When Linda and I were one
> Then I was like a fat raccoon
> A-bathing in the sun.[8]

III

But as Company B rode so confidently toward Philadelphia, hoping to overtake the brigade before morning reveille, Colonel Grierson was preparing to break camp. About ten o'clock that evening he ordered Colonel Blackburn to take the First Battalion of the Seventh Regiment and make a rapid march to Newton Station on the Vicksburg railroad. The main column would follow within an hour.

Blackburn characteristically had volunteered for this dangerous assignment. In the darkness his huge, high-stepping horse pranced along the forming column of his four companies. *Saddle up, boys, and fall in lively!* He had a personal word for almost every one of the 200 men; he told the non-commissioned officers exactly what the battalion was expected to accomplish during the coming eight hours.

As soon as the battalion was ready to march, Blackburn rode out ahead with Sergeant Surby and two other scouts. After the warm day the temperature had dropped sharply so that the long woolen Confederate coats worn by the Butternut Guerillas felt quite comfortable. "The night was a beautiful starlight one," said Surby, "the roads in good condition, and meeting with no enemy, nothing occurred to interrupt the stillness that reigned until midnight."

For a time Blackburn rode back and forth between the scouts and the battalion's advance. He was wary of ambush in the darkness, knowing that warnings of a Union invasion must certainly have spread miles before them on this road. He moved his advance guard a quarter of a mile out in front of the first company, and strung out moving pickets at hundred-yard intervals in front of them with orders to scour each byroad and crossroad in search of lurking enemies. Far ahead of the guard rode the Butternut Guerillas, Surby and his two companions alternating on the point.

Around midnight Surby was riding with George Steadman, the third scout being somewhere ahead of them in the starlight. "In coming to a point where the road forked, I was at a loss which one to take," Surby said, "and to decide the question, sent George Steadman back to a house to inquire."

While awaiting Steadman's return, the sergeant rode slowly along the road to the right, halting his horse crosswise in the trail, which was shadowed by a thicket of scrub oaks forming a narrow triangle between him and the left road of the fork. Unknown to Surby, the third scout was halted almost exactly opposite on the other road, waiting for his companions, and likewise unaware of Surby's presence.

After a few minutes Steadman came trotting back from the farmhouse, reining up his horse as he came to the fork, searching the darkness for Surby. To let Steadman know where he was, Surby called out: "Is this the right road?" Steadman was startled by the voice, Surby being indiscernible in the shadows of the trees. Hesitating a moment, Steadman then turned his mount slowly into the right fork.

Steadman, according to Surby, "came up within a few feet of me and peering into my face a moment, without saying a word, wheeled his horse and galloped off." A moment later a revolver cracked. Two other shots followed in rapid succession, then a volley from carbines or rifles. When Surby saw fire-sparks flying from a stone on the road beside him, he knew that he was the target.

Lashing his horse, the sergeant dashed into the thicket between the branching roads. Briars swept his hat away, scratching his face. He knew that Steadman could not have fired all the shots.

"I . . . was of the opinion," he said, "that we were ambushed from the point of timber between the two roads, and that the enemy had let us pass, and were firing into the advance of our column."

A moment later as he moved his horse cautiously into the other road, he met his second scout. Both men were holding their revolvers at ready, but luckily they recognized each other. "We struck out," said Surby, "and circled about a mile, striking the middle of the column, and soon learned that I was the sole object of all the firing. It appears that Steadman, when he rode up, did not recognize me, but hastily retreated to the fork of the road, and commenced firing at me with his revolver, causing the advance to hurry forward, who in turn began to fire with their carbines. Loss sustained, one hat."

Around three o'clock in the morning, as the column was approaching Decatur, Lieutenant-Colonel Blackburn ordered Surby to take his two scouts and enter the town. Blackburn wanted to learn whether or not there was an enemy force at Newton Station, and if so, their exact position, the number of men, artillery strength, and any other information which could be obtained.

When the scouts entered Decatur they found no one in the quiet streets, and Surby decided to enter a house. Halting in front of an old-fashioned country inn with pigeonhole windows cut half way up its slanting roof, he dismounted and left his horse with one of his men. He approached the nearest door, knocking loudly, but no one answered. He tried another door, and this time a voice inquired: "Who's there?"

"A Confederate soldier," replied Surby. "On important business."

The door opened. "Come in," said the voice in the darkness.

Surby stepped inside what appeared to be a combination sitting room and bedroom. He wrote afterwards in his account of the incident: "I begged to be excused for disturbing them at so unreasonable an hour. . . . The old gentleman, who proved to be the proprietor of the establishment, scraped out a few coals in the fire place, which threw a lurid light across the room, drew forth a chair, and told me to be seated. At the same time he sprang into bed again, from beneath whose covering I could see a pair of sparkling, roguish black eyes, tresses black as the raven's wing, a mischievous mouth, belonging to a young and charming woman. Can it be possible, thinks I, that she is married to this old man."

The sergeant's thoughts were interrupted by a mild query from the gentleman, demanding the nature of his visitor's business. Surby quickly replied that he was a scout from Van Dorn's command, stationed at Columbus. He explained that the Yankees were raiding toward Decatur, and that he was carrying messages to Confederate forces guarding the Vicksburg railroad. He wanted to know where these forces could be found.

Suspecting nothing of Surby's trick, the innkeeper replied that the nearest force would be at Newton Station, about ten miles south. A hospital was there, he said; about a hundred sick and wounded soldiers occupied it. Some infantry might be there, also.

Surby asked if any soldiers had been past Decatur recently, and was told that a considerable force of cavalry had passed going east, but that had been a few days ago. Thanking his host for the information and apologizing to his hostess for intruding, Surby prepared to leave. He wrote, in concluding this scene: "A sweet voice invited me to call if I came that way again. I promised, and, bidding good-bye, left them to slumber."[9]

Entering the houses of the conquered was an exhilarating experience for Yankee cavalrymen. When on night patrol they saw every dark silent house as a challenge in this strange southern land of soft feminine voices and hard masculine violence. For Grierson's men, sometimes the drama turned to farce, as Stephen Forbes recorded in his diary:

I entered the yard, struck the dog over the head with my saber, and knocked at the door. A very tremulous voice within managed with some difficulty to articulate the question: "Who is there?" "A Federal soldier," I replied, "and I want to get in." A moment of hurried bustling and smothered frightened talk, and the door opened reluctantly on an old man *en dishabille* with a candle in his hand, who immediately began the most profuse professions of welcome and happiness at my visit, while his face and stammering speech indicated the utmost consternation. He told me that he truly rejoiced to see me, while his hand shook so with fear that he could hardly hold his candle upright, and ludicrously asked me to come in and sit by the fire in a voice as if he was begging for his life, while there was not a live coal in the fireplace.

I allayed his fears as far as possible and proceeded to search his house, but to my infinite dismay was greeted at the threshold of the first door by a series of faint shrieks and the sight of the fairer portion of his family in a most charmingly distressful situation. I was very nearly overwhelmed with bashfulness, and if there had been a guerilla present, I think I would have thanked him to have shot me instantly for my baseness. As it was, I retreated with all haste, and completed my search elsewhere.[10]

IV

While Grierson's advance raiders were marching swiftly and unchallenged toward the Vicksburg railroad on April 23, the attention of the Confederate commanders remained fixed on the Mobile & Ohio. General Ruggles, directing the pursuit of Colonel Hatch's diversionary force, wired General Pemberton in Jackson that the enemy was "falling back before our cavalry."[11] Ruggles was still unconvinced by the rumors that a large enemy force had slipped through his district. He estimated Hatch's probable strength at two thousand men, exactly the same as the enemy force he had reported at Pontotoc three days earlier, leaving no margin for the rumored Yankee cavalry in the Macon area.

Instead of falling back before the Confederate cavalry, Colonel Hatch's actual force of 500 men was marching slowly northward "by all points of the compass," destroying bridges and capturing horses and mules. "We soon accumulated 600 head of horses and mules," said Sergeant Lyman Pierce, "with about 200 able bodied negroes to lead them. As the colored women and children could not be taken along, they expressed their feeling towards us by running out to the road, as we passed, with a bowl of milk or a pone of corn bread and slice of meat."[12] The Second Iowa Regiment camped that night near Tupelo.

Confronted by destroyed bridges and flooded creeks everywhere he turned, the luckless Colonel Barteau was not able during the day to come close enough for another fight with Hatch. He bivouacked his men that evening three miles from Hatch's camp and conferred with General Gholson, who had arrived to take command not only of his state troops but of the entire campaign as well. Lieutenant-Colonel Cunningham of the Second Alabama, still sulking because Barteau had refused to yield to his seniority, announced that his men and mounts were too exhausted to continue farther with the pursuit.

General Pemberton in his Jackson headquarters, having received no reply from General Joseph Johnston to his request for cavalry assistance, was telegraphing directly to Richmond: "I have so little cavalry in this department that I am compelled to divert a portion of my infantry to meet raids in Northern Mississippi. If any troops can possibly be spared from other departments, I think they should be sent here."

Ominous reports of enemy gunboats passing Vicksburg came in during the day, and Pemberton wired General Loring at Meridian not to leave the railroad. "Keep me hourly informed, as troops may be required here at any time."[13]

Pemberton would have been discouraged indeed, could he have foreseen that within twenty-four hours several miles of the very wires that carried these messages would be ripped and tangled into an inextricable snarl.

ACTION AT NEWTON STATION

While Grierson's raiders were approaching Newton Station in the early morning of April 24, a hundred miles to the west General Ulysses Grant was boarding the flagship of Admiral David Porter for a reconnaissance run along the Mississippi. He was going down for a close look at Grand Gulf. Tomorrow or the next day he would have to give the order that would send the first wave of infantrymen in a river crossing against that well-defended bluff, twenty-five miles below Vicksburg, the point which he had selected weeks ago as the necessary foothold for his encirclement from the south.

This would be Grant's eighth try at Vicksburg; he knew it would be his last, win or lose. He believed that he had planned this assault as thoroughly as any military campaign could be planned. He was counting heavily on the cavalry raids in eastern Mississippi to throw his enemy, General Pemberton, off balance. He remembered Pemberton from the

Eighth Day
Friday, April 24

PHILADELPHIA

DECATUR

VICKSBURG RR
NEWTON STATION
GARLANDVILLE

MONTROSE

time when they had served in the same division during the war with Mexico. Pemberton always liked his fighting to be neat and tidy, with well-defined lines, and would be thoroughly fretted by enemy cavalry disarranging his rear. And if Grierson's cavalry could reach and wreck the rail line between Jackson and Meridian, Pemberton would have good cause to fret.

Grant's principal concern today was General John McClernand, one of his three corps commanders. McClernand already had marched his corps into position at Hard Times Landing across from Grand Gulf, and only last night had practically demanded of Grant that he issue immediate orders for the attack. McClernand was bound to lead the first crossing, being the glory hunter that he was — McClernand the political general, the Yankee Democrat who had sold President Lincoln a deal, and had almost won command of the Vicksburg campaign over Grant. Against orders he had brought his wife down on the eve of the big crossing, had invited the governor of Illinois for a grand review, a Roman carnival — McClernand, a man with sharp eyes, a fox nose, and a face hidden under an untrimmed brush of beard.

When Admiral Porter's flagship swung around a bend in the river, there against the sun was Grand Gulf two miles away, a bluff honeycombed with defenses, twelve big guns on its frowning brow. Somewhere up there was Grant's old friend and neighbor, General John S. Bowen, a Missourian who had chosen to fight on the side of the South.

Admiral Porter insisted that Grand Gulf was too strong to be captured; a few hours earlier a Confederate informer had told him the garrison was 12,000 strong. Grant was stubborn. He had rejected an alternate plan for landing below Grand Gulf because the ground was too swampy south of the bluff. He wanted dry, hard ground for a base, no more of that oozing mud in which his armies had bogged themselves on other attempts to reach Vicksburg. If the Navy guns could silence the enemy batteries, he was sure that his river-borne infantry could land and hold at Grand Gulf.[1]

As the flagship turned and headed back towards his new headquarters at Smith's Plantation near New Carthage, Grant was probably thinking about the wounded. McClernand had not planned a line of transportation to take care of the casualties. Sherman would not have overlooked that necessity.

The only man Grant could trust, General William T. Sherman, was opposed to the entire plan of attack. Sherman had told Grant frankly that to cross the river and begin a campaign without a supply base was against all the rules of warfare. He recommended that the army return to Memphis to try again by land from the north.

Grant shut his mind to that, even though it meant he was siding with McClernand, the man he distrusted, against Sherman, the man he respected. But today, as soon as he landed and returned to his headquarters at Smith's Plantation, Grant's first thought was of Sherman, waiting patiently up at Milliken's Bend. He sent Sherman a long message. "My impressions are that if an attack can be made within the next two days, Grand Gulf will easily fall." Then he admitted that there were no preparations for taking care of casualties. He was sending a surgeon up to the Bend tomorrow to consult about the "best policy to pursue for caring for our sick and wounded."[2]

This would probably mean a delay of three or four days. But perhaps by that time news might have come of cavalry raids against the Vicksburg railroad. Hurlbut's last message from Memphis had assured him that Grierson would cut the railroad by Wednesday or Thursday, and today was Friday.[3] He would like to catch Pemberton on his front while he was busy tidying up his back yard.

II

Lieutenant-Colonel William Blackburn's battalion was six miles from Newton Station when the sun rose. In a few minutes they reached a creek ford, halting briefly to unbit and water horses. This would be the big day, the day of action. In Sergeant Surby's words, "Colonel Blackburn ordered me to proceed lively with my two men to the station, reconnoiter, and report what force was stationed there, what time the train would arrive, and so forth."[4]

The three Butternut Guerillas went off at a gallop, the sound of their horses' hooves muffled in the red soil. In less than an hour, as they topped a rise in the road, they saw the town suddenly in front of them, the single track of the railroad slicing through the few scattered buildings. They took cover quickly, Surby studying the landscape. He saw no camp but several men were walking aimlessly around a large building near the railroad station. They appeared to be unarmed and he saw no pickets anywhere. He guessed that the men were convalescent patients and that the building was the hospital mentioned by his Decatur informant of last night.

"I told the men we would proceed and see a little more before reporting. We started leisurely along and stopped at a house just at the edge of town; found a white man, called for a drink of water, and asked him how long before the train would be in. He said it was due in three quarters of an hour. I ascertained that no force was stationed here. Was obtaining other information, when my ears were startled by the whistle of a locomotive. It seemed a long way off. I then inquired what train that was. The man said it was the freight train coming from the east, due at nine o'clock A.M."[5]

Realizing that there was no time to lose if they hoped to capture the freight train, Surby sent one of the scouts back at a gallop to inform Colonel Blackburn. If the battalion could not be brought up immediately there would be no chance to seize the freight train, and they might also lose the passenger train.

With his remaining scout, Surby hurried down into the town, halting and fastening their horses to a hitching rail at the tiny railroad station. He was determined to capture the telegraph station to prevent warning of the raiders' presence being flashed to any nearby Confederate forces. But the station office was closed and they could see no telegraph instruments through the dingy windows.

As Surby and his companion came around the end of the building, they saw several convalescent Confederates coming out of the hospital a hundred yards away. Confident that Blackburn's column would be arriving within a few minutes, the sergeant drew his revolver and walked slowly toward the rebels. "Remain inside!" he shouted. "Don't come out on peril of your lives!"[6]

In a few moments the cavalry came charging down the street beside the railroad tracks. Blackburn was waving his hat and cheering. Less than a mile to the east, above the pine forest, a black streamer of smoke marked the slow approach of the freight train.

Blackburn immediately sent pickets scattering through the little town to block the roads and approaches. He ordered his company commanders to conceal their troops from view of the oncoming train; the men were dismounted and the horses were quickly led back behind the buildings. Two men were sent on the double to each of the sidetrack's switches, with instructions to hide in the tall grass beside the railroad. They were to spring up and throw the switches if there should be any attempt on the part of the engineer to take sudden flight.

In a moment the oversized cowcatcher of the squat little freight engine emerged from the pines. It was a noisy train, the wheels pounding, the cars rattling, the locomotive puffing and blowing with its weight of twenty-five loaded cars. Blackburn stood beside the station, inconspicuous in the shade, watching its slow approach. The engineer was forcing the engine to a squealing stop. A brakeman dropped off a side-step, moved in a slow trot to the switch, turned and locked it in place. The train crept slowly onto the rusted tracks of the siding.

This train, like most other southern trains after two years of war, was approaching disintegration, there being no railroad equipment factories in the South. Wheels were badly worn on ramshackle cars; engines wheezed out their power through leaky boiler pipes. And along the tracks, crossties were rotting, rails breaking, bridges sagging. Empty woodpiles forced frequent stops along the way while trainmen gathered fuel from the forests. The standard pre-war speed of twenty-five miles an hour had dropped to ten, and few engineers would take a train out after dark.

But this train was loaded with ordnance and commissary supplies for Vicksburg, with new railroad ties and bridge timbers and planking. It could still move. It carried death for the Union men before Vicksburg. It was precious to the Confederacy, necessary for the continuing defense of Vicksburg.

If the engineer glanced at the railroad station, he saw only Colonel Blackburn in his dusty, mud-caked blues, and the three scouts near him in their Confederate disguises. The town itself must have seemed deserted. Unseen horses nickered, answered by others. The engine began to slow, its wheel flanges clanking. Steam and smoke swirled across the front of the little sunlit station.

On a signal from Blackburn, the cavalrymen in a sweeping charge swarmed out on foot from behind the buildings. Within a few seconds they had captured their first train.

Meanwhile, Sergeant Surby had informed the colonel of the second train, and as soon as the freight's crewmen were under guard the soldiers were once again ordered out of sight behind the buildings. Blackburn and the three scouts resumed their studied poses beside the station.

In a few minutes the Jackson-Meridian passenger train — it was a mixed freight and passenger — was whistling for Newton Station. "On she came rounding the curve," Surby wrote, "her passengers unconscious of the surprise that awaited them. The engineer decreased her speed. She was now nearly opposite the depot. Springing upon the steps of the locomotive, and presenting my revolver at the engineer, I told him if he reversed that engine I would put a ball through him. He was at my mercy, and obeyed orders. It would have done any one good to have seen the men rush from their hiding places amid the shouts and cheers which rent the air of 'the train is ours.' "[7]

The mixed train consisted of one passenger car and twelve freight cars, four loaded with ammunition and arms, six with commissary and quartermaster's stores, and two with household goods belonging to families fleeing from Vicksburg. The train's sudden stop startled the passengers in the rear coach; they looked out upon a depot and a town that one moment was empty of life, and then in a flicker of time was crowded with the movement of a hundred blue-clad men. When the passengers began tossing their valuables out the car windows on the side opposite from the station, everything fell into a water-filled ditch. "A few revolvers, some papers and a considerable amount of money was unceremoniously thrown out. Some of the men, who never let anything pass unobserved, accidentally picked up a few articles. One old wallet which was floating on the water contained about eight thousand dollars in Confederate greenbacks."[*8]

III

Newton Station swirled with dust, smoke, steam, and confusion. Capturing two trains so effortlessly within a few minutes of each other had lifted Colonel Blackburn's travel-worn men into a

---

* Twenty years later, Sergeant Surby said that William Ponder, Company A, Seventh Illinois, had given him a wallet found beside the train. The wallet contained $2500 in Confederate fifty-dollar greenbacks. Before the raid ended, this money was to prove itself quite useful to Surby. — *National Tribune*, Washington, D.C., Sept. 6, 1883, p. 1.

state of giddiness. They were beginning to get out of hand, smashing in the doors of the cars, breaking the windows of the depot office, scampering off in pursuit of personal loot before the official pillaging could begin.

Blackburn restored order by rallying the troopers on the depot and forming them into their regular platoons. A systematic inspection of the trains was then begun. While this was going on, one of the Vicksburg refugees begged that his household goods not be burned, and Blackburn assigned a squad to remove the Southerner's furniture from the car.

When he discovered that both trains carried several hundred loaded artillery shells and other explosives, Blackburn had them moved down the tracks some distance from the hospital. Then he sent fire details into action, and within a few minutes each car was ablaze. The heated shells began exploding, not all simultaneously, but in ragged volleys, booming like an artillery duel at close quarters.

At this moment Colonel Grierson's main column was only a short distance from Newton Station. Being completely unaware of the captured trains and the burning ammunition, Grierson assumed that Blackburn had walked into a trap and was being shelled by artillery. *Trot, gallop, march!* he ordered.

"And on they came," said Sergeant Surby, "expecting battle, but instead, found the men had charged on a barrel of whisky, which they were confiscating. I did not see a man that had more or less than a canteen full."[9]

Grierson naturally was delighted by Blackburn's unexpected haul, but he wasted no time in getting on with the real business of the raid. He dispatched Major Mathew Starr with two battalions of the Sixth Regiment to the east with orders to burn bridges and trestlework, cut telegraph poles, and destroy the lines all the way to Chunkey River. Captain Joseph Herring of Company K was sent with a battalion of the Seventh to the west on a similar mission.

While these two expeditions were destroying bridges and telegraph lines, Grierson kept the other troopers occupied in the town. They burned a building containing 500 small arms and a considerable quantity of Confederate uniforms. With wrecking tools obtained from the depot, they tore out rails and heaped them on piles of crossties, warping them by fire. They exploded the two locomotives. Adjutant George Root of the Seventh Regiment set himself up at a table in the hospital, and seventy-five hospitalized Confederate soldiers filed by to receive paroles which would keep them from being returned to duty until Federal prisoner exchanges were arranged. After permitting the hospital's surgeon to remove food and other supplies from the storeroom in the depot, Grierson ordered that building burned.[10]

By two o'clock Grierson was convinced that the Vicksburg railroad had suffered a severe blow, and that days would be required to restore transportation and communication over the several miles of charred pilings and twisted wires on each side of Newton. He ordered his buglers to sound rally call, and the smoke-blackened, bleary-eyed cavalrymen began assembling into companies.*

Where now could they go, now that their mission was accomplished, these men who had scarcely been out of saddles for three days? They sat in the midday sun with eyelids drooping, smelling of sweat and whiskey and woodsmoke, waiting the order to march on mounts going lame with worn and thrown shoes, with nosebags empty and muscles spent to the limit of endurance.

They knew they must move swiftly from this desolate town. The enemy lay at every compass point and would surely pursue them now with renewed fury. Some of Grierson's officers were fairly certain they would not be marching eastward, for during the work of destruction at Newton Station their commander had advised them to make inquiries of the Confederate convalescents and the townspeople concerning eastbound roads, and to pass remarks within earshot of the rebels which would lead the listeners to believe the Yankee raiders would flee to the east.

---

* The Jackson *Appeal* for April 28, probably minimizing the damage, described it as follows: "Two bridges, each about 150 feet long, seven culverts and one cattle cap, constitute the injury done. Twenty freight cars were burned at Newton, and the depot buildings, and two commissary buildings. The telegraph wire was taken down for miles, and cut in pieces. In many instances the wire was rolled up and put into the ditches and pools. But few poles were destroyed. We can hear of but little outrage having been committed upon the persons of noncombatants or upon their property, except by the seizure of every good horse, and of the necessary forage and provisions. They had to depend upon the country for these. The safe at the railroad depot was broken open and the funds abstracted. The money was returned, however, by their commanding officer, with the exception of fifteen hundred dollars that, it was claimed, some of the men had stolen."

Would they turn back north into a countryside filled with aroused citizens and pursuing Confederate soldiers? It seemed unlikely, and no one was surprised when the advance company of the column wheeled away from the railroad and marched off at a slow pace, southward, facing again toward the unknown heartland of the enemy.

IV

Before Grierson's cavalrymen marched out of Newton Station, General Pemberton, only fifty miles away in Jackson, received a telegraphic flash of the raid. For the first time since the Yankee raiders had invaded Mississippi, the general could pinpoint their position on a map. He was astounded by their audacity, he was gravely concerned for his supply and communications lines, and he was determined on immediate revenge.

Alarming rumors also were coming in from Grand Gulf on this day. Grant's army was in movement around Hard Times Landing. But Grant's soldiers could wait; the broad waters of the Mississippi would hold them off for a time. Nothing seemed to stop these Yankee cavalrymen raiding in the east.

Pemberton evidently believed they would actually march on towards Jackson. In his orders to General John Adams directing the latter to take two infantry regiments and a battery of artillery to meet the raiders at Morton, Pemberton assumed that the enemy would have already reached Lake Station, ten miles west of Newton.

Significantly, General Adams was delayed in leaving Jackson by lack of transportation. Not until four o'clock in the afternoon did the two infantry regiments depart by rail, leaving the battery and its six pieces of artillery waiting for another train. Adams did not reach Morton until well after dark, and he spent the night forming his force of one thousand men to do battle with the raiders, supposedly heading westward along the Vicksburg railroad.

Satisfied that General Adams could block and defeat the invaders before they reached Jackson, Pemberton dispatched a series of messages to other parts of the state, hoping to prevent escape of the cavalrymen no matter which direction they might take. Because of the severed wires at Newton, he could not reach General Loring at Meridian, but he was rather certain that

Loring would have heard of the raid from the other end of the line. To prevent escape to the northeast he wired General James Chalmers at Panola: "Move with all your cavalry and light artillery via Oxford to Okolona to intercept force of enemy now at Newton." To block the northwestern routes, he ordered General Lloyd Tilghman at Canton: "Send one half of your command, under a reliable officer, to intercept the enemy should he attempt to retreat by Carthage."

And to further seal the trap, should the Yankees be so foolhardy as to flee toward the south, Pemberton also telegraphed General Franklin Gardner at Port Hudson, Louisiana: "A raid of the enemy, some 700 strong, reached Southern Railroad this morning, and it is possible they are making their way to join Banks.* Send all your disposable cavalry in direction of Tangipahoa, to intercept him."[11]

And so began the rapid draining away to the east of Pemberton's reserve strength, in pursuit of less than a thousand elusive cavalrymen, while Grant across the Mississippi was preparing to strike him hard on the west with a force of thirty thousand.

V

By mid-afternoon of the 24th, Grierson and his brigade were five miles below Newton Station, caught up in a wave of frightened citizens fleeing in wagons, in buggies, on foot. Some were carrying loads of bacon, flour, even household goods and valuables. From those overtaken the raiders seized such food stocks as they could carry in their haversacks.

Grierson would have preferred marching until well after dark, leaving far behind him the broken railroad — a sure rallying point for his enemy. But it was obvious that the column must halt, and on a plantation along the Bogue Falema he ordered a short bivouac.

After a three-hour rest they resumed march in the cool of the late afternoon, reaching the outskirts of Garlandville just before dark. "At this point," Grierson said, "we found the citizens, many of them venerable with age, armed with shot-guns and organized to resist our approach." He ordered a charge, but the old men

---

* General Nathaniel P. Banks, commander of the Union Army's Department of the Gulf.

of Garlandville met it bravely, firing blindly into the Yankee advance. One raider was severely wounded, a horse fell dead under another. But the charge swept on through the town, capturing several armed citizens. "After disarming them," Grierson continued, "we showed them the folly of their actions, and released them. Without an exception they acknowledged their mistake, and declared that they had been grossly deceived as to our real character. One volunteered his services as guide, and upon leaving us declared that hereafter his prayers should be for the Union Army. I mention this as a sample of the feeling which exists, and the good effect which our presence produced among the people in the country through which we passed."[12]

A different version of the little skirmish and its after-effects was reported a few days later by the Paulding (Mississippi) Clarion: "After leaving Newton Station, the federals proceeded to Garlandville, in Jasper County. This neighborhood being one of the richest in this part of the State, suffered severely from their depredations. As they approached Garlandville, three shots were fired at them, resulting in the killing of one of their horses and severely wounding one of the men. . . . The parties who fired on them (Cole, Marshal, Levi, and Chapman) escaped. . . . A company of about fifty men, armed with double-barrel guns, were made up at Paulding on Saturday to defend the place."[13]

Before leaving Garlandville, Grierson ordered his officers into the houses to search for food. "Lieutenant Samuel Woodward," said Grierson, "entered a house where the lamps were lighted, the supper on the table, the corn bread actually *steaming* hot from the stove, and everything else correspondingly fresh. Not a soul was to be seen, nor would come for calling nor could be found about the premises." The lieutenant summoned Grierson, and the colonel and his staff "sat down and ate the supper at their ease; but never learned for whom it was prepared."[14]

With the volunteer guide riding ahead to assist the Butternut Guerillas, the column turned southwestward, marching slowly across prairieland and through dark forests of pine, then down into darker bottomlands of tall water oaks and sweetgum. The men desperately fought away drowsiness; none of them had slept more than five hours of the last seventy-two. Many were sound asleep now as they rode, slumped forward over saddle horns.

Even the tireless Sergeant Surby succumbed. His horse, being ahead of the column, wandered astray, and when Surby awoke he had no idea how long he had been asleep. He found the road but had lost his sense of direction. Dismounting, he searched in the darkness for hoofprints, feeling for toe and heel marks of the horseshoes. "Mounting my trusty steed I put him on the track," he said, "with a slack bridle and smart canter. . . . After traveling about two miles I was rewarded by overtaking the rear-guard to the column. I assure you I felt relieved."[15]

At last they halted for the night camp on C. M. Bender's Plantation, two miles west of Montrose. It was almost midnight, and for the first time in forty hours the horses felt the relief of saddles being unstrapped for removal.

VI

Captain Forbes and the men of Company B met trouble at Philadelphia, where Colonel Grierson had stopped on the previous day to make a speech to the hostile citizens. If Grierson had won any converts to the Union cause, they were not in evidence when Company B reached the town.

As they approached Philadelphia about noon, Captain Forbes decided to stop and feed before entering the town. He ordered his bugler to blow the halt but the three scouts, Charles Martin, William Buffington, and Isaac Robinson, were too far ahead to hear the call. They rode on alone in their Confederate disguises, stopping at the next house to obtain information about the town. Three genuine Confederate soldiers met them at the door.

"You're Federal spies!" one of the rebels cried. Denying the charge, the scouts attempted to stall, expecting Company B to appear at any moment on the road. But they were unsuccessful in prolonging an argument. The Confederates drew their arms and a quick gunfight followed.

Hearing the firing, Captain Forbes immediately ordered his men to horse. "We galloped down the road," said Sergeant Stephen Forbes, "and within about half a mile, as our horses bolted suddenly to the roadside, we saw one of our men, dead on his back in the middle of the road."[16] He was William Buffington. Corporal Martin, his arm bleeding, came crawling out of the brush, and behind him was Isaac Robinson uninjured. The Confederates had fled at the approach of the company.

"We left our dead soldier," said Captain Forbes, "stretched on a Southern porch, under solemn promise from the householder that he would decently bury him — a pledge which I had afterwards the satisfaction to learn was honorably fulfilled."[17]

They rode angrily into Philadelphia, skirmishing with a company of home guards. The fight, according to Stephen Forbes, resulted in the capture and parole of about thirty of the guards, "the destruction of their firearms, the appropriation of their very welcome dinner, and the rapid consummation of several horse trades highly advantageous to the federal company, just then very much in need of a remount. As the horses of these home guards had been brought together to overtake Grierson, we gladly took them at their owners' estimate of their fitness for this task — which was also our own."[18]

But as they continued southward toward Decatur the men of Company B grew increasingly wary. "The guerilla and the bushwhacker and the ambush by the roadside, familiar to us from two years' service in the field, were in all our minds as we rode that day through the thickety woods, scanning every cover and watchful of every turn in the road."[19]

That night they marched without a halt, hoping to overtake the brigade on the morrow, moving closer and closer to what was now the enemy's main point of concern — Newton Station on the Vicksburg railroad.

VII

Until five o'clock on the afternoon of the 24th, General Daniel Ruggles at Columbus persisted in the belief that his cavalrymen were successfully chasing the main body of Yankee raiders out of Mississippi. His only concern was for the Mobile & Ohio bridges, and during the day he had mounted two guns on a railroad car which he kept moving up and down the tracks parallel with Colonel Hatch's retreat.

But Colonel Hatch's Iowans were finding it too difficult to extricate themselves from the persistent Barteau to attempt any forays against railroad bridges. As the Iowans approached Birmingham, Hatch divided his regiment, sending six companies to the left while he and the remaining companies, their thirty-one prisoners, the train of captured horses and mules, and the volunteer Negro drivers moved on toward the town.

Meanwhile, Colonel Barteau and his Second Tennesseans were making a forced march along with General Gholson's state troops, and at 11:30 in the morning they overtook Hatch's four companies, driving in the rear guard. The guard recovered quickly, however, dismounting and forming a line across the road.

Gholson, eager to gain some glory for his state troops, pushed Colonel Smith's regiment up front and they charged three times against the Colt's revolving rifles of Hatch's infantry-trained horsemen. A fourth attack from the flank finally broke the Yankee rear guard, but there were dead and wounded Confederates lying on the road and among trees. The retreating Iowans had not lost a man.

Colonel Hatch in the meantime had dismounted the remainder of his men and formed a fighting line based around his two-pounder cannon. Keeping to the saddle, he took his position in the center of the line and waited.

Barteau's Tennesseans charged on this formidable defense and were repulsed. They rallied and tried a flank movement. But Hatch checkmated this by falling back too rapidly to allow his enemy to pass his flank. Once more Barteau tried the center and failed. By this time the fighting had moved back to Camp Creek, and as soon as Hatch was across he burned the bridge.

The gallant Barteau and his Tennesseans could do no more. Their ammunition was all gone. With ten more rounds they might have won the day, ten rounds being all that Hatch's men had left for their deadly revolving rifles.

A few hours after the fighting ended at Birmingham, while Barteau and Gholson were still burying their dead, General Ruggles received the first startling news of the enemy raid far south at Newton Station. If Ruggles believed that these raiders had reached the Vicksburg railroad by passing through his district, he was not going to admit it officially. He got off a hasty message to Pemberton: ". . . Enemy completely routed at Birmingham. . . ."[20]

PINEY WOODS COUNTRY

Scattered among the pines of Bender's Plantation, the breakfast fires of Grierson's two regiments spun out lazy streamers of blue smoke; there was a cheerfulness in the sweet smell of roasting pork looted from Mr. Bender's smokehouses. For the first morning in days, the men ate leisurely, propped against tree trunks. Their hardtack was all gone but they wiped greasy fingers on soiled trousers and trooped off in small groups to the sandy creek below the camp to strip and swim.

The word had gone around that the brigade would not march until eight o'clock, and only necessary duties were assigned. Pickets and scouts were out, of course, and over at the plantation's stables a farriery detail was hard at work shoeing horses.

On such a pleasant morning it is probable that Colonel Grierson and his staff met for their conference on Mr. Bender's broad front veranda. Undoubtedly they reviewed the raid on Newton Station with the usual jesting remarks and easy humor of men who have suddenly been relieved of a heavy burden.

Ninth Day
Saturday, April 25

VICKSBURG RR
NEWTON STATION
GARLANDVILLE
MONTROSE
RALEIGH

But Grierson reminded his officers that although the deed was done they had yet to escape from it. Until yesterday they had in their favor all the advantages of surprise. But surprise was no longer possible, regardless of the direction in which they moved. And the enemy by this time, having more or less correctly ascertained their strength, could probably dispose troops of sufficient numbers to make escape impossible.

Combining what he knew of Grant's battle plans in relation to the timing of the cavalry raid with information obtained from captured documents, from prisoners, and from civilians, Grierson was fairly confident that a fight was in the making at or near Grand Gulf. "I . . . knew from previous conversation with the General [Grant], and afterwards by letter from an officer of high rank and in close relations with him, of his general contemplated movements, that the objective point was Vicksburg and that all his operations would lead to getting a foothold on firm ground, and then to fight it out for a final capture of that stronghold. From my study of maps and knowledge gained otherwise of the country, I needed nothing more to convince me as to the approximate route Grant's forces would eventually take."[1]

A glance at his map showed Grierson that the distance from their present location in the Piney Woods country to Grand Gulf on the Mississippi River was well over a hundred miles, crow's flight. And the route was parallel with Pemberton's bristling defenses along the railroad from Jackson to Vicksburg. Would it be possible for less than a thousand cavalrymen, cut off from their base and supplies, to march this distance deep in enemy territory and join Grant for his big river crossing? It was a bold proposal, indeed, but Grierson seems to have convinced his officers that it could be done.

Some one evidently remarked on the poor condition of the horses; a few of the men already were riding mules. Mules were slow, Grierson agreed, but they would take all of Bender's anyhow and travel leisurely during this day's march, with squads scouring the byroads and woods for hidden horse herds. The entire day would be devoted to replenishing mounts. At eight o'clock that morning the raiders marched slowly out of Bender's Plantation, bound westward.[2]

II

"They took all Mr. Bender's mules," reported the Paulding *Clarion*, "and two of his negroes, and consumed a large amount of his corn and meat. Before leaving Mr. B[ender]'s they gave him a receipt for three thousand rations of meat and forage, signed by Wm. Prince, Colonel, Seventh Illinois cavalry."[3]

This receipt was probably one of Prince's sly jokes; he could have easily paid the plantation owner in Confederate money captured at Newton Station.

After leaving the plantation the column moved at a very slow rate of march. Halts were frequent and the horses were trotted only when it was necessary to relieve fatigued muscles. The pines grew closer together, the straight trunks bare of limbs to extraordinary heights. Through the forest the road twisted aimlessly, some places so narrow that two horsemen could not ride abreast, the trail's sandy texture covered with a carpet of brown pine needles.

The needles silenced the horses' hooves, and in the light filtering through the trees the column must have seemed a ghost company, the men's heads and shoulders moving rhythmically up and down without a beat to mark the measures. The only sounds were the occasional snortings of the horses, the infrequent commands, and the soughing of the pines.

Here the farms were small, and houses were few along the way. Sometimes they passed log cabins with pine groves almost to the doors, the tree trunks scarified in V-shaped slashes, gummy resin oozing into wooden cups. Pine fumes drifted from stills boiling turpentine somewhere down in the forests.

This was the Piney Woods country, poor white country, the people owning few slaves or none, loyal neither to the Confederacy nor the Union, wanting only to be left alone. By 1863 Confederate conscription laws had aroused many of the Piney Woods dwellers to covert disloyalty. Small bands of deserters were already operating as bushwhackers against conscripting agents, and in one county an attempt would soon be made to withdraw from the Confederate government.[4]

At Garlandville Colonel Grierson believed he had discovered sentiments disloyal to the Confederacy, although he had incorrectly interpreted them as pro-Union sympathies. And on this first day in the Piney Woods country his discerning scout, Sergeant Surby, also learned to his surprise that some Southerners were not his enemies.

Along the road to Pineville Surby halted his scouts in front of a double log-house. Five women of varying ages were sitting on the doorstep, but not a man was in sight. As Surby approached he could read fear in the women's faces. At first he believed they had been warned of disguised Yankees, but soon learned that they feared him as a Confederate conscriptor.

The women lied in a chorus: *Our husbands are all in the army at Vicksburg.* No, they had no milk, only water. *I suppose you are conscripting. Well, you'll find no men around here. You'd better conscript all the women, too. We have no one left to care for us. We don't own any blacks.*[5]

But Surby discovered later from a chance remark that at least two of their men were hiding out in the woods, and when he convinced the women that he and his scouts were Yankees instead of conscript agents, they brought out not only milk, but bread, butter, and pies. The oldest of the women, according to Surby, opened a chest and showed him a Union flag which she had hidden away.

Fascinated by this reception, Surby lingered until the column's advance caught up with the scouts. Then they rode away hurriedly, continuing through the small village of Pineville where there was no evidence of resistance. A short distance beyond the village the sergeant found the first large plantation since leaving Bender's, and he sent a man back to recommend it for the noon bivouac.

In a few minutes Lieutenant-Colonel Blackburn arrived with the advance company. When he and Surby rode up to the veranda entrance, they were informed that the plantation owner, Elias Nichols, was down in the cornfield a mile distant.

Surby rode down to the field alone and found Nichols seated on a stump, a large leatherbound whip across his knees. About twenty-five Negro slaves of both sexes were working in the field, swinging hoes as they moved along the corn rows.

Surby unslung his carbine but Nichols showed no surprise as he watched him approach across the field. "Any luck hunting?" the planter called cheerfully.

"I'm not on that kind of business," Surby replied.

Nichols glanced at Surby's carbine, then at his revolver. "How is Pemberton getting along at Vicksburg?" he asked.

"I reckon Vicksburg is safe against the whole northern army," Surby replied. "I was sent to ask you to come up to the house."

The plantation owner called one of the Negroes, an old man with woolly gray hair, and handed him the whip. He then walked along beside Surby's horse as they turned back toward the house. "Whose command you belong to?" Nichols demanded suddenly.

Anticipating the question, Surby replied easily: "Williams' from Tennessee, stationed at Jackson. General Pemberton sent us out to gather commissary stores and pick up deserters and conscripts."

They swung around the barn and Nichols gasped in astonishment, completely unprepared as he was for two regiments of cavalry. Grierson's men had already helped themselves to his corn and fodder. The plantation owner began grumbling loudly about the impertinence of soldiers who had not asked permission to use his corn, besides he had none to spare — not that the Confederate vouchers were not good enough, he was willing to do his share, but he didn't have more than he needed for his own use.

Surby made a path for him through the scurrying horsemen. Nichols began remarking on the fine uniforms, some captured, he allowed, being as they looked like Yankee blues, healthy-looking fellows, fine arms, too.

"Best equipped cavalry in the Confederate service," Surby assured him, as he dismounted in front of the house. Noticing Colonel Grierson's horse hitched to the veranda railing, he led Nichols through his own front door and into the room where Grierson was waiting with Blackburn and some of the other officers. Quite solemnly, he introduced Elias Nichols to "Colonel Williams from Jackson, Mississippi, formerly from Tennessee,"[6] and it was some time before the planter discovered the true identities of his visitors.

During the long halt at Nichols' Plantation the raiders saw their first ill-treated slave, a field hand who had been recaptured by his master after attempting to run away. He was found imprisoned in a log hut, manacled and chained to a ring in the floor. Colonel Blackburn ordered the irons cut loose and told the slave to join the brigade as a horse herder if he still wished to escape to freedom. The Negro accepted with profuse thanks.

Before resuming march, Grierson sent several detachments back to the north with orders to make rapid feints toward the railroad, but to avoid if possible any skirmishing with the enemy. He informed the detachment leaders that the column would proceed only a few miles farther along the road toward Raleigh, probably would camp for the night at the next large plantation. His object in sending out these troops was to create an impression that he intended to strike the railroad again, this time near Jackson. While the Confederates were preparing to receive him there he could make his dash westward toward Grand Gulf to join Grant's landing party on the Mississippi.

At two o'clock the regiment began filing slowly out of Nichol's Plantation. "They robbed Elias Nichols of all his mules," said the Paulding *Clarion,* "took a carriage, several of his negroes, and a greater part of his corn and meat."[7]

The road now ran straight south, following the Leaf River valley, the country becoming more rugged, with occasional ridges and deep ravines. At dusk they halted on the plantation of a physician, Dr. Mackadore.

Once again Grierson and his officers could dine comfortably and leisurely, ending the dinner with a discussion of their situation. The day had been almost too peaceful, but all were fully aware that a hornet's nest was certainly in full swarm a few miles to their north. "About nine o'clock," wrote Sergeant Surby, "Colonel Grierson requested Colonel Blackburn to select one of the scouts and report with him. In a few minutes Colonel Blackburn appeared with scout Samuel Nelson."[8]

Describing Sam Nelson* in his autobiography, Grierson said: "He had a peculiar impediment or sort of stutter in his speech which enabled him to think twice before he answered once any question put to him; altogether his make-up with his long hunting rifle, powder horn, etc., was most admirable."[9]

Nelson was instructed to proceed north to the railroad at Forest Station, some twenty miles away. His orders were to cut

---

* Grierson evidently confused the names of the scouts, George Steadman and Samuel Nelson. According to Sergeant Surby, who knew both men intimately, Steadman was quite small and wiry, not large and muscular like Nelson. From Surby, who was in charge of the scouts, we learn that it was the robust, hesitant talker, Nelson, who was ordered to Forest Station. Grierson's description is certainly that of Nelson rather than Steadman.

the telegraph line on the Vicksburg railroad; he was to bring back a piece of the wire as proof of accomplishment. And if he could find any bridges or trestlework before daybreak, he was to set fire to them. Grierson then handed Nelson a sheaf of Confederate money; he might need to return some of it to the rebels before he found his way back to the column.

At the conclusion of the interview, Grierson shook hands with the scout. "I bid him God's speed," he said, "and I thought to myself that in any event the rebels would not get the best of that singular looking but bright and sharp individual."[10]

III

Late in the morning, Captain R. C. Love, commanding a Confederate cavalry picket stationed at Brandon twelve miles east of Jackson, was surprised to receive a telegram sent direct from General Pemberton's headquarters and bearing the general's name:

CAPTAIN R. C. LOVE, Brandon, Miss.:

Ascertain where the enemy is, and go in that direction. You will not stay at Brandon, but if enemy is at Raleigh, go there and get on his rear, and plant ambush and annoy him. See if something can be done.

J. C. PEMBERTON.[11]

Captain Love wasted no time. Impressed by this order out of channels, he sent an immediate compliance reply, gathered up every available cavalryman and mount in the vicinity, and marched off on the double along the road that ran to Raleigh.

At that hour, then, Captain Love's Confederates and Colonel Grierson's raiders were marching directly toward each other, only thirty-four miles separating their forces. Pushing his men hard, Love was far down into the longleaf pine forests by nightfall. After an hour's halt to feed and rest, he resumed the march, intent on reaching Raleigh before dawn. Around midnight, sometime after his column reached a crossroads and turned south, his advance scouts picked up a lone northbound traveler.

They hustled him back to the captain.

The traveler was Grierson's scout, Samuel Nelson.

Corporal Nelson fortunately possessed a slight Southern accent, his home being in Gallatin County, Illinois, separated from Kentucky only by the Ohio River. When Captain Love demanded to know who he was and what he was doing on the road in the middle of the night, Nelson explained in an exaggerated drawl that the Yankees had pressed him in for a guide, had kept him two days, released him on parole, and that he was then on his way to see a friend who lived at Forest Station.

Love wanted to know when and where Nelson had left the Yankees.

"Garlandville," Nelson replied, "yesterday at noon."

"What force do the Yankees have?" asked Love.

"About eighteen hundred," Nelson said, doubling the brigade's strength. He added that they were well armed.

Captain Love indicated that he believed he could furnish the Yankees a fight. He then asked if Nelson knew the nearest route to Garlandville, and which direction the Yankees had taken from there.

Nelson directed the Confederate captain so as to lead him away from Mackadore's Plantation, telling him that the Yankees had gone eastward toward the Mobile & Ohio Railroad.

Love seemed to be satisfied with this information, and told the scout that he could continue to Forest Station.

As he continued northward Corporal Nelson rode slowly along the side of the Confederate column, attempting to estimate the enemy's strength. But the men were scattered, and in the thick darkness of the forest-bound road he could not be certain whether they consisted of squads or companies. He could not believe there were as many as 1,800, yet the Confederate officer had bragged he would give the Yankees a fight after being told *they* numbered 1,800.

Riding until the sounds of the Confederates had died away behind him, Nelson turned his horse aside and waited quietly for several minutes. Satisfied that the rear guard had passed, he began retracing his path. He knew that as soon as the rebels reached the main road somewhere to the east they would discover signs of the brigade's passage, and then would immediately turn in pursuit. His orders to proceed to the railroad seemed less important now than the danger of these night-riding rebels. It was up to him to outrun them to Mackadore's Plantation and give Colonel Grierson warning of their coming.[12]

IV

In addition to sending Captain Love in search of the Union cavalry force which had devastated his eastern supply line, General Pemberton followed up his actions of the previous day, leaving nothing undone which might ensnare the tricky enemy.

General John Adams had reached Lake Station only twelve miles from Newton at 2:20 o'clock in the morning, reporting that telegraph operators were at work restoring the wire in the long break. Pemberton advised Adams to send messages to General Loring at Meridian, General Simon Buckner at Mobile, and General Johnston in Tennessee, notifying them of the raid on Newton Station and requesting them to send troops to help track down the raiders.

Adams put the messages through by courier to the other end of the severed line, wiring copies back to Pemberton. When Pemberton saw Adams' telegram to Buckner, his edgy temper flared up. The telegram read:

GENERAL BUCKNER:

All is lost unless you can send a regiment or two to Meridian. General Pemberton directs me to urge you to send.

JOHN ADAMS, BRIGADIER-GENERAL.[13]

Pressed as he was, Pemberton took the time to write a blistering reprimand to Adams: "You say in your dispatch to General Buckner 'all is lost, unless &c.' Correct it. I never authorized you to use such an expression."[14]

His intense concern with the petty details of his command, details which hourly increased in number as the enemy prepared for the big strike, was beginning to tell on Pemberton. His generals at Grand Gulf and Vicksburg were asking for reinforcements, but he reminded both of them sharply that cavalry raiders on his rear were doing far more damage than Grant's army across the river. The commander of his arsenal in Jackson also sent him an urgent inquiry concerning the condition of the broken railroad. Seven hundred thousand musket percussion caps and 30,000 pounds of powder from Alabama arsenals were somewhere on the way to replenish the depleted stores at Grand Gulf and Vicksburg. But Pemberton could not tell his arsenal commander when the tracks would be repaired. Perhaps the enemy cavalry might even strike the road again at some other point.

Late in the afternoon a message arrived from General Loring, dispatched from Enterprise, a town on the Mobile & Ohio ten miles below Meridian: "Enemy appeared here at 1 o'clock and demanded the town. They were represented as 1,500 strong. Colonel [Edward] Goodwin was here with the Thirty-fifth Alabama, who defied them. I hastened here with two regiments; enemy have fallen back at last accounts 3 miles. I am now on the road pursuing them. . . ."[15]

After reading this, Pemberton was fairly confident that he now had the Yankees cornered. Loring would block an escape through Alabama and Adams would stop them if they turned back to Newton. And if they attempted to flee all the way to Baton Rouge, units drawn from the Mississippi River defenses would surely bring them to bay.

V

The force of 1,500 Yankee cavalry believed by Loring and Pemberton to be near Enterprise was of course the will-o'-the-wisp Company B, Captain Henry Forbes and his thirty-four horsemen. Grierson's brigade at that hour was all of fifty miles to the west, marching leisurely through the Piney Woods country.

Shortly after dawn on April 25, Captain Forbes and his men galloped down the road from Philadelphia into Newton Station, where the fires kindled by Grierson's men still drifted smoke over the scorched metal undercarriages of the trains. The little town bore the look and smell of devastation.

Outside the hospital the paroled convalescents were waiting to receive the new visitors; instead of offering resistance they politely answered all of Captain Forbes's questions. The raiders' rear guard, they said, had departed late yesterday afternoon, about fifteen hours past.

Company B, then, had gained only six hours on the main column after riding hard for twenty-four hours.

And which direction had the raiders taken? The convalescents were certain they intended to turn east; the commanding colonel and several of his officers had made repeated inquiries concerning the roads in that direction. It was true they had marched southward from Newton; travelers from Garlandville had already brought stories of a skirmish there. The Yankees were said to have continued eastward on the road to Paulding which would take them across the Mobile & Ohio at Quitman.

Thus did Colonel Grierson's carefully planned deception mislead one of his own company commanders. Captain Forbes, of course, had more reason to believe than to doubt the rumors that the brigade was marching toward the east. Three days ago when Colonel Prince gave him orders to make the feint on Macon, Prince had said that it seemed highly probable the column would swing eastward after raiding the Vicksburg railroad and move into Alabama for a retreat northward to the Federal lines.

After listening to varying stories in Newton, Captain Forbes was convinced that Grierson had indeed marched eastward. He decided there would be no point in following the brigade directly. It seemed more sensible to cut off the southward loop, which he believed Grierson to be making, by turning directly east from Newton, crossing the Mobile & Ohio at or near Enterprise, and joining the brigade beyond the railroad as it passed up to the north. Enterprise appeared to be the logical crossing point since all his informants agreed that the town was without defenders.

At once Company B filed off to the east on the road to Enterprise, every hoofbeat taking them in the opposite direction from their comrades in Grierson's brigade.

We spent the day in this move, until at about one o'clock we were within six miles of the town. All rumors agreed that there were no rebels in Enterprise.

The town lies on two benches, the lower of which is not in sight until the upper one has been crossed. We rode confidently in sight of the upper bench, when looking down to the right toward a fringe of woods about three quarters of a mile distant, we saw a party of perhaps forty Negroes, who had gathered in the rear of our little column, scampering down a lane as fast as their old mules and hacks could carry them. What they were running from we never knew, for we never saw one of them again.

Perhaps they had seen two or three horsemen who were dashing madly about through the town; for about this time we ourselves discovered them. We kept straight ahead at a walk, until we discovered to our left front what appeared to be a stockade, with a sentinel bearing a musket, at its corner. Halting a moment, we borrowed a pocket handkerchief from a wash hanging in one of the door-yards, fastened it to the end of a saber, and under this as a flag of truce rode down to demand a conference.[16]

Captain Forbes ordered his lieutenant, William McCausland, and the first file of four to follow. Although he waved the white flag continually, several shots were fired at them from the sentry gate as they approached the stockade. But they kept moving ahead.

Back with the company on the slope, Sergeant Stephen Forbes watched his brother Henry riding unhesitatingly forward, the town beyond drab under the cloudy sky. Was this the place where the prison train had stopped a year ago, where the rebel recruits coming over from their camp had almost taken the cars by storm? *Where one of our guards benevolently ransacked the town in search of something to eat for us, finally obtaining three dozen cookies for which they charged us one dollar and twenty cents?*

Stephen remembered the rebel recruits swarming over the prisoners' car. *In their open-mouthed eagerness to catch a glimpse of a dozen "live yankees," collecting in crowds about the car and even climbing the roof and peering through the cracks, from whence the guards could only dislodge them by using their bayonets . . . As they looked to me from the car window, there was only a surging sea of butternut rags and dirt, above which rolled and bobbed a tumult of faces composed mostly of old hats and open mouths, while the whole mass was kept in a state of constant agitation by the efforts of a swaggering, good-natured rumshop blackguard whose cavern of a mouth gave vent to alternate floods of ribaldry and tobacco juice, and the occasional remarks of the sportively inclined of our party.*[17]

There had been, on that other day, barrels and barrels of sugar and molasses lying beside the railroad, and now Stephen Forbes, sitting straight in his saddle with his hands gripping the sweated bridle leather, must have looked around wonderingly for the barrels, the one feature of the colorless landscape that had marked it in his memory.

Then three finely mounted Confederate officers appeared, one carrying a white kerchief fluttering at the end of an infantry ramrod. Captain Forbes halted, awaiting the approaching enemy.

The Confederate carrying the white kerchief wore a gold sash around his waist; his horse pranced nervously to within a few feet of Captain Forbes. The man glanced once at the company drawn up in a column of fours on the slope beyond. His voice came firmly, yet disinterestedly courteous, soft and Southern, the words stilted in the old chivalric form: "To whom are we indebted for the honor of this visit?"

"I come from Major-General Grierson," replied Captain Forbes sternly. "To demand the surrender of Enterprise."

Betraying no surprise, the Confederate officers held their horses steady, the eyes of all three fixed on Captain Forbes's austere face, as if waiting for a limiting clause to follow the blunt request. After a moment of silence, the spokesman replied: "Will the Captain put the demand in writing?"

"Certainly," replied Forbes quickly. "To whom shall I address it?"

"To Colonel Edwin Goodwin, commanding the post."

"Very well. I shall give the Colonel one hour to consider the demand for surrender."[18]

My informants were either lying or mistaken, Captain Forbes was thinking. *This town is garrisoned.*

He finished scribbling the surrender demand: "One hour only for consideration, after which further delay will be at your peril." Glancing up, he saw that the rebel carrying the white flag had also written a message. Their horses came closer, the notes were exchanged.

"Will the Captain await the reply here?" asked the Southerner.

"We shall fall back to the main body," replied Captain Forbes, "and there await the reply."

The Confederates swept off their hats in a gesture of farewell, turned their mounts about, and galloped back toward the town. Captain Forbes nodded to Lieutenant McCausland. "Right about, gentlemen! And let's pray that we find the main body." They rode at a slow canter back to the company, the captain unfolding the Confederate officer's note and reading it hurriedly: "Colonel Goodwin's compliments to General Grierson, commanding United States forces, and asks permission to consider his demand for one hour."

Forbes slipped the paper inside his saddlebag. He hoped he would be lucky enough to pass it on to Grierson; the colonel would appreciate his promotion in rank.

We never officially knew what the Confederates' reply was, as for reasons best known to themselves they failed to make it reach us. Perhaps it was lack of speed. We fell back, very cheerfully, four miles, and fed, and resumed our retreat, which was diligently continued all night. We learned afterwards from the Southern papers that our reply was forwarded six miles on our track that evening with an escort of 2,000 infantry, under the impression that we were at least 1,500 strong.

Once more we were out of the lion's mouth, but woefully and inextricably entangled in his den. We rode on towards the sinking sun and — planned. Should we run north? Should we attempt Pensacola, Mobile, Vicksburg?* We determined on one more despairing effort at a stern chase of the regiments. We had lost another forty miles. The nearest point where we were certain of the whereabouts of our command was Garlandville.[19]

Garlandville was twenty miles away, the roads bad, the streams unbridged, but by dusk they were approaching the town, the men so long without sleep they had lost all fear and caution.

We made rapid work, and passed through this place in the early dusk. Here was a home guard of sixty men (the Garlandville Avengers) who had sworn to fight at sight any Yanks they might encounter. Our scouts fell in with one of these guards and actually accompanied him to warn his companions that we were Alabama cavalry, fearing that they might mistake us for Yankees and give us trouble![20]

As the company marched through Garlandville where yellow lights gleamed in the windows and mounted armed men lurked in the shadowy streets, the riders were unnaturally silent, their exhausted nerves and muscles grudgingly taut against this new danger. They wondered if fortune would desert them now — an alert rebel suddenly discovering a telltale Yankee symbol, a spray of lanternlight revealing a trouser-leg too blue beneath its dust, or a carelessly spoken word in an accent strange to Southern ears.

They were out of Garlandville suddenly, every man of the little company resisting an urge to flee in a wild gallop. But they marched calmly on, and in a few seconds were excitedly talking among themselves, the news coming down quickly through the column from Captain Forbes. Grierson had marched to the west!

While they were passing through Garlandville the disguised scouts, posing as Alabamans, had made certain of Grierson's route. Cheered by the news and the knowledge that the hard flight from Enterprise had probably saved their lives and brought them back within a day's ride of the brigade, the men's energies were renewed for another night march, their third in succession.

---

* According to Stephen Forbes, they also considered breaking up and scattering, riding north by twos and threes, in the hope that though some might be taken, the rest would escape. "A consultation was held quietly by the leading officers as we rode along. . . . Should we return to Grierson's trail and make another effort, under new disadvantages, at a direct pursuit? We stood three to one for the last alternative, and so we kept on to Garlandville." — Stephen A. Forbes, "Grierson's Cavalry Raid," *Illinois State Historical Society, Transactions,* 1907, p. 112.

Not until midnight, when his scouts reported a plantation well off the main road, did Captain Forbes call a halt. They stopped at Dr. Hodge's for "several hours," reported the Jackson *Appeal* of April 28. "Some of them entered the doctor's enclosure and required his daughters to furnish them provisions, which was done to the extent of cooked articles on hand. The rose bushes and flower beds of the young ladies were also sadly despoiled by the unwelcome visitors, but beyond this, our informant says they did no damage, nor did they insult the ladies. The doctor was absent."[21]

And what were the feelings of the young daughters of plantation owners toward these invading Yankees? The visit of Captain Forbes and his company with the Hodge sisters apparently is unchronicled by any of the participants, but another planter's daughter, Miss Cordelia Scales of Oakland Plantation, recorded a similar experience in a letter to a friend. (See also p. 52.)

"Grierson's Thieves," she called the raiders. "I can't write of these; it makes my blood boil to think of the outrages they committed. . . . Capt. Flynn & Col. Steward* protected us. One of them [Grierson's men] sent me word that they shot ladies as well as men, & if I did not stop talking to them so & displaying my Confederate flag he'd blow my damn brains out."

In another letter, Miss Scales was equally indignant:

I must tell you about the Yankees as you are so anxious to know how they behaved. You may congratulate yourself, my dear friend, on being slighted by them. They came & stayed in our yard all the time . . . they took corn, fodder, ruined the garden & took every thing in the poultry line. I never heard such profanity in all my life & so impudent, they would walk around the house & look up at the windows & say, "wonder how many Secesh gals they got up there." I did not have my pistol & Ma would not let me go where they were, but one evening she was so worn out she sent me down to attend to the skimming of some wine & other household matters, when she thought they had all left. Just as I got out in the yard, two Cavalry men & six infantry came up & surrounded me. Pa was not at home. Ma & Sis Lucy were looking on & were frightened very much for they knew I would speak my mind to them if they provoked me.

The first Lt. asked me if we had any chickens.

I told him, "no."

"Any milk?"

---

* Two Union officers admired by Cordelia Scales, who referred to them as "Irish Democrats." They were with the 90th Illinois Infantry.

I said, "no," — that some of his tribe had been there that morning and got everything in that line. He smiled & said "they did not pay you for them did they?" I told him a few pretended to pay by giving us federal money, that I preferred leaves to that.

He said "why federal money dont seem to be in demand."

I said "not down this way sure."

The second Lt. a red-headed ugly pert thing commenced to laugh about our men running from Holly Springs & said "our men never run, Miss," I told him, no, we all knew what a orderly retreat they made from Bull Run, Manassas, & Leighsburg, that it did their army a great deal of credit & that I hope they felt proud of it.

One of the pickets remarked then "Oh! hush Tom you dont know how to talk to Secesh gals."

I turned to him & thanked him that we were all ladies in the South.

The 2nd Lt. got very mad at what I said about their men running — said, " I can inform you, Miss, I was in the battle of Leighsburg & our men did not run far."

I told him I knew they did not, they ran as far as they could and then jumped in the river.

The first Lt. broke out in a laugh & said "Ah! Tom shes got you now," & turned to me & said, "I admire your candor very much. I had much rather see you so brave than for you to pretend to entertain Union sentiments."

Just as I was walking away and congratulating myself that they had not cursed me one of them said "She is the damnest little Secesh I ever saw" & another "she is a damn pretty gal, I be-dog if she aint." I could write you a newspaper about them but I reckon you are tired now & it makes me mad to think about them. Goodbye little darling I will write you more news next time."[22]

"CAPTAIN FORBES
PRESENTS HIS COMPLIMENTS"

The pickets came alert, set carbines at ready, and then out of the darkness one of them sounded the familiar call: "Halt! Who goes there?"

Scout Samuel Nelson replied with the password of the Butternut Guerillas, identifying himself by name. As soon as the pickets signaled him past, Nelson urged his lathered horse into a trot, moving up through the graying light to the front veranda of Dr. Mackadore's plantation house.

Colonel Grierson was still asleep, but when the officer of the guard heard Sam Nelson's story he immediately awakened the brigade commander. In a few moments Grierson was listening to the scout's hasty report of the encounter with Confederate cavalry. As soon as Nelson had finished, Grierson questioned him carefully about the enemy's location, the time of the meeting, the number of soldiers.

Nelson could not be certain of the number; he told how he had set the raiders' strength at 1,800, a number

*Tenth Day
Sunday, April 26*

RALEIGH
WESTVILLE

135

which did not appear to cause the rebel captain to have any qualms about a possible meeting with them. But Nelson was certain he had not passed more than a regiment in the darkness.

In his official report Grierson estimated that his scout had met the rebel cavalry about seven miles below the railroad. "He succeeded in misdirecting them as to the place he had last seen us," the colonel said, "and, having seen them well on the wrong road, he immediately retraced his steps to camp with the news. When he first met them they were on the direct road to our camp, and had they not been turned from their course would have come up with us before daylight."[1]

Grierson immediately ordered the buglers to sound boots and saddles. His plan for cutting the telegraph line at Forest Station was, of course, abandoned, and Nelson was sent to report for duty again with Sergeant Surby; the Butternut Guerillas would have plenty of work to do out in front of the column this morning.

Before the regiments marched, Surgeon Archibald Agnew reported to Grierson that he had three men who were unable to travel farther. One of them was the man wounded in the charge through Garlandville, the other two were seriously ill. Grierson settled the matter promptly, arranging to leave the men under the care of their host, Dr. Mackadore, a physician.

Another and more vital problem facing Grierson this morning was the shortage of provisions. With the best of luck they would need four days in which to reach the Mississippi River. This would be their tenth day out of La Grange, and the five days' rations issued at departure were long since gone. Such meat and corn as they had been able to take from the sparsely furnished plantations in the Piney Woods had been cut fine among the 900 haversacks and 1,000 nosebags of the two regiments.*

To handle the problem of food supply during the raid, Grierson had selected a young farm boy from his Sixth Regiment, appointed him acting commissary sergeant, and attached him to

---

* The usual haversack rations for a day, according to Private Henry Eby of the Seventh Illinois, consisted of "a quantity of the genuine, indispensable, hard-as-a-rock-Uncle-Sam-hardtack, sometimes animated hardtack, a slice of bacon, sometimes animated; a small package of browned coffee, a small quantity of sugar tied up in paper and tucked away in a corner." — Henry H. Eby, *Observations of an Illinois Boy in Battle, Camp and Prisons,* Mendota, Ill., 1910, p. 69.

headquarters staff. His name was William Pollard and he carried out his duties like a veteran forager. Sergeant Pollard always rode into a plantation with the advance, detailing men to guard the doors of each smokehouse, barn, and kitchen, allowing no one to pass without permission from a commissioned officer. After surveying the food and forage supplies available, Pollard would then assign men to issue each company its share of hams, shoulders, cornmeal, corn, and hay.[2]

But as the brigade moved deeper into the Piney Woods, Sergeant Pollard was finding his commissary post a more and more frustrating duty. Officers and men alike were beginning to grumble over the lack of coffee, a commodity virtually unknown in the South since the coastal blockade had become effective. Almost every one of the raiders carried a tin pail, usually made from an emptied quart fruit can, in which to make his coffee. "This rude little kettle," wrote one cavalryman, "was seen hanging to every saddle on the march, and three or four or half a dozen times a day, if opportunity offered, small fires were started and water set on for making coffee."[3]

The men refused to drink Secesh coffee made from parched peas and corn ground together, or from dried chicory and okra seeds. They detested this wartime beverage of the South as much as they disliked the Union Army's "desiccated vegetables"—potatoes and shredded carrots and turnips dried and pressed hard and intended to be cooked by boiling.

But the raiders had learned how to mix Mississippi cornmeal with salt and water in their tin pails and bake the mixture on a hot flat stone, or at the end of a stick, or wrapped in a corn husk. Nor did they object much to the fat pork and molasses diet of the Piney Woods country, and they cheerfully roasted in the hot ashes of their campfires the mountains of sweet potatoes unearthed by Sergeant Pollard and his persevering foragers.

As they marched out of Mackadore's Plantation, however, their haversacks carried almost as much corn as their horses' nosebags, and the old joke about the solicitous general undoubtedly was going the rounds:

"How are you getting along, boys?"

"Pretty well, General, only them blamed mules are eating up all our rations."

II

Shortly after departing from Mackadore's Plantation at six o'clock in the morning, Grierson's raiders began crossing Leaf River. Before the rear guard passed over, a fire detail had heaped piles of leaves and brush around the supports, and as soon as the last horseman was across, the bridge was blazing. What hopes Grierson had held for the return of Captain Forbes and Company B went down with the bridge, but he decided to burn it as a necessary delaying action against the Confederate cavalry reported by Corporal Nelson.

Ahead of the column, Sergeant Surby and the Butternut Guerillas turned northwestward with the twisting road, leaving the reed brakes of the river bottomlands and climbing into hills where sedge grass and pines struggled for supremacy on the red soil. Occasionally a gaunt, long-snouted hog would dart across their path. The farms were small, fields of young cotton, corn, and sugar cane lay unfenced around log cabins that were little more than hovels.

It was about eight o'clock when the scouts sighted the first houses of Raleigh scattered along the top of a narrow red ridge, the first town of any size they had seen since leaving Garlandville two days before. "On entering the place," said Sergeant Surby, "I discovered a man hastily mounting his horse and riding away at full speed. . . . He was requested to halt, but paying no attention, kept increasing his speed."[4]

After ordering his men in pursuit, Surby began patrolling the town alone while awaiting the advance squad. Within a few minutes, the scouts galloped back with their captive. He proved to be the county sheriff, and he was carrying in his saddlebags three thousand Confederate dollars in county funds. As soon as Lieutenant-Colonel Blackburn arrived, Surby turned the sheriff and the money over to him and took the lead again, following the road which now veered back to the southwest.

Rain began dripping from the dark skies during the noon bivouac; by midafternoon the fall had increased to a steady drenching downpour. But in spite of weather and lack of forage in this lonely grassless land of everlasting pines, Grierson urged the regiments to set a lively rate of march. In contrast to yesterday's leisurely pace, he seemed now to be obsessed with a desire for speed.

As the column moved steadily westward, the rear guard burned every bridge they crossed. This precaution, together with the heavy rain flooding the streams, kept the brigade doubly secure from a pursuing enemy.

Soon after nightfall the downpour slackened to a drizzle. They passed through Westville unopposed, moving on through the darkness a couple of miles to Williams' Plantation. Strong River was only two or three miles farther, and Grierson ordered the Seventh Regiment to proceed and cross, set a bridge guard, and halt at the first plantation beyond. As Colonel Prince was to remain with Grierson for a staff conference, Lieutenant-Colonel Blackburn took command of the Seventh, marching across Strong River to Smith's Plantation.

The Sunday night meeting of Grierson and his officers is not recorded in detail, but it appears from subsequent events that it marked the beginning of an intense rivalry between Colonel Prince and Colonel Grierson, a rivalry that was to end in bitterness and a threat of court-martial. Tired and wet as they all were, they probably gathered around one of their unwilling host's fireplaces, drying their uniforms and damp socks, smoking cigars and sipping rebel wine.

Grierson was pleased with their progress in such unfavorable weather; they had covered about forty miles that day, leaving only sixty miles between them and Grand Gulf on the Mississippi River. Sometime tomorrow, however, they would pass out of the Piney Woods into more thickly settled country and could expect to meet more resistance, both from civilians and enemy soldiery. The New Orleans & Jackson Railroad was only twenty miles to the west. It would probably be guarded at certain points, but if the raiders' arrival was unexpected they might be able to damage trestles and tracks considerably. And before reaching the railroad, they must again cross the Pearl River, a much more formidable stream here than the first place they had crossed it — above Philadelphia, three days ago.

Grierson had been informed by a captured deputy sheriff that the Pearl was unbridged. A public ferry, with a bottom large enough to float several horses at a time, was the only means of crossing. It was highly probable that this ferry was under Confederate guard, and there was no other crossing for twenty-five miles north or south. The importance of securing the Pearl River ferry at the earliest possible moment was apparent to every man on Grierson's staff. "Though tired and sleepy, there were those who did not rest or sleep longer than to feed their horses and prepare supper. As the citizens were arming themselves, and the news [of our approach] was flying in every direction, it was a matter of life or death that Pearl River should be crossed and the New Orleans and Southern railroad reached, without any delay."[5]

"After feeding," Grierson reported laconically, "Colonel Prince, of the Seventh Illinois Cavalry, with two battalions, was sent . . . forward to Pearl River to secure the ferry and landing. . . . With the main column, I followed in about two hours."[6]

III

Under the same clouds which darkened Corporal Sam Nelson's dawn arrival at Mackadore's Plantation, Captain Henry Forbes's Company B struggled to wakefulness several miles to the east, on the soft lawn of Dr. Hodge's country estate.

Sergeant Stephen Forbes had drawn the last guard detail, stationing himself against a rail fence beside the long entrance drive which led up to the house from the main road.

It was a carelessly fastened horse, however, which really kept watch for us. Becoming entangled in his halter strap, he pulled down the rail fence to which he was tied, with a crash which wakened the solitary sentinel, who had gone to sleep with his gun in his hands. . . . I can vouch personally for the truth of this statement, for I was the sentinel. . . .

After a rapid breakfast by the light of our camp fires we started for the hardest and most discouraging ride of the raid. Approaching Raleigh, we repeated in substance the exploit at Philadelphia, surprising, by a headlong charge, a company of home guards which had gathered at the village inn, breaking up their guns and taking their captain with us as a prisoner. We were now but seven or eight hours behind the regiment, and hope began to dawn, until we came to a stream swollen with recent rains. The column had crossed on a bridge, which was now a wreck of blackened timbers. Grierson had given us up for lost and was burning his bridges behind him. Five times that day we swam our horses across overflowing streams, and once were compelled to make a long detour to find a place where we could get into the water and out again.*

---

* It is probable that this detour prevented an encounter with Captain R. C. Love's Confederate cavalry, also pursuing Grierson over these same roads.

And then a greater danger loomed ahead of us. Some thirty or forty miles farther on was Strong river, and a few miles beyond that was the Pearl, neither of which we could hope to ford or swim; and we were losing time, by reason of the burned bridges, instead of gaining on Grierson. Some way must be found to reach him before he destroyed Strong river bridge or we were lost.[7]

In the hope that three men could move faster than thirty-five, Captain Forbes halted and asked for volunteers to ride on and overtake the column. Stephen urged his horse forward out of the formation, followed by two privates, John Moulding and Arthur Wood.

"You men will leave all your arms and other encumbrances," said the captain, "excepting a pistol apiece and a few loose cartridges in your pockets." He rode quickly down the file of the company, looking over the horses. Selecting the three freshest mounts, he ordered a quick exchange with the volunteers.

Although it was only five o'clock in the afternoon, the low clouds persistently drizzling rain would bring early darkness to hinder tracking the brigade over the winding and diverse roads. But the three volunteers waved cheerily and galloped off through the green pines.

"I never expected to see one of them again," Captain Forbes said afterwards, "feeling sure they would be picked off as stragglers."

Stephen and his two companions kept their horses moving steadily, following the trail marked by the passing regiments, the tall pines closing out all the world except the narrow road ahead. Just before darkness closed in they saw a group of saddled horses down in the woods. No riders were in sight. "We listened for shots as we hurried by," said Stephen, "but they did not come."

Suddenly the pines broke away and the hoof marks they were following vanished in a grassy field. "Puzzled at first, we presently suspected a countermarch, and following the trail back through the thickening dusk about half a mile, we found where it branched off to the left. If we had been a little later we should have been completely lost. Black night now fell, with drizzling rain, and we dismounted now and then to make sure, by feeling the road, that we were still on the track of the regiments."[8]

Once or twice Stephen thought he heard voices and marching horses ahead, but when he dashed forward in the solid blackness,

141

his mount sliding and stumbling on the slippery clay surface of the road, he found nothing but the bitter frustration of one who pursues a mirage.

Then he was sure, coming down into bottomland with the smell of rotting mud and a sluggish river, and his companions heard the voices, too, and the nickering horses, and they saw a lantern flickering like a yellow firefly far down in the trees.

They spurred their tired horses into an extra burst of speed.

"Halt! Who comes there?" The voice came out of a Mississippi canebrake, but to Stephen Forbes's ears it was sweet—for it rang with the clean, hard tones of the Northern cornlands.

Ignoring the command, he and his two companions did not slacken their speed, but answered the challenger as they rode by with a shout: "Company B!"

A moment of silence, and the pickets responded with a cheer. "Company B has come back!"

"The cheer," said Stephen Forbes, "was caught up by the rear company, it ran down the column, cheer upon cheer, faster than our horses could run."

They reached Grierson just as the colonel was turning his horse onto the Strong River bridge. "Company B has come back!" some one shouted in the darkness.

Pulling his reins up tight, Stephen halted beside Grierson. "Captain Forbes presents his compliments, and begs to be allowed to burn his bridges for himself!"[9]

It is easy to picture that dramatic moment — the drenched and mud-stained nineteen-year-old sergeant sitting erect upon his spent horse, the colonel grinning at him through his black, spade-shaped beard.

Grierson assured Sergeant Forbes that the bridge-burning detail for Strong River would be augmented into a guard detachment to await the arrival of B Company. He congratulated the messengers on their speedy ride. Half an hour later and the bridge would have been in flames. He asked after Captain Forbes's health, and the outcome of the Macon venture. When Stephen informed him of the long march to Enterprise, Grierson was astonished that they had been able to overtake the main column.

The colonel would have liked to hear more details of Company B's adventures, but time was pressing. He ordered Sergeant

Forbes and his two companions to remain with the Strong River guard, and then turned his horse back upon the bridge, moving with the column towards the more formidable Pearl River. As the hoofbeats rumbled in uneven measures over the muddy planking, Grierson was probably wondering if the raiders' luck and good timing had held long enough for Prince to secure the ferry.

IV

Colonel Grierson would have been gratified to know that the raiders' luck had held for his detached Iowa regiment under Colonel Hatch, which had finally returned to the base at La Grange.

Luck had run out during the march, however, for ten of the Iowans, an unusually low number considering their two hard fights and the persistent enemy skirmishers hindering their advance on the march south and dogging their rear and flanks on the return north. Six of the unlucky ten had been captured in the Palo Alto fighting; three had been wounded. The tenth was Hatch's orderly, Charles Ellsthorp. When the regiment came within fifteen miles of La Grange, the colonel sent Ellsthorp ahead with a message to the Federal picket line. "On his return," said Sergeant Lyman Pierce, "he was mortally wounded by a ball from a squirrel rifle in the hands of a guerrilla, who stole up to the roadside for the purpose of committing the murder."[10]

The Iowans had captured fifty-one Confederates, and in his report Colonel Hatch estimated they had killed or wounded not less than one hundred of the enemy. They captured 300 shotguns and rifles, and 200 horses and mules. "I left camp with 70 rounds of ammunition, and had 10 on reaching it," he said. "The fight at Palo Alto, and diverting the enemy from Colonel Grierson has undoubtedly given him thirty-six hours' start."[11]

On this same day, General Pemberton acknowledged the damage done by Hatch's cavalrymen by claiming a victory over them and then immediately pleading for more help in a telegram to General Johnston in Tennessee:

All mounted men are actively engaged endeavoring to intercept enemy; none stationary. Enemy, who were at Okolona, driven back. Defeated them at Birmingham, killing some twenty and wounding many others. Have no cavalry of any importance to operate against the Newton Station party; am mounting some infantry. Hope to intercept them. These raids cannot be prevented unless I can have more mounted men."[12]

General John Adams at Lake Station was in turn pleading for more men from Pemberton. He reported the enemy raiders, 800 strong, were fifteen miles south of him and he expected them to attack either Forest or Lake momentarily. He could not defend both stations without another regiment.

Adams' fairly accurate estimate of Grierson's location, however, was passed over by Pemberton, who was still peeved with Adams because of the latter's "all-is-lost" telegram to General Buckner. Pemberton was inclined instead to accept yesterday's reports from Enterprise, placing Grierson's raiders in that vicinity.

In fact, Pemberton was so confident on this unusually calm Sunday that Grierson was somewhere in eastern Mississippi, attempting to slip back to the north, that he wired General Chalmers a repeat of the order sent on Friday (and then amended on Saturday): "Move with all your cavalry and light artillery via Oxford, to Okolona, to intercept force of enemy."[13]

At the hour of this order, Grierson's raiders were only thirty miles south of Pemberton's own headquarters in Jackson, almost 200 miles from Okolona!

Captain Forbes's bluff at Enterprise had indeed thrown a blind across the eyes of the Confederates, and at the same time had raised the raiders' wonderful timing and luck to the quality of high magic.*

---

* Lieutenant Thomas W. Lippincott, Company I, Sixth Illinois Cavalry, was convinced that Grierson performed his magic with a daily timetable of combined operations, and possibly a secret communications system, with General Grant. Many years after the raid he wrote to Grierson as follows: "Major Starr rode much by my side at the head of Company 'I' and several times he told me Grant was going to do so and so *today*. He never told me what he was going to do tomorrow or at any future day it was always *today*. . . . I knew if he knew it he must have got it from you and it impressed me deeply . . . I conclude . . . that you knew . . . the data [of Grant's plans] before you started and that you depended on information obtained through rebel sources to inform you of the success or failure of each. . . ."

Grierson replied that "no one knew my plans any more than they did those of Gen. Grant — nor did each of us have predetermined or definite detailed plans before starting on our hazardous undertakings." — T. W. Lippincott to B. H. Grierson, March 6 and March 24, 1886; B. H. Grierson to T. W. Lippincott, March 13, 1886 (Grierson Papers).

ACROSS THE PEARL TO HAZLEHURST

It would be interesting to know the thoughts of thirty-year-old Colonel Edward Prince as he led his battalions through darkness toward the Pearl River ferry. Was Prince resentful of Grierson's order sending him forward to secure the ferry? Or had he volunteered for this assignment, as the New York *Times* later reported after interviewing him? Did he feel that his regiment, the Seventh, was bearing the brunt of the entire raid, drawing all the dangerous missions while Grierson's old regiment, the Sixth, was always kept back in reserve? Or was his growing bitterness toward Grierson only a personal matter, the envy of an officer forced by circumstances to take orders from an equal in rank?

Two years ago, sitting in his comfortable law office in Quincy, Illinois, Edward Prince probably would have laughed at anyone who might have suggested that he would make a good cavalry officer. But now, was he not proving his abilities as a leader by driving ahead of the brigade through black

Eleventh Day
Monday, April 27

HAZLEHURST ⊢○———╳⊶○ WESTVILLE

145

and disagreeable weather toward what might well be the most dangerous undertaking of the raid?

Prince must have known that some of his junior officers distrusted him, disliked his imperious demeanor which sometimes broke through his outwardly easy-going manner. But none of them had been as successful in civil life as he, not even Grierson who had failed in business, some said because he spent too much time tinkling away on a piano or blowing a tin horn. Prince may have wondered if Grierson would end up the same way in military service; Grierson didn't seem to give a continental damn for cavalry drill or tactics.

Edward Prince had been zealous in studying cavalry tactics, so adept at mastering the intricate maneuvers of drill that in the early weeks of the war the Governor of Illinois appointed him Cavalry Drill Master at Camp Butler, with the rank of lieutenant-colonel. Perhaps Prince resented the fact that it was Grierson who had recommended him for his full colonelcy, "out of respect for his education, ingenuity and resolution," Grierson had said. But Prince did not know that some of his classmates at law college had warned Grierson against him: "I was informed by some of Prince's college class mates that sooner or later his meanness would be shown."[1]

It is possible only to conjecture as to the causes that aroused Colonel Prince's jealousy of his commander; the next few days and weeks would reveal the emotion in full flower.

On this April night, Prince's thoughts came back to the present when he smelled suddenly the stench of stagnant mud that was the Pearl lowlands, and almost at the same time saw in the cloud-ridden sky a faint touch of dawn. He could hear one of the scouts returning the advance guard's challenge up ahead, and waited impatiently for the man to approach and report.

The ferry, said the scout, was tied up on the opposite side of the river; he had found no evidence of enemy soldiers on this side. Prince immediately passed an order back through his companies: Advance as quietly as possible. If the the ferry was across the river, the rebel guard would be there, and he hoped to capture the boat without arousing them. He would have to act quickly before daylight revealed the raiders' presence.

Prince pressed his horse forward to ride with the advance; they turned a bend in the muddy, down-sweeping road. In front

146

of them lay the river — flat, sleek, and blacker than the ragged rim of trees and the square, box-like house of the ferryman on the opposite bank.

It might be possible for a man on a powerful horse to swim across, Prince thought, and he called for a volunteer. Private William Douer of I Company rode up out of the darkness. Prince told him to swim across and steal the ferryboat.

Private Douer spurred his big horse down the muddy slope; a second later, horse and rider splashed into the deep water, the swift current grasping and swirling them downstream before the animal could begin to swim. It was too much river, and Douer had to turn back.

At that moment, across the stream, a lantern light suddenly appeared in the ferryman's house. Prince watched it anxiously, a yellow diffused glow in the drizzle of rain, moving jerkily along the shore. Then a voice came from across the river: "You-all want across?"

Prince wondered if he could imitate that Dixie inflection. He megaphoned his hands. "First Regiment, Alabama Cavalry from Mobile!" he shouted. And to put the man on the defensive he added: "It's harder to wake up you ferrymen than it is to catch the damned conscripts!"[2]

The ferryman shouted back a muffled apology, and in a minute the cavalrymen heard the splashing of a pole. The flat-bottomed boat came up suddenly out of the river. A Negro leaped ashore, spinning a heavy rope around a stake thrusting out one side of the landing.

Only twenty-four horses and men could be crossed at one time, and Prince anxiously watched the sky brightening as two platoons of I Company went over on the first trip. He had no information concerning the strength of the Confederate guard across the river, and he was afraid he might arouse suspicion if he questioned the ferryman too closely.

Prince's worries over an enemy guard vanished with the return of the ferry and a lieutenant from Company I. There were no Confederate soldiers at all on the other side of the river; the lieutenant had made a thorough search and had found no evidence of anyone except the ferryman's family and a few Negroes.

Immediately after the second boatload had crossed, one of the second battalion's rear-guard pickets came riding up with a captured rebel. The man confessed to being a courier racing to warn the ferryman that the Yankees were coming. Prince had saved the ferry by half an hour, proof that the raiders' luck and timing still held.

At daybreak, while Prince was preparing to load the last company and post a guard at the landing, the main column came trotting down the muddy trail that cut through the river approaches. Colonel Grierson was riding with the advance, and though his first act probably was to congratulate Prince for securing the ferry, he later failed to do this in his official report: "As soon as Colonel Prince had crossed his two battalions, he was ordered to proceed immediately to the New Orleans Railroad."[3]

Grierson now took command of the river crossing himself. From a Confederate courier captured after Prince's departure from Williams' Plantation, Grierson had information of an enemy gunboat carrying two six-pounders several miles upstream, and as soon as Captain Smith arrived he was ordered to take a pair of his mounted guns two or three miles up the river and lay behind the bank to engage the boat if it should steam down and attempt to break up the river crossing.

Only one thing had gone wrong that morning. A deputy sheriff captured the day before by Sergeant Surby and the scouts had escaped, taking with him a prized horse belonging to Grierson's orderly. If Grierson considered the sheriff's escape of minor importance, two of the Butternut Guerillas certainly would not — before this day was done.

As soon as the ferrying of the Sixth Regiment appeared to be operating smoothly, Grierson and some of his officers crossed over to the ferryman's house. "Our troops were taken for the First Alabama Cavalry from Mobile," Grierson wrote afterward. "I receipted to the ferryman for the passage of the command in the name of that regiment, and as the crossing was slow, accepted an invitation to breakfast with my officers at a fine home near the ferry. The breakfast was well served, the ladies were all smiles, when up came some blunderhead and blurted out something to me about the 'Sixth Illinois Cavalry,' and what they were doing. The countenances of the hosts changed and some persons immediately left the room."[4]

Sometime during his stop at the ferry, Grierson decided to send

a fake telegram to General Pemberton's Confederate headquarters in Jackson, then only twenty-five miles away. Grierson
may have recalled how Morgan's Confederate raiders had pulled
that same trick repeatedly in their northern forays against the
Yankees, and possibly he thought it was high time the score
was evened.

It is not clear whether Grierson gave the message directly to
Colonel Prince or sent it to him by messenger after Prince's
departure from the ferry for the New Orleans & Jackson Railroad. All that can be determined definitely from the various
accounts is that Sergeant Surby later received the message directly from Colonel Prince. At any rate it was a clearly worded
and shrewdly timed message: "The Yankees have advanced to
Pearl River, but finding the ferry destroyed they could not cross,
and have left, taking a northeasterly direction."[5] It was designed
to scare the buttons off Pemberton, make him see visions of
Yankees galloping into his very headquarters before nightfall.

II

The crossing of Pearl River in the single flatboat was a tedious
operation requiring almost eight hours, but the delay probably
saved Company B from being cut off again from the main column
and stranded in the Piney Woods.

Misfortune had overtaken the company shortly after Sergeant
Stephen Forbes and his two companions had started their successful ride to overtake the brigade. Stopping at a small farm
to feed, Captain Henry Forbes had accepted the services of the
owner who volunteered to guide them by a shortcut through the
woods to the main road which Grierson was traveling.

Whether he was blundering or treacherous they never certainly
knew, but he led them after dark into an old tornado track, or windfall,
as it is called; and there, twisting and turning, this way and that,
through the tangle of fallen tree trunks, they lost, not only their way,
but all sense of direction likewise. Some of the men begged, in his
hearing, to be allowed to kill the guide, and terror reduced him to
temporary idiocy. There was nothing to do but to bivouac in the rain
and wait for morning to come. Every one went to sleep, guards and all,
and when the captain awoke at dawn, their guide had abandoned
them and their prisoners had escaped, bearing with them, of course, news
of the company's numbers, whereabouts, and predicament. By a rapid
scout after daylight they discovered the trail of the column and once

more rode steadily on in the hope that their messengers of the day before had not failed in their mission.[6]

About midday, Company B finally reached Strong River where Sergeant Stephen Forbes, his two companions, and the detachment left by Colonel Grierson were anxiously waiting. The men celebrated their reunion by galloping on to the Pearl, arriving at the ferry landing at two o'clock — as the last companies of the Sixth Regiment were crossing.

Captain Forbes went over with the next load to report in person to Colonel Grierson. "We were now once more with friends on the west side of the Pearl," said the captain. "We had been absent five days and four nights; we had marched fully three hundred miles in ten different counties, had captured and paroled forty prisoners, confronted and evaded several thousand of the Confederate troops at Macon and Enterprise; slipped through the home guards of six county towns, been twice misled and once lost; had had but eighteen hours of sleep, while rations for man and horse had been for the most part conspicuous by their absence. We simply had not had time to eat. The men who did this work *were a year and a half from the plow-tail,* and their chief claim to consideration is that they were representative men — fair types of our American citizen-soldiery."[7]

Colonel Grierson gave a detailed account of Captain Forbes's exploits in his official report of the raid, concluding as follows: "He was obliged to march 60 miles per day for several consecutive days. Much honor is due Captain Forbes for the manner in which he conducted this expedition."[8]

In his *Record of Services,* Grierson added: "I still have the soiled scrawl so hastily penciled, 'Col. Goodwin's compliments to General Grierson commanding United States forces, and asks permission to consider his demand for one hour.' "[9]

III

Colonel Prince and his Second Battalion meanwhile were driving ahead out of the valley of the Pearl toward Hazlehurst, fourteen miles west of the river, on the New Orleans & Jackson Railroad. The drizzle had stopped, but clouds rolled across the sky and a warm wind from the Gulf of Mexico brought perspiration through the men's woolen uniforms.

The familiar longleafs thinned and disappeared before an army of scrub pines; the small fields were gray and yellow and stony under strips of cotton and corn; the undulating land was marked with ridges and gashed by deep narrow gulches.

Once again the Butternut Guerillas were patrolling the front, and about four miles from the ferry crossing they began picking up fleeing civilians who had received news of the Yankees' approach. Some of them were armed but none suspected the true character of the scouts until too late. "One small man," said Sergeant Surby, "with sandy whiskers and foxy eyes, trying to look as savage as a meat-axe, had secured in an old belt around his waist two large old flint-lock dragoon pistols, and slung over his shoulder a large leather pouch and powder-horn, and on his left shoulder, with his hand resting on the stock, an old United States musket, flint-lock."

As the scouts approached him, the man brought his gun to carry arms, greeting the disguised strangers with a grin. "I've jist bid the old woman good-bye, and told her that she need not expect me back until I had killed four Yankees."

Using a trick which had been successful several times before, Surby dismounted and approached the rebel, complimented him on the efficient appearance of his arms, and asked permission to inspect them. "Without any hesitation he passed over his musket to me; the other men in the meantime had his pistols. I informed him he was a prisoner, and would soon have a chance to see the General."

Two miles farther on the scouts came upon a dozen men, some mounted and some seated on pieces of timber in front of a small building which resembled a blacksmith shop. The men watched the scouts approaching, curiosity rather than fear or animosity upon their faces. As soon as he halted, Surby discovered that the place was being used as a gunsmith's shop. "They had flocked here," he said, "with their old shotguns, muskets, rifles and pistols, some of which looked as if they were made in the year one."

The rebels inquired if the scouts had seen any signs of the Yankees. Surby replied that they had not; but he had heard they were supposed to be advancing toward Pearl River. As soon as his men were properly disposed around and inside the building, he gave a signal; the scouts drew their revolvers and the rebels were quietly informed that they were prisoners of the Union Army.

Seizing all the weapons in the gunsmith's shop, the Butternut Guerillas proceeded to destroy them by striking the stocks on the ground, breaking them off at the breech, and twisting the barrels until they were "no longer fit for anything but to shoot around corners." They were thus busily engaged when Colonel Prince arrived with his first battalion.

"Colonel Prince handed me a written dispatch and ordered me to send two of my men with it to the station [Hazlehurst] to be handed to the telegraph operator." With his six available scouts, Sergeant Surby hurried forward to the outskirts of Hazlehurst. Halting beside the railroad and telegraph line, Surby and four men dismounted to await the return of George Steadman and Lycurgus Kelly, selected for the mission to the Hazlehurst telegraph station.

Under a blackening sky that threatened a thunderstorm, Steadman and Kelly rode slowly into the town. Hazlehurst's false-fronted, unpainted pine-board buildings clung in a narrow strip along the single line of rail track, resembling a western frontier town rather than a southern village. Few people were moving in the muddy street or along the planked sidewalks.

The railroad station and telegraph office was a square, buff-colored building surrounded by a string of freight cars, a water tank, and what seemed to be a protective guard of stores and warehouses and dwellings, so close were these other structures to the depot.

As Steadman and Kelly dismounted and hitched their horses to the rear railing, they saw half a dozen Confederate officers and soldiers lounging inside the station, obviously awaiting the arrival of a train. The scouts glanced at each other but did not hesitate; ignoring the rebels, they moved directly into the telegraph office, Steadman waving Colonel Grierson's faked report to Pemberton with an exaggerated flourish.

The telegraph operator read the message with evident excitement, then asked the scouts several questions concerning their military unit and commanding officer, all of which were answered to his satisfaction. He turned to his instrument and began tapping out code over the line to the operator in Jackson.

Thunder was rumbling in the dark sky when the scouts stepped out upon the station platform. A hotel sign across the street reminded Steadman that he was hungry, and he suggested that they trade some of their Secesh money for some Secesh food before riding back to inform Surby he could cut the wires.

They were half way across the street, skirting the deeper mudholes, when a horseman came galloping around the corner of the hotel. Steadman lifted one hand in a casual greeting. His arm froze in mid-air. The horseman had pulled up sharply, staring at the scouts, his face flushing in sudden anger.

The rider was the deputy sheriff who eighteen hours ago had been captured by them only to escape later during the night from Williams' Plantation. He was riding the horse stolen from Grierson's orderly, and now began to brandish a saber also stolen at the same time.

"Help! Stop the Yankees!" the sheriff shouted in a voice high-pitched from sudden excitement. He shifted the saber awkwardly to his left hand, withdrawing a pistol from his belt with his right. His horse, feeling the bridle loosen, began to twist and stamp in the mud.

The scouts drew their revolvers and began backing toward the station. Standing in his stirrups now, the sheriff continued bellowing: "Help! Help! Stop the Yankees!" He did not fire his pistol, and the scouts guessed it was empty.

But his urgent clamor brought the Confederate soldiers out of the station just as Steadman and Kelly reached their horses and began jerking the hitches loose. The scouts were mounting when several Confederates came pounding around the depot.

Steadman fired his revolver above the rebels' heads and sent them scurrying to cover, while he and Kelly lashed their horses into a gallop, using the line of side-tracked freight cars for a screen as they sped out of the town.

Coming up to Surby and the other scouts, they shouted a warning to cut the telegraph wires. Surby sent a man up the nearest pole and then listened to Steadman's excited account of the adventure in Hazlehurst. The sergeant wasted no time. He sent one scout on the double to report the incident to Colonel Prince and ordered the others to follow him on a charge back into Hazlehurst. As they galloped into town, a sweeping gust of wind dashed big raindrops into their faces. The citizens of the town had taken cover from the storm, leaving the streets deserted.

Rain was pouring in torrents when they dismounted and surrounded the station. Surby led the way inside, expecting resistance from the Confederate soldiers, but they had all vanished, along with the telegrapher and the deputy sheriff. Only two old men remained, sitting quietly on a bench in the waiting room. From them Surby learned that a train would soon be coming in from the north.

"The usual precaution was taken to secure it [the train]; but after waiting half an hour beyond the time for its arrival the command became careless, and no further attention was given it, supposing that news had reached the next station of our approach."

During the wait for the train some of the men found several boxes of eggs, hams, sugar and flour stored in the railroad depot — a whole commissary waiting to be cooked up to serve the battalion. A detail was assigned to carry the food across the street to the Hazlehurst Hotel.

But in the midst of this activity a train whistle suddenly shrilled; the engine, boiling smoke and sparks, darted around a curve and began slowing for the Hazlehurst stop. At least a hundred Yankees began charging on the railroad, waving carbines.

The engineer reacted swiftly. In a moment he reversed his engine, and with a loud chugging and shrieking the train began to retreat, disappearing around the bend in a cloud of smoke and steam.

They had lost the train, but a good dinner was waiting in the hotel. And while they dined, the tall-tale spinners could amuse themselves and their listeners by inventing stories about what they had missed by not capturing the train. Sergeant Surby liked the one about the "eight millions in Confederate money, which was *en route* to pay off troops in Louisiana and Texas."

As soon as the first groups had finished eating, details were assigned to search the town for hidden military stores. They found 500 loaded shells, several cases of ammunition, and a large quantity of commissary and quartermaster supplies in the freight cars, marked for shipment to Grand Gulf and Port Gibson. No arms were discovered in any of the business houses or residences, and since the railroad station was too near private buildings to be burned separately, Colonel Prince decided to set fire only to the freight cars. He ordered other squads out to cut telegraph wires and to pry up a few sections of railroad track.

While the cars were blazing at their highest, another windstorm swept in suddenly, showering sparks over Hazlehurst's buildings. Flames burst upward from the roof of a drugstore on the east side of the depot, quickly spreading to two other buildings. This brought the timid citizens out of their homes to fight the fire, and for the next half-hour Yankees and Southerners worked side by side to extinguish the blaze and save Hazlehurst.

In the midst of the firefighting, ammunition and shells in the freight cars began exploding, and just as had happened at Newton Station the loud noise was heard by Colonel Grierson approaching with the main column. The companies came charging into town, too late for the fun, too late for a hotel dinner, astonished to find the boys of Prince's Second Battalion scattered around the smoking, half-burned buildings, with water pails instead of carbines in their hands, laughing and swapping jokes with the townsfolk of Hazlehurst.[10]

It was, as the Augusta (Georgia) *Chronicle* ruefully reported, "a gala day."*

IV

Half an hour after the excited engineer had backed his train out of Hazlehurst in time to escape capture, he was bringing his locomotive to a stop in Crystal Springs, ten miles north. He leaped down from the cab and raced into the telegraph office. Thus did General Pemberton learn of the raiders' presence in Hazlehurst early in the afternoon of April 27, some hours before Grierson gave the order to march out of the town.

To discover that enemy cavalrymen — which only last evening he had so assuredly placed at Enterprise a hundred miles to the east — were now suddenly only twenty-five miles to his south was a shocking surprise to the commanding general. Pemberton's

---

* "Their boldness and impudence in some cases were remarkable. A couple of their scouts were sent into Hazlehurst an hour or two before their raid upon the place, who walked boldly into the telegraph office and penned a dispatch to Jackson, stating that the Yankee raiders had turned to the northeast. Their true character, however, being recognized, there was some talk of arresting them, when they — the Yankees — drew their pistols, defied the officers and men of the town, mounted their horses and rejoined their commands, then within two or three miles of the place, after which the whole force entered the town in squads of fifty and a hundred — several hours' interval between the van and rear guards — as leisurely and with as much nonchalance as our country people would ride into town on a gala day." — Augusta (Georgia) *Chronicle*, May 8, 1863.

first thought was of Vicksburg's security. An enemy cavalry force at Hazlehurst was little more than a day's striking distance from the long railroad bridge across the Big Black River. If that bridge went, Vicksburg would be isolated, cut off completely from the Jackson supply depots.

For months the bridge had been under secure guard, but Pemberton hastened to warn his Vicksburg commander, Major-General Carter L. Stevenson, of the new danger from Grierson's raiders: "It seems to me probable the intention is to reach Big Black Bridge," he said. "Movements should be made to prevent it." Later in the afternoon he sent a second message to Vicksburg: "I suppose you have field artillery at Big Black Bridge; if not, you must put some there."

Another message was dispatched to Colonel Thomas Dockery, commanding troops at Big Black Bridge. "General Stevenson will send cavalry to co-operate with you. Vigilance should be increased. A guard of a company should be kept at each end of this bridge and trestlework."

And a fourth order went to Colonel James Jackson, commanding the Twenty-Seventh Alabama Infantry at Edwards Depot a few miles east of the bridge: "Move your regiment at once up to Big Black Bridge."

Three days earlier upon learning of the raid upon Newton Station, Pemberton had ordered General Franklin Gardner to send all his disposable cavalry from Port Hudson to Tangipahoa, Louisiana, to block a possible southern flight by Grierson's raiders. As the telegraph line was now cut at Hazlehurst, he was forced to dispatch a courier to the Tangipahoa cavalry commander: "Move up north with your command, and be guided by such information as you receive en route."

Pemberton also notified General Gardner of the reappearance of the raiders: "You must make every effort to intercept them. They were today, 12 o'clock, at Hazlehurst, on New Orleans & Jackson Railroad."

Even Barteau's Second Tennessee Cavalry, fatigued from their long futile pursuit of Hatch's Second Iowans, was not overlooked by the frantic Pemberton. Cut off from northeast Mississippi by broken telegraph lines, he wired Colonel A. E. Reynolds at Forest Station: "Send a courier to Barteau to continue on down as rapidly as possible to Hazlehurst on the New Orleans & Jackson Railroad."

Pemberton also found time to send his daily plea for help to General Johnston in Tennessee, informing him of the raid on Hazlehurst: "I cannot defend every station on the road with infantry," he said. "Am compelled to bring down cavalry from North Mississippi here, and the whole of that section is consequently left open. Further, these raids endanger my vital positions."

And before the day was over the commanding general also remembered to warn General John Bowen at Grand Gulf that the raiders *might possibly* be making for that point. "Which way the enemy will move," he added, "is only a matter of conjecture. Port Gibson or Big Black Bridge most probable." Bowen was ordered to send Colonel Wirt Adams' cavalry out to meet the enemy. "Follow them up without delay. Annoy and ambush them if possible. Move rapidly."

General Bowen obediently but reluctantly ordered Wirt Adams toward Hazlehurst, although this would leave Grand Gulf and Port Gibson without the mobility of a cavalry defense.* To Grant's former friend and neighbor, John Bowen, the enemy was not a small force of cavalry raiding in the hinterland; the enemy was Grant's army preparing to lunge at him from across the big river. He made this clear in a message that evening to Pemberton's headquarters: "I have the honor to report that all the movements of the enemy during the last twenty-four hours seem to indicate an intention on their part to march the army still lower down in Louisiana."[11] Bowen was referring to Grant's forces; he did not even mention the raiding Yankee cavalry which so perturbed his commander, Pemberton.

V

Not until seven o'clock in the evening did Colonel Grierson give the forward command for the march out of Hazlehurst. The little railroad town had provided food for the entire brigade, as well as hay and grain for the horses. Grierson now felt that the major problem facing him was to elude any Confederate forces moving to snare him somewhere along the forty miles which lay

---

* Port Gibson, where Colonel Wirt Adams' cavalry was stationed, was five miles east of the Grand Gulf fortifications.

between him and Grand Gulf. His best chance of success, he believed, was to confuse the Confederates, to conceal his real objective from them as long as possible.

As Sergeant Surby observed,

the enemy's scouts had been sent out, and were watching our movements; couriers were flying in every direction, spreading the news, forces were concentrating and sent to intercept us, hem us in and annihilate us, as they boasted, and felt confident of accomplishing. They certainly had every advantage on their side — a perfect knowledge of the country — every road, public or private — every stream of water, small or large — the fordable places and bridges — forces above and below us on the railroad, in our front at Port Gibson, Grand Gulf and Port Hudson — following in our rear — retreat was impossible, even if such an idea had occurred to us, we having destroyed our only hope in that quarter — bridges and ferries.[12]

Grierson rode out of Hazlehurst in the advance with his Sixth Regiment, keeping a slow pace to Gallatin, a county seat doomed by the railroad which had bypassed it in 1857 in favor of Hazlehurst. About sunset the first company was sent charging into Gallatin. A few shots were exchanged, but in the gathering darkness no casualties were inflicted by either side, and the Gallatin defenders quietly disappeared while the two regiments marched through the town without further incident.

Six roads met at the courthouse, but instead of taking the northwesterly route which led to Grand Gulf, Grierson deliberately turned southwest on the road to Natchez. This was the beginning of a series of planned diversions which he hoped would deceive both his pursuers and any enemy forces which might be on his front.

A mile or two beyond Gallatin the scouts met an ox-drawn wagon train. They turned off into the woods, riding alongside until they were satisfied it was a military train, then hurried back to give the information to Grierson. He sent the advance company of the Sixth Regiment dashing ahead with orders to surround and capture the wagons.

After a brief flurry of firing in the darkness, the small escort troop of Confederates surrendered. The train proved to be a prize catch for the Sixth; it contained a 64-pounder Parrott gun, machinery for mounting it, a wagon load of ammunition, and 1,400 pounds of powder, all en route to Grand Gulf.

Grierson ordered the gun spiked and the carriages and ammunition destroyed. As he did not wish to be burdened with prisoners, he paroled the rebel soldiers and instructed them to return to their homes.

The column finally halted at Thompson's Plantation, near Hargraves, going into camp just before midnight. As Grierson prepared for his first sleep in forty-eight hours, he wondered what was delaying Grant's plans for crossing the Mississippi. None of the civilians or prisoners he had talked with that day had heard anything of an attack anywhere along the big river.

VI

From across the river "near Grand Gulf, Mississippi," General Grant was sending a report to the general-in-chief, Major-General H. W. Halleck, in Washington: "I am now embarking troops for the attack on Grand Gulf. Expect to reduce it to-morrow."[13]

At the same time, Grand Gulf's cavalry defense, under Colonel Wirt Adams, was marching swiftly away from the river, under Pemberton's orders to meet and ambush Grierson's raiders.

COLONEL ADAMS SETS AN AMBUSH

HAZLEHURST

UNION
CHURCH

BYHALA

The Sixth and Seventh Illinois Regiments began moving out of Thompson's Plantation at six o'clock in the morning, continuing along the road to Natchez. Grierson was not yet ready to turn north for Grand Gulf; he wanted to feel out the country for the presence of enemy forces before revealing his final direction of march.

Grierson's map indicated no through roads to Grand Gulf anywhere between Gallatin and Natchez, but he had learned from prisoners captured the night before that several dry weather trails cut across northward to the Mississippi River, the best route running through Fayette. He would let chance and the presence of the enemy determine his choice. His first anticipation this morning was to capture rebel scouts who might give him more information as to the location and strength of the Confederates and some news of a river crossing by Grant's army.

But his scouts brought in only a few guerillas and armed citizens, who professed to know nothing of any Confederate force closer than the river, or of any battles with the Union Army there.

By ten o'clock Grierson had decided the column had moved far enough along the Natchez road. He ordered a halt and sent his orderly back to bring up the regimental officers for a council.

Grierson frankly admitted to his officers that he was mystified over the absence of rebel resistance; either the Confederacy was a hollow shell or the enemy was laying a trap for them somewhere. He was also puzzled over Grant's delay in crossing the Mississippi. The big campaign for Vicksburg should have begun, according to plans, at about the time the raiders hit Newton Station and wrecked the Vicksburg railroad.

Undoubtedly, Grierson was tempted to swing to the right at the next side road and march on toward Grand Gulf. It would be a feather in their caps if they came up to the river in time to play a role in Grant's troop landings. But perhaps Grant had changed his plans. Grand Gulf was strongly manned, with Wirt Adams' always dangerous cavalry somewhere in the vicinity, and if Grant had postponed or changed his plans the brigade would be so outnumbered on all sides that defeat or capture would be inevitable.

After some discussion with his staff, Grierson finally made his decision. He would throw one battalion in a sudden feint back east to the New Orleans & Jackson Railroad. Bahala appeared to be the closest town.* The battalion would ride in fast, do as much damage as possible, then circle back to rejoin the column. As soon as the detachment returned, the brigade would turn north under cover of darkness while the rebels were still looking for them along the railroad.[1]

Four companies from the regular First and Third Battalions of the Seventh were selected for the expedition. Captain George W. Trafton of Company G was given command as acting major, and Richard Surby and George Steadman of the Butternut Guerillas were assigned as scouts.[2]

The battalion moved out toward the east about eleven o'clock, and before the rear guard disappeared among the trees, Grierson gave the forward command for the main column. He planned to march slowly along the Natchez road toward Union Church until

---

* Bahala later changed its name to Beauregard in honor of the Confederate general.

161

he came to a suitable plantation where he could dispose his men in some sort of battle formation and await the return of Trafton's expedition.

At two o'clock in the afternoon the column halted at Snyder's Plantation, two miles outside Union Church. Horses were unsaddled and mules unpacked. The usual feeding details went into action, moving a bit slower than usual under the hot April sun.

"While feeding," Grierson later reported in one terse sentence, "our pickets were fired upon by a considerable force."[3]

In a short time the camp was all in confusion, men running as fast as they could in every direction, carrying saddles, leading horses on the gallop, gathering up carbines and sabers and buckling on belts, while the air was filled with cries and oaths and quick impulsive exclamations and sharp stern orders and shouts of "Get out of my way there!" "Catch my horse!" "Who's got my gun!" "Fall in here, men, quick! Dry up that noise and load your guns!" "Gallop — March!"

The column came in sight, a crowd of greylooking horsemen galloping and shooting in a cloud of dust and smoke, passing by on the road in our front.[4]

For the first time since leaving La Grange, after eleven days of marching through Confederate-held territory, the Sixth and Seventh Regiments were now challenged by an enemy force.

"A beautiful roll of smoke sprang from the line of carbines with a roar, and a sheet of balls swept through the rebel line bringing it to a sudden halt and sending it back in confusion."[5]

Grierson sent the First Battalion of the Sixth in pursuit, while the remainder of the command fell into battle order. No more than 150 Confederate cavalrymen had shown themselves in the charge, and the First Battalion drove them back over the two miles to Union Church, a quiet little country village clustered around a church on high ground commanding the rolling, forested country sloping away on all sides.

At the edge of the town Grierson's men dismounted, the horseholders withdrawing with the mounts to a thick grove of oaks.* "The dismounted men went through the village of Union Church by sheer weight," Grierson recorded. "Whole picket-fences were torn up and overturned by a rush. Right and left went everything that came in their way."[6]

Remounting on the other side of the town, the Union cavalry-

---

* Every fourth man served as a horse-holder when cavalry dismounted for an attack on foot.

men skirmished with the rebels until nightfall, pushing them back three miles. When the fighting stopped, the raiders had one man out of action, slightly wounded. At least two Confederates were wounded; they were brought in with several prisoners. "It proved to be a part of Wirt Adams' Mississippi cavalry," said Grierson. "After driving them off, we held the town and bivouacked for the night."[7]

II

Shortly after General Pemberton ordered General John Bowen at Grand Gulf, on April 27, to "collect Wirt Adams' cavalry and send them out to meet the enemy,"[8] a message was received in Natchez, fifty miles down river, by Captain S. B. Cleveland, commanding a detachment of Adams' troops. Cleveland's orders were to march east along the road to Hazlehurst until he either met the Yankee raiders or formed a junction with Adams' main column coming down from Grand Gulf.

Captain Cleveland departed late in the afternoon of the 27th, marching most of the night, and it was his detachment from Natchez which attacked Grierson's pickets on Snyder's Plantation at two o'clock and then retreated through Union Church during the afternoon of the 28th.

In the evening, as soon as Grierson's Sixth Regiment withdrew into Union Church, Captain Cleveland sent a courier fifteen miles west to Fayette where a military telegraph connected with the Mississippi River forts. The courier carried a message addressed to the telegraph operator: "Notify Colonel Adams, Grand Gulf, General Stevenson, Vicksburg, and General Gardner, Port Hudson, that the enemy are at Union Church, on the Natchez and Hazlehurst road. Tell the operator at Natchez they may look out for them there. I have been skirmishing with them for some hours this evening. Cannot ascertain their strength. They have four pieces of artillery. . . ."[9]

Colonel Adams, of course, was far from Grand Gulf, making a forced march across country with two companies and two mounted pieces. His remaining five companies were marching at regular cavalry pace to Fayette to await further orders there. Adams' intentions were to get behind Grierson, flush him out with his two fastest and best mounted companies, and then ambush him if possible with the others.

About the time Captain Cleveland was sending his communication to the Fayette telegraph operator, Colonel Adams was turning into the Natchez road several miles east of Union Church to pick up Grierson's trail. From farmers along the way, the rebel leader soon learned that the Yankee cavalry force was stronger than he had expected. He sent scouts some distance ahead, and before midnight they brought back news of the skirmish at Union Church. Adams decided to halt before Grierson's pickets discovered his presence. He then sent a courier by side roads to notify Captain Cleveland to stand his ground until the five companies at Fayette could be moved into position.

Wirt Adams and Benjamin Grierson had met before on the battlefield, in fights around Corinth and Iuka, and each man held considerable respect for the abilities of the other. Yankee soldiers fighting in the West rated Adams second only to Bedford Forrest; they called Adams' cavalrymen "a bunch of wild riders."

Sergeant Forbes had been face to face with the belligerent Mississippian when he was captured near Corinth in June, 1862, by Adams' cavalrymen and taken immediately to the colonel's headquarters for questioning. "He was inclined to be very impressively severe," said Stephen, "but I talked so independently that I aroused his wrath greatly, and he even so far forgot his position as to threaten violence, saying that they had a short way of disposing of young men like me who wouldn't listen to reason."[10]

Wirt Adams was a grandiose commander when in action, sitting tall in the saddle with his great gray cloak around his broad shoulders, his bearded chin thrust up, the wide nostrils of his aquiline nose quivering, his eyes flashing. President Jefferson Davis had offered him the postmaster-general's office in the Confederate States cabinet, but Adams wanted to fight—on horseback. "He rode continuously and fearlessly through the whirlwind of war," said one of his admirers. "Handsome as Philip the Fair, he stood six feet in the stirrups, the noblest paladin of the South who rode to war. At the court of Philip Augustus he would have led the nobles; at the court of England, he would have led the barons, and with the Crusaders, he would have ridden abreast with Godfrey Bouillon or Richard Coeur de Lion."[11]

Now this knight-errant of the Confederacy found himself with a chance to avenge some of the bitter defeats his colors had suffered. The unholy invaders lay only a few miles over the wooded hills; with the morrow he would have enough men to go eagerly to battle.

Sometime before midnight, however, Colonel Adams changed his plans. He became convinced that he stood no chance of holding the Yankees with only his two companies on the east and Captain Cleveland's small detachment on the west of Union Church. The five companies at Fayette must be brought into battle reach before morning. He decided to ride with a fast squad to Fayette and personally spur the companies there into a forced march down to the Natchez road.

As Adams was also expecting reinforcements from along the New Orleans & Jackson Railroad, he left a lieutenant and a few men behind to inform any approaching Confederate troops as to his location and battle plans. With his column he then turned off into the woods and began a flanking movement around Union Church. He would join Captain Cleveland, leave all except an escort squad with him, and then speed on to Fayette for the reinforcements. Tomorrow, if everything went well, he would have an ambuscade waiting for these abolitionist Yankees somewhere on the Natchez road.

III

Not long after Colonel Adams vanished into the woods with his small column, the lieutenant left behind to act as a liaison heard horsemen approaching from the east. He ordered two men to mount immediately, and the three rode out along the dark road to meet what they expected would be Confederate cavalry. But they could see only one lonely rider moving cautiously toward them in the starlight. They cocked their weapons, the sharp clicks of the hammers echoing along the tree-bordered road.

"Who comes there?" the stranger challenged.

"Friends," replied the rebel lieutenant.

"Advance one and give the countersign."

"We don't have any countersign. Who are you?"

"Scout for Colonel Falkner's First Mississippi Cavalry. We been traveling all day and all night to catch Colonel Adams and reinforce him."

One of Adams' men laughed. "I reckon we can rest our guns, boys," said the lieutenant. "All right. We belong to old Wirt

Adams' cavalry. And tomorrow we're goin' to give the Yanks hell."

The lone scout moved closer. "Is Colonel Adams nearby? Colonel Falkner would like to see him."

"Colonel Adams went up to Fayette to get reinforcements. He left me behind to tell anybody coming up just to camp here till morning. He's aimin' to fix up ambush for the Yankees on yonder side of Union Church."

"Ambush?"

"That's right. If the Yankees think they're goin' to make Natchez, they're sure goin' to get slipped up."

The scout nodded solemn agreement, then said he would ride back and meet his advance troop. "I'll tell 'em you're here, so we won't have any accidents in this dark."

"We'll wait here," said the lieutenant.

A few minutes later, blue-uniformed soldiers swarmed in on the three Confederates from both sides of the road. Colonel Adams' men were prisoners, but their captors did not bother to question them further. The easy-talking lieutenant had already told the Yankees everything they wanted to know.[12]

The lone scout in Confederate butternut who met, questioned, and arranged the capture of Colonel Adams' well-informed liaison lieutenant was Sergeant Surby, returning with Captain George Trafton's battalion which during the morning had been detached from Grierson's main column for the feint against Bahala.

As soon as Surby turned his prisoners over to Captain Trafton and informed him of Wirt Adams' night movement and of his intentions to draw Grierson into ambush, Trafton ordered the scouts to speed up the march into Union Church.

Between three and four o'clock in the morning, the scouts sighted the first friendly picket fires, and a few minutes later the battalion was inside the lines. They rode through the quiet streets of Union Church, past lawns filled with sleeping cavalrymen sprawled upon the grass without blankets on this warm starlit night. As soon as he found Grierson's headquarters, Captain Trafton halted the column, ordering the men to dismount and find feed for their horses. The captain adjusted his belt and saber, then turned and walked rapidly over to Grierson's guard. He asked the man to wake the colonel immediately. The stars were already losing their brightness in the lighting sky.

IV

From various sources [said the Jackson (Mississippi) *Appeal* for April 28], we have particulars of the enemy's movements from the north line of Mississippi, through the eastern portion of the State, almost to the Louisiana line. The route chosen for this daring dash was through the line of counties lying between the Mobile and Ohio, and New Orleans, Jackson and Great Northern railroads, in which, as they anticipated, there was no organized force to oppose them.

The penetration of an enemy's country, however, so extensively, will be recorded as one of the gallant feats of the war, no matter whether the actors escape or are captured. The expedition, we learn, was under command of Col. Grierson, of Illinois, who has already acquired considerable reputation as a dashing leader in West Tennessee. He boasted that he had no fears of his ability to extricate his command from the dangerous position it seemed to be in, but gave no indication as to the route he should take to get out of the country. . . .

Whether they will move thence to Natchez . . . can only be conjectured; but we still incline to the opinion so confidently expressed some days ago, on first being advised of their presence at Newton, that Baton Rouge will be their haven, if undisturbed.[13]

General Pemberton was not so certain that Grierson's cavalry was heading for Baton Rouge. A few hours after the *Appeal* published its prediction, however, he notified General Franklin Gardner at Port Hudson that the enemy was en route to Natchez, adding, "I wish you to make your dispositions, if possible, to ambuscade them in case they should approach you, going to Baton Rouge." Gardner complied with this mild request by sending Colonel H. B. Granbury with the Seventh Texas Regiment, Major James De Baun with a company of Wingfield's partisan rangers and a section of Bledsoe's battery, to form a concentration point at Woodville, thirty-five miles below Natchez.

Sometime during the morning Pemberton authorized Colonel Wirt Adams to take command of all cavalry pursuing Grierson, and then, in an effort to build up Adams' reserve strength, he sent numerous detailed orders to the eleven scattered cavalry units along the New Orleans & Jackson Railroad. Captain R. C. Love had finally reached Hazlehurst, after being thrown off Grierson's trail two days before by scout Samuel Nelson; Pemberton instructed Love to gather up all cavalry in that area and proceed westward to join Wirt Adams. In characteristic fashion, Pemberton prodded the captain: "Hire horses and citizens and act promptly."

Major M. R. Clark, commanding a training camp at Brookhaven, twenty miles below Hazlehurst, was warned to watch out for a visit from the enemy. "The principal object will perhaps be to parole prisoners," said Pemberton with what turned out to be remarkable divination. "It will be well in that event to send all the men you cannot arm to the country, if only a few miles."

By noon, information was coming into Pemberton's headquarters confirming reports that the enemy cavalry had taken the Natchez road out of Gallatin. Convinced that Grierson was driving for Natchez, Pemberton wired the quartermaster captain in command there: "Enemy believed to be moving toward your city. Communicate with the mayor. My cavalry have orders to fall on rear and flanks."

Later in the day, Pemberton decided to send a reassuring message to General John Bowen at Grand Gulf: "Have reason to believe enemy are striking for Natchez or Baton Rouge."

Bowen's reply was a shock to the commanding general: "Transports and barges loaded down with troops are landing at Hard Times, on the west bank."

Grant was moving at last.

Pemberton's first reaction was to telegraph President Jefferson Davis in Richmond. He wanted Davis to know that Grant was coming, but all he asked for was more cavalry to protect the rear approaches into northern Mississippi. He then sent his daily plea to General Johnston in Tennessee, informing him that the enemy was preparing to attack Grand Gulf. "I must depend upon the Army of Tennessee to protect the approaches through northern Mississippi."

Grant was coming across the big river to strike a hard blow for Vicksburg, but Pemberton could not put out of his mind the enemy raiders under Grierson still loose in Confederate-held territory. While he was busily preparing emergency orders and scraping up reinforcements for his desperate generals in the forts along the Mississippi, he interrupted himself long enough to direct the commander of the Twentieth Mississippi Regiment stationed in Jackson to mount three companies and have them ready to depart by train at 9 P.M., to join in the pursuit of Grierson's raiders.[14]

FOX AND HOUNDS

At 2:30 on the morning of April 29, the last men and horses of three companies of the Confederate Army's Twentieth Mississippi Mounted Infantry were loaded aboard a train in the New Orleans & Jackson depot in Jackson. General Pemberton's orders for these troops had set their departure time at 9 P.M.; they were five and one-half hours late in beginning their pursuit of Grierson's raiders.

Commanding this battalion of mounted infantry was a fiery, enigmatic, incorrigible Tennessean — Colonel Robert V. Richardson. During the past two months, General Joseph Johnston, commanding Confederate armies in middle Tennessee, had been attempting to arrest Colonel Richardson for persistent abuse of conscript laws and for his unorthodox actions as leader of the First Tennessee Partisan Rangers in enemy-occupied western Tennessee.

During the past month the Union Army's General Stephen Hurlbut (Grierson's corps commander) had also been pursuing Richardson not as an enemy

Thirteenth Day
Wednesday, April 29

UNION CHURCH   BYHALA   BROOKHAVEN

169

officer but as an outlaw acting "without and against Confederate orders."[1] Hurlbut declared he would bring the freebooting colonel to a drumhead court-martial.

And within the past fortnight, General Pemberton had sent a Confederate major through the lines into western Tennessee with orders to arrest Colonel Richardson and attempt to salvage the Tennessee partisan rangers for the Southern cause. Pemberton's emissary discovered, however, that Grierson's Sixth and Seventh Illinois Cavalry Regiments had captured or made casualties of the better part of Richardson's rangers in a running fight east of Memphis, only two weeks before Grierson started his raid from La Grange. Richardson himself was reported to be severely wounded. And it was said that the partisan leader was last seen fleeing across the Mississippi River in a canoe, carrying a fortune in Federal money stolen from Tennessee citizens loyal to the Union.*

While this extensive search was under way, Richardson himself appeared suddenly in Jackson, Mississippi, a balding, thin-nosed man with large, wide-spreading ears and a pointed beard. He reported to Pemberton's headquarters with all the bland innocence of an erring schoolboy. And in his petulant schoolmaster fashion Pemberton certainly must have scolded Richardson, although he does not appear to have placed him under arrest before giving him command of the Mississippi mounted infantry, with orders to overtake and fight Grierson.

Just how Richardson persuaded Pemberton to give him a new command so quickly is not made clear in the official records. Originally the general had intended to assign Lieutenant-Colonel W. N. Brown as commander of the Mississippi mounted troops ordered out of Jackson to pursue Grierson's raiders.[2] But at the last moment Pemberton chose Colonel Richardson. Perhaps Richardson told him of the blood-feud he had to settle with Grierson and the Sixth and Seventh Illinois Regiments. Perhaps Pemberton decided that this fire-eating rebel with revenge in his heart would

---

* Richardson was accused of pocketing fines and bounties collected from conscripts, and of using strong-arm recruiting methods. On March 6, General Joseph E. Johnston telegraphed Richmond: "One R. V. Richardson, claiming to have authority of the War Department to raise partisan rangers in Mississippi and West Tennessee, is accused of great oppression. If he has any authority, I respectfully recommend that it be withdrawn." — OR, ser. I, vol. 24, pt. 3, p. 654.

drive himself and his men with such furious purpose that even the slippery Grierson could not escape him. At any rate, Colonel Robert V. Richardson received his orders early in the evening of April 28, and promptly at 9 P.M. arrived at the Jackson railroad station, eager to take up the chase of his old enemy, Grierson.

When I got to the depot I was chagrined and surprised to find that the three companies of the Twentieth Mississippi Mounted Infantry, who were to constitute a portion of the forces subject to my orders in the movement projected against the enemy, with horses, were just beginning to be placed on the train.

About 2:30 A.M., April 29, 1863, the men and horses were all aboard. I inquired for the conductor, and learned that he was in bed at his chamber. I sent him an order to get up and proceed with his train immediately, or I would send for him a file of men. After a short time, he came. He then inquired of the engineer whether he could pull the train, who replied that he could not, because there were too many cars in the train.

The conductor and engineer then said that three cars must be taken from the train. This was done. Now they said they had not wood enough to run the train to the next station, and they had no lamps. I inquired whether or not they had an ax to cut wood; they replied they had none. About daybreak they started with the train, and did not reach Hazlehurst until 11 A.M. In spite of all efforts, these men were churlish, and seemed to be laboring to defeat as far as possible the movement of troops. They claim their privilege of exemption from military service as employes of the railroad company. It should not be granted to men who are so unmindful of the public interests.[3]

II

While Colonel Richardson was arguing with the reluctant trainmen in Jackson, Colonel Grierson in Union Church was listening to Captain George Trafton's account of the capture of Wirt Adams' garrulous liaison lieutenant who had revealed Adams' plan of ambush. Grierson congratulated Trafton for his bag of twenty-one prisoners and requested that the lieutenant be brought up for questioning. The young Confederate was much less communicative than he had been with the Butternut Guerillas, but Grierson learned enough to be convinced that Adams was waiting somewhere to the west with a large force of cavalry.

After ordering Adjutant George Root to set up a parole table on the veranda of the house which he was occupying as headquarters, Grierson summoned the regimental officers for a council.

Grierson outlined his plans briefly and to the point. Of course, he had no intention of marching into Wirt Adams' ambush. Nor would he wait here for a fight. "I had previously hoped to join General Grant in the vicinity of Grand Gulf or Port Gibson, yet the heavy firing from the gun boats heard by us satisfied me that it would be impracticable to undertake to do so, as it was very evident he had not at that time effected a landing with his troops. To delay an indefinite time to effect a junction would be too hazardous with my small command, in view of the large forces — over 20,000 men — sent out from various points to intercept and destroy us."[4]

The last place the enemy would expect them to move would be back to the New Orleans & Jackson Railroad; therefore, that was where they should go. But first they would "fool the enemy by a strong feint," and throw Wirt Adams off balance. "I made a strong demonstration toward Fayette with a view to impress upon the enemy the belief that we certainly intended to go to Natchez or Port Gibson."[5]

Grierson ordered Colonel Loomis' Sixth Regiment to make the demonstration. Colonel Prince would take the opposite direction with the Seventh, moving slowly across country to the Brookhaven road until the Sixth could overtake them.

Before leaving Union Church, Grierson used a theatrical trick to further deceive his enemy. He arranged for one of the prisoners, a prominent citizen of the county, to be brought into the room he was using as headquarters. "This gentleman," Stephen Forbes later wrote, "was permitted to overhear conversations and orders, made merely to deceive him, all implying a march for Natchez the next morning; and later a guard, instructed to be negligent, permitted him to slip away and escape."[6]

At six o'clock the Sixth Regiment was moving west on the Fayette road for a strong demonstration against Adams' men under Captain Cleveland. Shortly afterward the Seventh marched out as if to follow the Sixth, then made a wide sweeping turn through the woods until the column faced east. The Butternut Guerillas, in full strength again under Sergeant Surby, rode a few hundred yards ahead of the Seventh's advance company, following obscure trails through thick forests of oak and magnolias. "Considerable dodging was done the first three or four hours' march," said Surby. "I do not think we missed traveling toward any point of the compass."

Not long after the raiders struck the Brookhaven road they met a train of ox and mule teams hauling hogsheads of sugar; the wagons had loaded at the Brookhaven railroad station and were destined for the Mississippi River forts. The train was destroyed after the men had replenished their haversacks.

As the advance companies approached Brookhaven in the early afternoon, they encountered increasing evidence of excitement among the citizenry. Volunteer enemy scouts and spies were frequently seen dashing off into the thick woods ahead. Eight unarmed Confederate infantrymen, bound for Port Hudson from home furloughs, and five armed citizens were captured, but many more escaped by vanishing among the trees before they could be overtaken.

Two miles outside Brookhaven, while still under cover of the forest which surrounded the town, the column halted and Sergeant Surby went forward to reconnoiter. From the edge of the woods Surby looked out upon a "very pretty location," the rooftops of the houses shimmering under the bright sun. Two or three hundred men scattered in small groups were moving restlessly about the streets. None was in uniform, few appeared to be armed, but it was obvious that Brookhaven was expecting an immediate visit from Grierson's raiders. A mile to the south on a high oak-shaded hill were several rows of tents, revealed in white splashes of sunlight, and beyond the tents some long low frame buildings — a military training camp.

But where were the rebel soldiers? Surby could see only one or two, lolling in the shade.

The sergeant hurried back to report to Colonel Grierson. "We ascertained that about five hundred citizens and conscripts were organized to resist us," Grierson said in his official report. "We charged into the town."[7]

The Seventh Regiment made the charge into Brookhaven, the Sixth swinging to the right to overrun the tent camp. As they swept out from the trees the men of the Seventh formed in columns of fours. Somewhere to their left a rebel watch fired a single shot to warn the Brookhaven defenders that the Yankees were coming.

But the sudden rush of 500 sunburned, bearded, dusty, mud-stained Yankee cavalrymen, waving carbines and swinging sabers, took the heart out of Brookhaven's poorly armed citizens.

173

"There was much running and yelling," Grierson said, "but it soon quieted down into almost a welcome."[8]

And when the Sixth Regiment dashed up the oak-timbered hill into the Confederate training camp, they found only a few guards and convalescents who surrendered without a fight. General Pemberton's message of the previous day addressed to Major M. R. Clark, commanding the camp, had been obeyed to the letter. More than a hundred unarmed conscripts had been sent back into the Piney Woods to protect them from being captured and paroled.

Even so, after all the prisoners were corralled into the main street under heavy guard, they totaled 216. Adjutants George Root and Samuel Woodward must have been dismayed as they faced the prospect of laboriously writing out by hand so large a number of the tediously worded statements to be signed by each prisoner. But in this war a parole was almost as effective against an enemy soldier as a bullet, and Grierson ordered that the task be completed if the brigade had to remain in Brookhaven until dark.*

While Adjutants Root and Woodward were preparing papers

---

* A few months later, Colonel Grierson would not have bothered to parole anyone. Already, in the spring of 1863, the parole and prisoner exchange cartel between the Union and the Confederate governments was beginning to disintegrate. The Federal government had been reluctant in the first place to enter into a written agreement with the South, for fear the action would appear to be recognition of the Confederacy as a legitimate government.

One of the first difficulties to arise concerned paroled Confederates whom the Yankees wanted to use in the far West to guard camps or fight Indians — "galvanized Yankees" they were called. A second difficulty arose over the apparent willingness of many conscripted Union soldiers to welcome capture so that they could be paroled and returned home. Then in December, 1862, President Jefferson Davis, enraged over General Benjamin Butler's activities around New Orleans, had declared Butler an outlaw and proclaimed officially that all of Butler's officers were to be considered criminals subject to execution and not eligible for parole. The Union Army countered this action by treating partisan rangers, such as Colonel Robert Richardson, in the same manner. Two of Colonel Richardson's officers were captured in January, 1863, and put on trial for murder, arson, and robbery. Richardson's subsequent protest to the Union authorities is an indication of the bitterness developing over the parole question:

"This pretended trial of Bass and Scarborough is one of the many gross and wanton violations of the military law of nations. If this proceeding is not immediately stopped and these men treated as prisoners of war or if they are punished capitally or cruelly treated as prisoners of war I will retaliate tenfold . . . U. S. officers and soldiers have been stealing negroes, horses, mules, money &c.; they have plundered houses, broken open bureau for the long lines of prisoners, Captain John Lynch took two companies a short distance down the railroad track to burn several sections of trestlework. Other companies from the Sixth Regiment destroyed the deserted training camp. In Brookhaven the Seventh Regiment fired the railroad station, a dozen freight cars, and a small bridge.

As had occurred two days before at Hazlehurst, flames from the burning railroad station threatened to spread to nearby dwellings, and the raiders once again had to turn firefighters. "Our own soldiers," said Sergeant Stephen Forbes, who was in charge of one of the fire squads, "climbed to the roofs of the houses and kept them wet by pouring water over them until the fire had burned down."[9]

When this excitement was ended and it was apparent that the scrivening adjutants were not nearly finished with their wearisome parole business, Lieutenant-Colonel William Blackburn decided to treat his First Battalion — which had led the charge into Brookhaven — to a hotel dinner. Blackburn paid for the meal with his thick roll of confiscated Confederate money, and Sergeant Surby, who was a special guest with the other Butternut Guerillas, reported that the landlord expressed a wish that the Yankees would come every day "if they all acted like 'we'uns' did."[10]

It is probable that the raiders found some genuine Union sentiment in Brookhaven, a town founded by a Massachusetts Yankee some years before the war, and which would later form a new

drawers, searched the person of ladies and insulted women; they have burnt houses and assassinated unoffending men, women and children all over the land, and yet when they have been captured although we had every reason to avenge these injuries they have been promptly paroled except when necessary to retaliate. No unusual trials have been resorted to to scare prisoners and extort from them the oath of allegiance to a belligerent government. Your command has pillaged my own premises and grossly insulted my wife and very nearly shot one of my children and have threatened to burn my houses. I wish to notify you and your command that if I can get hold of the demons who have perpetrated these acts or who shall perpetrate them again, or who shall order or execute these threats, I will not treat them as prisoners of war but as outlaws and enemies of mankind."

General Grant, recognizing the fact that the North outnumbered the South two to one in manpower, was always opposed to the parole system, and when he went east after the fall of Vicksburg to command the armies driving on Richmond, he forbade further exchange of prisoners altogether. — OR, ser. II, vol. 4, p. 267; OR, ser. II, vol. 5, pp. 158-59.

county around itself as county seat in 1870, a county which the Brookhaven citizens successfully insisted should be named Lincoln for President Abraham Lincoln. The New York *Times* account of the Brookhaven raid reported that "the people were much terrified by the idea that the whole town would be burned, but when they found all private property perfectly undisturbed, they seemed to entertain a very different opinion of the Yankees to what they did only a few hours previously."[11]

III

"As we rolled into Hazlehurst," reported Colonel Robert Richardson, "a citizen approached us in an excited manner, and said 1,000 Yankees were within a quarter of a mile of the place, approaching it. I did not much believe the report, but, as a measure of precaution, I ordered the train to be run back on the road about a mile. I then ordered the men to form on each side of the railroad, and 20 horses to be taken from the train, and sent out a scout in the direction of the reported advance of the enemy. The scouts returned in a half hour, and reported the enemy not to be found as reported."

At the time Colonel Richardson was directing this exploratory movement, Grierson's raiders were about twenty miles to his south approaching Brookhaven. It is more than likely that the rumor of the one thousand Yankees was a garbled warning passed along from some fleeing citizen who had seen Grierson's column during its zigzag turnabout from Union Church.

Richardson's information, however, placed Grierson several miles west on the road to Natchez, and he was not inclined to accept rumors counter to this. "I availed myself of every resource to get information as to the position and direction of the enemy," he said. "He was reported to have been that Tuesday morning at Union Church, and to have engaged Col. Wirt Adams' command there. . . . So far as I could judge, he was leaving the line of the railroad and was going to Natchez. . . . It seemed that the proper direction for me to go . . . was Union Church."

And so as Grierson's raiders were charging into Brookhaven twenty miles south, Colonel Richardson completed feeding his horses and ordered his Mississippi mounted troops to march westward for Union Church.

"I got there at 9 o'clock that night," Richardson continued, "and learned that the enemy had left there at 8 o'clock in the morning for Brookhaven, and that Colonel Adams had camped the previous night within 3 or 4 miles of the enemy, but had gone that morning toward Fayette, believing that the enemy intended to go to Natchez."

Richardson fed his horses, allowed his men two hours' rest, and then grimly set out for Brookhaven, an impetuous but tenacious hound after a clever fox. He had played this game before with Grierson, in Tennessee, and was not to be put off the scent by one sly maneuver. Before leaving Union Church, he sent a courier to Colonel Wirt Adams, "advising him of my design to follow the enemy, and advising him to shape his march so as to join me near Liberty."[12]

As for Colonel Adams, he had waited patiently in his carefully planned ambush below Fayette until midafternoon. At last he learned the bitter truth: Grierson had slipped away that morning in the direction of Brookhaven. Unaware that Grant's massed armies were preparing to attack Grand Gulf, which his cavalry was assigned to defend, and without waiting for orders, Adams telegraphed Pemberton from Fayette: "Shall now march to intercept [enemy's] movement toward Baton Rouge."[13] Adams' regiment, in full force again, marched that night along a parallel road south of the route taken by Richardson's troops. Had Grierson stayed in his camp near Brookhaven for another twenty-four hours, the two Confederate forces probably would have ended the raid right there.

Far to the south along the Louisiana line, other Confederate troops were also marching to intercept the raiders. General Franklin Gardner, annoyed by the recurring escapes of the Yankee raiders approaching so boldly from the north, decided to send a formidable force out from his Port Hudson command. He ordered Colonel W. R. Miles to march his famed Louisiana Legion to Clinton, Louisiana, and await further orders. Miles's Legion boasted a duty strength of 2,000 infantry, 300 cavalry, and a battery of artillery.*

---

* A Confederate Legion was an oversized regiment developed by a popular leader whose men refused to be transferred to any other organization. Basil Duke of Morgan's cavalry described the Legion as "something between a regiment and a brigade with all of a hybrid's vague awkwardness of conformation." — Basil Duke, *History of Morgan's Cavalry*, Cincinnati, 1867, p. 81.

Gardner's other pursuit force, Major James De Baun's Ninth Louisiana Partisan Rangers, meanwhile had arrived at Woodville, Mississippi, early in the afternoon. With only twenty miles separating De Baun's rangers at Woodville and Miles's Legion at Clinton, the escape roads from Mississippi to the Union lines at Baton Rouge were fairly well covered by the largest force yet assembled to block Grierson's raiders.

IV

It was on this day that Grierson's commander in La Grange, General William Sooy Smith, first learned of the successful raid upon Newton Station. Smith's informant, a spy who had come in from Jackson, led the general to believe that Grierson was fighting his way back to the north along the same route he had taken south, and Smith wired General Hurlbut in Memphis, suggesting that a relief force be sent down to aid the raiders' return.

Hurlbut immediately ordered three cavalry regiments to move toward Okolona, and then sent a message to General Grant informing him of Grierson's successful strike against the Vicksburg railroad.

All that day, from a tugboat in the Mississippi River, Grant had been watching Admiral Porter's seven ironclad gunboats cannonading the Grand Gulf defenses high above the river. Early in the morning the fleet had knocked out the two lower batteries mounting small guns, but the big ones on the highest promontory resisted obstinately, even though Porter pushed one of his boats to within a hundred yards of the hillside and dropped shells within the parapets.

By noon Grant knew that he had underestimated the strength of his enemy. The besieged Confederates were not only holding firm, they were returning shell for shell. Porter's ironclad boats were still afloat but their armor was riddled. The fleet's casualties were growing heavier by the hour.

"During this time," Grant said, "I had about 10,000 troops on board transports and in barges alongside ready to land them and carry the place by storm the moment the batteries bearing on the river were silenced, so as to make the landing practicable."

Perhaps it was the sight of this massed army of river-borne Yankees which inspired the gunners in the Grand Gulf batteries to withstand the continuous cannonading. At 1:30 P.M., after five hours of futile bombardment, Admiral Porter gave the signal to withdraw; the Confederate batteries had proved too much for the gunboats.

Convinced now that it was impracticable to take Grand Gulf directly from the river, Grant quickly adopted his alternate plan of landing in the swamps below. As soon as the sun was down over the Louisiana marshes, he sent the gunboats back to make a vigorous night attack, and while the guns set off a din of cannonading and drew the fire of the batteries, he slipped his troop-laden barges past the blockade to De Shroon's Plantation, four miles below Grand Gulf on the west side of the river. Grant's final act of this frustrating day was to send a confident message to General-in-Chief H. W. Halleck in Washington: "A landing will be effected on the east bank of the river tomorrow. I feel that the battle is now more than half won."[14]

Only fifty miles to the east of this scene of portentous events, Colonel Grierson also under cover of darkness was marching out of Brookhaven. Although he was moving south, following the railroad into the flats of Bogue Chitto Creek, he had not yet abandoned his original plan of swinging west to Grand Gulf. If only some news of Grant's movements would come! No one he had talked with in Brookhaven, however, had heard the slightest rumor of an attack along the river.

Grierson did not care to travel too far south as yet, and after a leisurely march he ordered the column halted eight miles below Brookhaven, at Gill's Plantation.

For the first time in forty hours, the men of Trafton's battalion removed saddles from their horses and sprawled on the ground for sleep. Could it have been possible for them to know that two strong columns of Confederate cavalry under Colonels Adams and Richardson were converging upon them from only twenty miles to the west, it is doubtful if these men would have wasted a moment of wakefulness in apprehension of the morrow.

THE TRAP BEGINS TO CLOSE

BROOKHAVEN

SUMMIT

Before dawn Admiral Porter's gunboats were out in front of Grand Gulf, resuming their cannonading of the previous day. During the first few minutes of the bombardment one of the boats slipped away almost unnoticed and steamed four miles down river to De Shroon's Plantation. Massed around the willow-framed river landing at De Shroon's was the fleet of transports and barges which only a few hours earlier had passed the Grand Gulf batteries under cover of darkness.

While the single gunboat stood by, three divisions of General John McClernand's corps completed re-embarkation on the barges, and the river crossing began, two hours later than General Grant had ordered.

Taking the lead, the low-slung convoy gunboat churned the Mississippi waters into a trail of foamy waves that slapped against the transports and barges behind. The men crowded against the low railings on the sides of the barges facing the shore upon which the landing must be made; they were generally silent, the unreal morning already filled with sound — the splashing of the river, the conflicting rhythms of the chugging twin-stacked transports, and the far-away booming echoes of Porter's fleet noisily distracting the attention of Grand Gulf's defenders.

The convoy gunboat began slanting eastward, the transports and barges following course in file. The deserted Mississippi bank loomed closer. When they came within a mile of the mouth of Bayou Pierre, the gunboat increased speed, swung into the front of the river village of Bruinsburg, and began lobbing shells at random into this unfortified area. The transports drifted past, so close to land that birds could be seen and heard among the heavy-leaved trees. A few minutes later the first men were wading ashore. Grant had not won his foothold on dry hard ground yet, but he had made his landing unopposed.[1]

Fifty miles to the southeast in the heart of southern Mississippi, Colonel Grierson was watching the dawn of the fourteenth day of his raid, unaware of this historic landing. Had he known of it he would have turned his column in that direction at once, fighting his way through if necessary to join General Grant in what every Union soldier in the west had long hoped would be the final campaign for Vicksburg.

Last evening Grierson had questioned his host, a plantation owner named Gill, but Mr. Gill had heard nothing of any fight with the Yankees along the Mississippi River. Now, as Grierson prepared to give his morning march orders, the plantation owner was talking with a group of the raiders who had just finished feeding and saddling their horses: "Well, boys, I can't say I have anything against you. You haven't taken anything of mine except a little corn for your horses, and that you are welcome to. I've been hearing about you from all over the country. You're doing the boldest thing ever done. But you'll be trapped, though" — and he shook a finger at them — "you'll be trapped, mark me."[2]

A few minutes later, Surby and his scouts rode out with instructions to reconnoiter south along the New Orleans railroad. Grierson's plan for the morning was to move slowly southward, burning trestlework and doing as much damage to the track as possible. Sometime today he would decide whether to cut back and dodge to the northeast for another attempt to find Grant's landing place, or whether to risk the long dangerous ride for Baton Rouge.

In the middle of the morning the column reached a small village bearing the name of the creek which the railroad followed south — Bogue Chitto. Grierson rode forward and ordered the Sixth Regiment to burn the railroad depot and eight freight cars on the switch track beside it. When Captain Joseph Herring came up with the Seventh Regiment's advance company, the colonel sent him down the line to destroy a section of trestlework which could be seen from the village. Within an hour a wide swirling cloud of smoke marked the destruction of several hundred feet of bridges and trestlework, and the raiders were marching south again. Grierson could now take some satisfaction from the fact that even if he should not be successful in extricating his brigade from the enemy's country, at least he had dealt heavy blows to two railroads. Transportation between Jackson and the supply bases of southern Mississippi and Louisiana would surely be interrupted for weeks.*

As he rode southward from the burning trestles, Grierson decided to raid the next town, Summit, before halting for noon feeding. He set the column moving at a faster rate, with frequent gallops under the hot sun, the horses' hooves raising clouds of yellow-brown dust. Longleafed pines became more numerous again, and the white plantation houses seemed untouched by war — their entrances landscaped with neat rows of trimmed cedars among the native pines.

Shortly after noon, the scouts sighted the town of Summit on a hill sloping out of the undulating plain.

II

While Grierson's raiders were moving on Summit, their old enemy Colonel Robert Richardson was approaching Brookhaven, twenty miles to their rear. At nine o'clock in the morning Richardson overtook Captain R. C. Love, who in response to Pemberton's orders had augmented his force with hired horses and civilians at Hazlehurst. Love had been pursuing Grierson for five days now, and for the second time had found himself thrown off the trail.

---

* The New Orleans & Jackson Railroad was unable to make full repairs on this section of track until after the war's end. "There was scarcely a bridge . . . that was not wholly or partly destroyed by fire or rendered unfit for use by decay." — Carlton J. Corliss, *Main Line of Mid-America, the Story of the Illinois Central,* New York, 1950, pp. 197-99.

Attaching Love's troops to his regiment of Mississippi mounted infantry, Richardson hurried on to Brookhaven. "We reached Brookhaven at 11 A.M.," he said, "fed, and rested three hours."

The smoking ruins of the railroad station and freight cars were immediate evidences of Grierson's passage, but Richardson was eighteen hours behind the raiders and no one could tell for certain where they might be at that moment. Rumors were strong, however, that the Yankees had marched south from their camp that morning, heading for Bogue Chitto, and Richardson ordered Captain Love to proceed immediately to that point.

"After I had ordered Captain Love, as my advance, to proceed to Bogue Chitto, I received information that the enemy had committed his depredations there in the forenoon, and had gone to Summit, to do the same thing, that evening."[3]

Richardson now believed he had a good chance to overtake Grierson by nightfall, but he needed Wirt Adams' regiment to insure a victory. He had heard nothing from Adams, but hoped that he might be somewhere west of Summit en route to Liberty, as Richardson had advised him. Before leaving Brookhaven, Richardson dispatched a courier to seek out Adams' column and notify the Mississippi colonel that if the two regiments could be brought into concerted action somewhere in the vicinity of Summit, Grierson might very well be trapped before morning.

III

Grierson's raiders in the meantime were marching quietly and leisurely into Summit. "The people seemed to expect us," said Sergeant Surby, "and there were no signs of excitement or fear displayed." Colonel Grierson believed this response to be positive rather than apathetic: "We found much Union sentiment in this town, and were kindly welcomed and fed by many of the citizens."[4]

In his autobiography, written long after the event, Grierson added a story of a lady who came down to her gate in front of her house and asked to see the Yankees' commanding officer. When she was presented to Colonel Grierson she told him her husband was an officer in the Confederate Army and that her whole heart was in the Southern cause, that she was a Southern woman through and through, but that this whole thing [the raid] beat anything she ever heard of, or had ever read of in history;

that if the North *should* win in the end and Grierson should run for President, her husband would vote for him or she would get a divorce.[5]

Whether this story is entirely factual or not, Grierson evidently found his reception in Summit to be more friendly than any yet given the raiders in Mississippi. He kept his brigade there all afternoon, although there was little for his men to do. They found a quantity of Confederate commissary supplies — sugar, salt, molasses and corn meal — which they loaded into several empty freight cars. The cars were rolled down the track away from the town and burned. The Summit depot was spared because it stood too near private dwellings; Grierson decided his men had done enough fire-fighting in Hazlehurst and Brookhaven.

After this work was finished the men prowled around the town. They forced the custodian of the town hall to open the doors for inspection, and found several old and useless muskets stored inside. Folded in a box beneath the weapons was a Confederate battleflag which had been brought back from Shiloh by the survivors of a local company. The prowlers appropriated it at once; Confederate battleflags were seldom come by with such ease.

Another group of explorers discovered thirty barrels of Louisiana rum hidden in a swamp behind the town. As Sergeant Surby observed, "it was no use trying to hide anything from the Yankees." News of the find spread rapidly, "and the swamp became a place of much resort," until Colonel Grierson heard about the hidden rum barrels.

"I discovered them before it was too late to save my men," he said, "and emptied the vile stuff as remorselessly as I did the canteens of whiskey of my soldiers at Shawneetown, Illinois, two years before."[6] According to Surby, the squad of men assigned to destroy the rum "with great reluctance stove in the head of each barrel, and thus did waste the balm of a thousand flowers."

And why did Grierson linger in Summit for so long? In the first place, he was still hopeful of receiving news concerning General Grant's movements. Secondly, he was attempting, through questioning as many persons as possible, to learn the whereabouts of enemy forces assembling to overtake or ambush his brigade. It is also probable there was disagreement among his officers as to what direction the column should take upon resuming march.

And for the first time during the raid, he appears to have reached a state of indecision.

Also for the first time, Grierson was completely duped while he was in Summit by a clever piece of rebel trickery. Eighteen miles below Summit, in the town of Osyka, the Confederate government had concentrated large stores of military supplies, a storage base selected because of its remoteness from the enemy and its accessibility to the river forts by rail and wagon train. Only thirty men had been assigned to guard the storehouses, an adequate force to prevent petty thieving but quite insufficient, of course, to cope with two enemy regiments. When Captain Thomas C. Rhodes, commanding the Osyka detachment, received warning of the raiders' approach toward Summit, he sent his second lieutenant, William S. Wren, north to meet them. Captain Rhodes ordered Lieutenant Wren to spread a rumor that Osyka was garrisoned by two regiments of infantry, one regiment of cavalry, and a battery of artillery.[7]

Lieutenant Wren's mission was a complete success. Sergeant Surby recorded that the Butternut Guerillas captured a courier and learned of a large force at Osyka. And Grierson himself said that "large forces were concentrated to meet us . . . at Osyka," a misrepresentation of the truth which he probably never discovered.

It is quite evident that Grierson was influenced by this manufactured story in his decision to turn away from the railroad and make a dash to the southwest for Baton Rouge. Late in the afternoon he discussed the plan with his officers; his final order was to cut across country avoiding main roads until they reached the Louisiana line. "Hearing nothing more of our forces at Grand Gulf and not being able to ascertain anything definite as to General Grant's movements or whereabouts, I concluded to make for Baton Rouge."[8] He also must have instructed the officers to keep their destination secret for the time being; not even the scouts were informed.

About five o'clock all companies were assembled along the road south of town for a brief inspection. The officers redistributed ammunition; some men still had their original forty rounds while others were in short supply. Lame mounts were cut loose, reducing the led horses to a small number.

An unexpected discovery during the inspection was the absence of three men from the rear guard company. The men had been present for roll call that morning at Gill's Plantation, but none of their comrades could recall seeing them in Summit. They were presumed to be stragglers and were so listed.

In the meantime, Grierson was contriving a small deception for the enemy. He had always enjoyed amateur theatricals — while teaching music in Jacksonville he had composed skits and music for minstrel shows — and he could not resist playing parts, particularly when he might thereby mislead the enemy. Now, acting the part of the interlocutor in a minstrel show, he asked questions of the citizens which would lead them to believe he planned to march directly south along the railroad to Osyka by way of the next town, Magnolia.

The sun was going down when the bugle calls sounded boots and saddles. To horse! "A straight line for Baton Rouge, and let speed be our safety!" were Grierson's final words to his officers.[9]

But instead of turning west for Baton Rouge, the raiders rode out of Summit south along the railroad. According to Grierson, the people of the town watched them march away "waving handkerchiefs with much genuine good feeling," but no doubt the Summit citizens were secretly wondering what would happen when these over-confident Yankees met their own soldiers in butternut and gray down at Osyka Station. Not until the column was well below the town did Grierson swing the point to the west along a secondary trail leading away from the railroad and Osyka.

Some of the scouts had calculated that New Orleans was only a hundred miles away. "Were we going there? That was the question," said Sergeant Surby.

"We . . . marched about 15 miles on the Liberty road," Grierson said in his report, "and halted until daylight on the plantation of Dr. Spurlark."[10] In later years one of Grierson's favorite stories of the raid was based on an incident occurring at Spurlark's Plantation.

There had been all these fourteen days of hard work and scanty rest and rations, wherein the officers had scarcely fared better than the men; at least the men were always first served. This night I was determined that my staff and I should have a good supper. I accordingly stationed a guard at the well-filled chicken coop, while the smokehouses and store-houses were opened as usual, and their contents dealt out to the men.

But perhaps some of the Louisiana rum was not yet worked off — I was suddenly made aware that the men, either by hustling away, or conniving with the guard, were devastating that chicken coop. I looked in, and saw the last chicken, and a hand grasping for it. Saber in hand, I went for that private. Over the hen coop, around the pig-sty, through the stable, behind the smokehouses, between the horses, and under the horses, dodging the trees, and jumping the briers, down the steps, and smashing the trellis — the hen squawking, I vociferating, the laughing officers cheering the novel chase, till over a picket fence went the soldier, dropping the fowl under my saber. It did not require much picking by this time, but I had earned my fricassee.[11]

While Colonel Grierson was enjoying himself in this quite unmilitary recreation, the Confederate colonel whom he had outwitted at Union Church was moving his regiment into camp only five miles to the west, beside the main road running from Liberty to Summit. Sometime during the day, Colonel Wirt Adams, waiting at Liberty for a rendezvous with Colonel Robert Richardson, had learned of Grierson's destructive march along the railroad. Adams had decided not to wait for Richardson, but to move toward Summit in the hope of cutting across Grierson's path. He had almost succeeded in this objective. Certainly during that night the Confederate and Yankee pickets must have been close enough to shout challenges at one another.

IV

Colonel Robert Richardson also had spent the afternoon endeavoring to close the trap on the Yankee raiders. About two o'clock in the afternoon he marched his regiment south from Brookhaven, "hoping to be able to find the enemy encamped [at Summit] or in the vicinity, and determined to make a night attack."[12]

He sent a courier toward Bogue Chitto to notify Captain R. C. Love of his plans. Love, who had preceded Richardson's march by about two hours, had already galloped on beyond Bogue Chitto, overtaking and capturing the three stragglers from Grierson's rear guard company. When Richardson and Love joined forces at dusk, three miles above Summit, the Tennessee colonel immediately interviewed the prisoners. The prisoners swore that they knew nothing of Grierson's destination beyond

Summit, and Captain Love seemed convinced that Grierson was planning to camp in or near that village. As the rebels were too far from town to see the Yankees marching out (at that very hour) Richardson decided to plan a surprise attack.

"All preliminaries were made for a night attack and surprise," he said.

Thus, while the raiders slept peacefully on Spurlark's Plantation, five miles to their west Wirt Adams' was resting his regiment for the night, and fifteen miles to their east Richardson's forces were cautiously surrounding the town of Summit. None of the three was aware of the location of the others.

And some distance to the south, large numbers of Confederate troops were losing sleep this night in movements designed to block Grierson before he could reach the security of the Yankee lines at Baton Rouge. General Franklin Gardner, having received warning that Grierson was heading south along the railroad, ordered Major James De Baun to leave Woodville with all available cavalry and proceed to Osyka by forced march. Woodville was fifty miles from Osyka, and De Baun covered about half this distance before halting late in the night near Liberty. Another dawn would find him moving directly across Grierson's path.

And from Ponchatoula, Louisiana, almost fifty miles south of Osyka, Colonel John M. Simonton was leading his First Mississippi Infantry on a night march towards the vulnerable supply base. Simonton sent a message to his commander, General Gardner, informing him that he was taking a battery of artillery and sixty cavalrymen with his infantry regiment. "Enemy reported at Summit, on railroad, advancing on Osyka. . . . My object is to protect Government property at Osyka, if possible. All quiet in my front. Our scouts well advanced. I make this move without orders, but could not communicate with you."[13]

For once, while Grierson's raiders slept, the Confederates were marching. The trap was beginning to close.

But General Pemberton in Jackson, overwhelmed by the news of Grant's successful crossing below Grand Gulf, issued no orders concerning the pursuit of Grierson.

THE FIGHT AT WALL'S BRIDGE

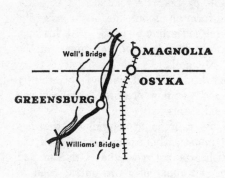

Colonel Robert Richardson completed the disposition of his Confederate troops around the town of Summit, at three o'clock in the morning, May 1, and gave orders to charge into the streets, to fire at will at the first sign of an encamped enemy. "We learned," said Richardson, "that the enemy had left about sunset on the previous evening, marching on the road to Magnolia . . . saying he intended to go to that place; thence to Osyka. . . . The commanding officer had been heard to ask a negro guide if he knew the way to Magnolia, and, upon an affirmative answer, had ordered him to take the lead."

Colonel Richardson did not suspect Grierson's neat deception, for he knew of the important Confederate tannery at Magnolia and of the large storehouse at Osyka, and naturally assumed that his old Yankee enemy was bent upon destroying these resources while en route to Baton Rouge. And even though his men and horses were worn from their two successive night marches, Richardson determinedly resumed his pursuit of

Fifteenth Day
Friday, May 1

189

Grierson. "I hoped to be able by taking a road east of the railroad to get in his front, and form an ambuscade." By sunrise the persistent Tennessean had formed a line of battle, with his men dismounted under cover of a thick undergrowth of timber, on the road between Summit and Magnolia. As there were no cavalry tracks on this road, Richardson believed he had successfully bypassed Grierson's camp and was now prepared to give him a reception that should even old scores.

He sent a scout west of the railroad to determine Grierson's exact position, and waited impatiently. About nine o'clock the scout returned with the disheartening news that Grierson had marched westward at dawn and apparently was on the road to Liberty.

Even the stubborn Richardson was now discouraged. He looked at his fatigued, bedraggled troops and ordered them into bivouac. "My men and horses had marched all night, and were wearied and hungry," he said. "I remained three hours to feed and rest, when I marched for Magnolia, hoping to be able by another night march to overtake and attack the enemy at or near Osyka."[1] In spite of Grierson's westward course, Richardson was confident that the Union leader planned to turn back and attack Osyka.

During this delay a courier from Colonel Wirt Adams reached Richardson's bivouac, and Richardson sent the messenger back to advise Adams to follow him down to Magnolia, where their forces might be joined to attack the enemy there or at Osyka. As Colonel Adams also believed that Grierson would attempt to destroy the Osyka stores, he was agreeable to this arrangement. During his march down the railroad behind Richardson, Adams overtook Lieutenant William Wren, the Osyka officer who had so successfully spread the false rumors of a large defense garrison at the supply base, rumors which had led Grierson to turn directly for Baton Rouge. After talking with Wren, Adams evidently became less certain that Grierson would swing back to the east and attack Osyka. At Wren's suggestion Adams ordered the young lieutenant to ride on the double for Williams' Bridge on the Amite River. It was a forty-mile ride, but if Lieutenant Wren could get through and burn that bridge, Grierson's raiders would find themselves stranded in the Louisiana lowlands with an unfordable stream between them and Baton Rouge.

II

"A cavalry raid at its best," said Stephen Forbes, "is essentially a *game* of strategy and speed, with personal violence as an incidental complication. It is played according to more or less definite rules, not inconsistent, indeed, with the players' killing each other if the game cannot be won in any other way; but it is commonly a strenuous game, rather than a bloody one, intensely exciting, but not necessarily very dangerous."[2]

So had Grierson's cavalrymen found this raid to be after two weeks of continuous marching through the heart of the western Confederacy. Of the nine hundred men in the two Illinois regiments, only one had been killed, Sergeant William Buffington of Company B. Four had been wounded, three had been left en route because of illness, and half a dozen stragglers who may or may not have been captured were listed as missing.

And on the dawn of this beautiful May day, the fifteenth day of the raid, there was nothing to indicate that their luck might change. "A gentle breeze floated through the trees," said Sergeant Surby, "causing a rustling among the green leaves of the oaks. Perched among the branches was the mocking bird, singing a variety of notes, the whole impressing the beholder with a sense of a Creator of all this beauty. . . . We little dreamed what a change would be produced in a few hours."

Lieutenant-Colonel William Blackburn, who probably more than any other officer in Grierson's brigade loved the game of cavalry raiding, had requested command of the advance on this day. "I charged him *particularly* to make a cautious advance,"[3] Grierson said afterwards, and Grierson himself rode near the head of the column with the Seventh Regiment, probably suspecting that the day might not end so peacefully as it had begun.

As the column moved rapidly southwestward along the thickly forested watershed between the Amite and Tickfaw Rivers, "marching through woods, lanes, and byroads," Grierson threw off two small expeditions in short feints eastward, designed to alarm Magnolia and Osyka and keep the rebels' attention off the main body of his troops. About nine o'clock, he ordered Lieutenant G. W. Newell, Company F, of the Sixth Regiment, to move off with a squadron on the flank in search of fresh horses. Lieutenant Newell's instructions were to rejoin the column during the noon bivouac, probably at or near Wall's Bridge on the Tickfaw River.

Following the cross-country course selected by Colonel Grierson, the scouts encountered only a few civilians during the morning. They captured one wagon filled with tobacco, a very welcome commodity which was immediately confiscated and distributed among the men in the advance.

Around ten o'clock the scouts emerged from the woods upon the main road running from Liberty to Osyka. "I at once discovered," said Sergeant Surby, "by the newly-made tracks, that a column had passed, and could not have been long before." He sent a scout back on the gallop to inform Lieutenant-Colonel Blackburn, and in a few minutes both Blackburn and Grierson came up to the road. They dismounted and examined the tracks carefully, attempting to estimate the size of the enemy force which was traveling in the same direction the column would have to follow in order to cross the Tickfaw River at Wall's Bridge.

Grierson ordered Sergeant Surby to advance with extreme caution. "Let nothing escape your observation on either side of the road," he said. "If you see anything suspicious, report back to me at once. And don't get more than half a mile from the advance."

"After receiving these instructions," said Surby, "I started, followed by my scouts."[4]

III

The tracks which Sergeant Surby was trailing so cautiously on the morning of May 1 were not more than an hour old. They were the tracks of three Confederate cavalry companies under command of Major James De Baun, a lithe, six-foot Creole from New Orleans, a man in his forties who looked younger than most of his troopers, a swarthy dark-haired fighter with piercing black eyes.[5]

Before dawn Major De Baun had urged his command out of their brief night encampment near Liberty, marching rapidly along the road toward Osyka. His orders of yesterday from General Gardner had informed him that Grierson's raiders were moving south along the railroad toward Osyka; he did not suspect that he had already cut across the Yankees' course, leaving them on the road behind him.

At 11:30 in the morning De Baun reached Wall's Bridge. His destination, Osyka, was only eight miles away, but as he was not certain of finding water farther along he ordered a brief noon halt beside the Tickfaw, sending seven rear guard pickets back half a mile as a routine security measure. The pickets rode leisurely away from the bridge past a cotton field, turned a sharp angle, and halted beside a graveled driveway which curved out of sight through a dense growth of live-oaks and silver poplars that almost concealed a white two-story plantation house standing 300 yards back from the road.

De Baun's pickets were hungry. Their breakfast before dawn had been scanty and they had almost nothing left for noon. The view of the well-kept plantation was tempting, and four of the seven pickets rode their horses up the driveway in search of food. The three men left behind dismounted. Two sat down on a log beneath the tall oaks at the drive's entrance; the third stretched out on the ground with his hat over his face.

Back at Wall's Bridge, Major De Baun watched the last of his men cross the bridge and join the others watering their horses in the river. At 11:45 A.M., fifteen minutes after he called the halt, two shots echoed suddenly, followed by irregular carbine firing. The sounds came from the west, from the road where his rear guard was picketed.

De Baun shouted a command to his men to get their horses out of the river and into the concealment of the thick woods. "I immediately ordered the bridge to be dismantled and the men ambushed," he said, afterwards, "posting men at the bridge to destroy it as soon as the rear guard would have reported."

But the rear guard did not report. De Baun waited ten minutes, standing impatiently at the bridge end and staring up the road which ran straight out through a natural lane of water oaks screening the cotton field to the right. Finally he ordered Captain E. A. Scott to proceed "up the road to ascertain, if possible, the cause of the delay."[6]

Captain Scott signaled his orderly to come forward with two horses. They mounted and rode rapidly up out of the lane of trees to where the road swung to the right in a wide angular bend around the field. Here the captain and his orderly turned to take a short cut across the field, but after they had gone a few yards, Scott pulled his mount up suddenly. He saw four horsemen in butternut riding slowly along the road toward them a quarter of a mile away. They were not De Baun's men but they did not appear to be Yankees.

IV

After receiving orders directly from Colonel Grierson, Sergeant Surby proceeded cautiously for half an hour. The woods were too thickety to use his Butternut Guerillas on flank; he kept them strung out in single file so that each scout was always in sight of the man behind and ahead of him, assuring immediate contact with the head of the column. The tracks and the horse dung were very recent, and Surby kept his eyes always on the road to his front. The sun was directly overhead, and Surby guessed that the rebels would probably halt soon for noon bivouac.

He passed a plantation entrance, the house concealed by a solid green growth of live-oaks and silver poplars. A few yards beyond this driveway he turned a sharp bend in the road. About 300 yards ahead of him on the roadside were three horses, saddled. He could see no men.

Surby halted and waited until three of his scouts caught up with him. He sent the first one back to report to Colonel Grierson and then went forward slowly with the others. "Revolvers ready at hand," he ordered, and as the scouts came up to the saddled mounts, they saw three Confederate soldiers — two sitting on a log, the third lying on the ground — their carbines stacked carelessly against the log.

The rebels had seen the scouts by now, but they made no move to challenge these three strangers in shabby butternut jeans.

Surby slowed his horse, keeping his revolver concealed. "Hello, boys," he said softly. "On picket?"

One of the rebels on the log grinned and replied: "Yes; been on about an hour and feel devilish tired." The man on the ground sat up and yawned. "Been traveling night and day after the d----d Yanks, and I'll bet my horse they will get away yet."

"That is just our case," Surby said. He was studying the terrain, thick forest on the left, a cotton field beyond slanting down toward a wooded bottom where the river lay, and there he guessed would be the enemy force, waiting. He noted a side road curving in to a white plantation house almost obscured by trees, and guessed then that this was a second entrance to the same plantation he had already observed around the angular bend of the road. Surby signaled the two scouts behind to cover him, then slid his revolver back into its holster, threw one leg over his saddle and stepped down.

At that moment, two shots followed by carbine firing exploded upon the somnolent noonday, the sound breaking from somewhere beyond the green foliage that screened the plantation house.[7]

A few minutes before this unexpected gunfire alarmed Sergeant Surby on the road and Major De Baun down at Wall's Bridge, the advance company of Grierson's column had come to a halt beside the main driveway to the plantation house. G Company, Seventh Illinois, was in the advance and the men halted gratefully there in the shade as soon as Surby's scout met them on his way to report to Colonel Grierson.

Only four hundred yards separated G Company from Surby and the Confederate pickets, but neither group was visible to the other because of the angular turn in the road. Captain George Trafton, in command of G Company, was also acting as battalion commander, and he had dropped back a few hundred yards with Colonel Grierson for a conference with the regimental officers, leaving Lieutenant James Gaston in command.

Lieutenant Gaston dismounted in the thick shadows of the live-oaks, probably wondering what lay beyond the screen of shrubbery through which the driveway led. He waited five minutes and there was no sound or sign of action from front or rear. Lieutenant Gaston then signaled the second lieutenant, William H. Styles, to come forward. He told Styles to take over the company while he rode in to the plantation house. With a dozen men behind him, Lieutenant Gaston rode gaily up through the curving driveway.

A few moments later Gaston and his men came suddenly into full view of the plantation house, brilliant in its whiteness against the abundance of enveloping vegetation. But a gate blocked farther passage. "As they rode up to the gate they were surprised at seeing four armed rebels standing around in the yard, their horses being tied outside the gate. The 'rebs' were surprised as well, and both parties showed a disposition to fight."[8]

Lieutenant Gaston immediately shouted a surrender order, but two of the rebels replied with quick fire, two resounding bursts, one carrying a load of buckshot that ripped through the blouse of one of Gaston's men, wounding him slightly.

After opening the driveway gate, the Yankees charged forward, Lieutenant Gaston swinging his saber, the men's carbines rattling a scattered volley. Gaston captured two of De Baun's men; the other two escaped by fleeing on foot around the plantation house and disappearing into the woods beyond.

The lieutenant had won his little skirmish but the gunshots had warned Major De Baun of the enemy's approach.

Back on the road, Sergeant Surby acted quickly when he heard the first shots. He decided there was no time for further questioning of the pickets. "Giving my scouts the sign, each of us covered his man with a revolver and ordered them to surrender and raise their hands over their heads, or we would fire. They complied at once, and I ordered one of my men to dismount and secure their arms, and then, directing them to mount, double-quicked them back to the head of the column."

Amid the confusion of G Company's alarm over the firing inside the plantation yard, Sergeant Surby met Lieutenant-Colonel Blackburn. Blackburn immediately ordered him to turn back and resume scouting. "I was ordered to proceed cautiously."

Summoning George Steadman, Uriah Fowler, and Arthur Wood to accompany him, Sergeant Surby advanced slowly around the bend of the road. As the four Butternut Guerillas passed the side entrance to the plantation house and neared the green-stripped cotton field, they saw two Confederates sitting motionless on horseback far down the open slope, a quarter of a mile away. "Those two men were looking very earnestly at us."

The sergeant ordered Wood to continue along the road while he and Steadman and Fowler cut across the field directly toward the horsemen. They had advanced about a hundred yards when one of the rebels stood up in his stirrups and shouted: "What in hell does all that firing mean?"

Surby cupped his hands and replied that reinforcements were coming and the pickets had fired on the advance. "Nobody hurt," he added.

The two Confederates laughed, and one replied: "Is that all?"

The scouts could see now that one of the rebels was a captain; he was waving his orderly forward to meet them.

"Fowler!" Surby said quickly. "Let him ride up between us. I'll manage him." They checked their pace and spread out to receive the galloping rebel.

He was very young, his face flushed from heat and excitement, and he was grinning when he pulled his horse up short between

Surby and Fowler. "How are you, boys," he drawled. "How much force have you got?"

Surby had turned his mount obliquely, shielding his left hand from the distant officer's view. He had his revolver cocked and pointed directly at the rebel orderly's chest. "Don't talk or make a move," he said quietly. "Fowler, take his arms before I blow him through."

Fowler moved in expertly, blocking the action from the Confederate captain who was now approaching slowly. As soon as the orderly was disarmed, Surby glanced around at Steadman; he was surprised to find Steadman dismounted and leading his horse toward the Confederate captain.

The two met about a hundred yards from Surby. Suddenly Steadman released his horse and caught the Confederate's bridle with one hand, swung his body in alongside the horse, grasping the man's revolver holster and demanding that he surrender. Steadman was over-confident. He was also the smallest of the scouts, and this rebel captain was a big man — and stubborn.

The captain made a quick movement to release the scout's hold on his holster. "Who and what in hell are you?" he cried.

Surby, who had been anxiously watching Steadman's careless procedure, spurred his horse into a quick lunging gallop across the field and came up just in time to persuade the rebel officer to change his plans for escape. "I noticed the gold bars on his collar which in the Southern army denotes captain. He proved to be Captain E. A. Scott."

Captain Scott was trembling with rage at his own stupidity, a reaction which Surby at first interpreted as fear for his life. "Don't be alarmed, Captain," Surby said reassuringly. "We're Illinois boys and we'll treat you right. Just follow me now."

Scott forced a smile. "I'm not afraid," he replied firmly. "But I should not have been your prisoner had it not been that I was deceived in your dress."[9]

Surby did not reply. When he faced back toward the plantation house he saw Company G approaching in column of twos. Lieutenant-Colonel Blackburn was riding alongside Lieutenant Styles, and as soon as Blackburn noted that the scouts were returning with prisoners he galloped his horse forward to meet them.

Blackburn sat high in his saddle, a huge man on a huge bay

stallion. His tight uniform was streaked with salt stains and dark patches of sweat; his sun-burned cheeks above his bluish beard were flushed with the eagerness of the hunter in the chase. "Sergeant!" he shouted. "Bring along your scouts and follow me, and I'll see where those rebels are hiding!"

Surby checked his reins, expecting Blackburn to halt, but the colonel continued past him at a slow trot down the sloping cotton field toward the wooded surround of Wall's Bridge. Restraining a spoken warning to his commander, the sergeant ordered Steadman and Fowler to conduct the prisoners back into the column, and then swung about. Lycurgus Kelly and Sam Nelson had just come up from the advance, and Arthur Wood had joined him during the scuffle with the reluctant Confederate captain. Surby motioned them to follow him, and the four galloped across the field after Blackburn.

"It seemed to me," Surby said afterward, "that this was a rash movement on the part of Colonel Blackburn, but he had ordered me to follow him, and it was my duty to obey."

The scouts overtook Blackburn at the edge of the field, and the colonel led the way out into the sandy road pitted with hoofprints. He halted for a moment in the bright sunlight, the four scouts drawing up beside him, facing down the shaded lane that led straight to the lonely bridge and the dark inscrutable undergrowth beyond. It was a relief when Blackburn clucked his stallion forward and broke the silence with the faint creaking of saddle leather. The river was visible now, below and to one side of the bridge, the stream's surface spotted with twinkling flashes of sunlight.

Then they were close enough to see the roiled waters where the enemy's horses had stood to drink, the muddy slope of the far bank disturbed and pocked with the passage of men and animals. The bridge lay directly before them, fifty feet long, wide enough only for one wheeled vehicle, the siding dismantled, the planks strewn hastily at either end. But the flooring was still intact.

Blackburn was in the lead when without warning, just as he reached the bridge: Wha-a-a-ng! The single report was followed almost instantaneously by a rattle of fire, the bullets whining and skipping through the leaves, echoes swallowed up by succeeding explosions.

Blackburn charged upon the bridge, his horse's hooves pounding hollowly. Surby and his scouts pushed close behind. The scattered firing suddenly concentrated into a volley. "It seemed as though a flame of fire burst forth from every tree." Blackburn's horse was whinnying in pain. The big bay twisted sideways and dropped abruptly, the bridge trembling and spraying dust from its floor seams. Surby's own horse was rearing. He felt a stab of fire running through his thigh.

While he struggled with his horse, Surby caught a glimpse of Blackburn. The colonel lay on the rough flooring, his hat gone, blood streaming from his forehead into his beard; one leg was caught under the dead stallion. Surby glanced quickly back over his shoulder; the long lane behind was empty. Where was G Company? He pulled his mount around, found the bridge half blocked by another dead horse; the dismounted scout was already up behind a comrade's saddle, in flight. Surby spurred his own horse after them.

He knew he was off the bridge at last, but he seemed to be floating painfully and slowly through stopped time. He looked down at his hand; he still gripped his revolver tightly but his thumb was sticky where it had brushed against his trousers. He could feel the blood trickling warm into his boot, and then faintness and nausea overwhelmed him. He barely had strength to pull off the road when he heard the horses pounding on the sandy clay, and looked up to see Lieutenant Styles leading a charging platoon of G Company. Lieutenant Styles was shouting and waving his saber, but to Sergeant Surby the sounds all seemed to come from very far away.[10]

When he heard the first firing from Wall's Bridge, Lieutenant William Styles was still in command of the column's advance, G Company. Styles had started the company forward after Blackburn trotted on ahead with the scouts, but he followed the curving road instead of cutting across the cotton field, thus spreading the gap between the advance and Blackburn's reconnaissance. For some reason the column behind G Company had been delayed in resuming march, and so Lieutenant Styles acted upon his own authority when he ordered the first platoon to follow him in a dash to aid Blackburn and the scouts.

The lieutenant's action was as brave and as imprudent as Colonel Blackburn's. Followed by the twelve men of his platoon, he charged upon the bridge, dodged around the dead horses, and reached ground on the other side. But Major De Baun's ambushed rebels, their weapons reloaded, had purposely held their fire to draw the Yankees in closer for a deadly volley. Seven horses went down, thrashing and screaming, and a swarm of Confederates rushed forward. Miraculously, only three of Styles's men were hit, but the rebels captured five others. The four survivors, including Lieutenant Styles, beat a hasty retreat across the bridge and were moving into the shelter of the trees when they heard the Seventh Regiment's bugler blowing battle calls beyond the shaded road.

At the first sounds of action from Wall's Bridge, both Colonel Grierson and Colonel Prince had come forward to the head of the column, and while Lieutenant Styles was charging the bridge, Companies A and D of the Seventh were sent forward on the double-quick across the cotton field.

The time was high noon, the battle commands echoing in heavy air that smelled of burned gunpowder:

Form fours! March!

C-L-O-S-E U-P!

A bugle interrupted the hoarse commands. A and D Companies halted in adjoining columns facing the road. *Prepare to fight — on foot!* The troopers dismounted, passing reins to the horse-holders, and formed in three lines. Behind them one of Captain Jason Smith's two-pounder mounted guns was rolling and bouncing across the cotton field, the captain galloping along in front.

Colonel Prince sent A Company to the left and D Company to the right of the bridge, with orders to form skirmish lines along the river bank. The two-pounder clattered across a ditch, skewed around into the middle of the road, showering sand on the batterymen. Captain Smith began shouting fire orders, and in a minute the shells were whooshing into the woods beyond the bridge. At first shock, De Baun's Confederates replied with rifle and carbine volleys directed upon the Yankee skirmishers, but Captain Smith's men brought up a second mounted gun and persistent artillery shelling quickly diminished the rebels' return fire.

A courier came speeding down from Grierson's position in front of the halted Sixth Regiment. A trumpet sounded Cease Firing, and then the Sixth's bugler was blaring the Charge. Down the slope by fours came the regiment, slowing and then spinning off in files at the road.

"They came galloping in with all haste with their guns smoking and some of them without their hats and fell into line. We could hear the sound of galloping horses in front and soon a perfect chorus of yells arose from behind the brush and with a quick sharp rattle a little cloud of smoke arose, whiz, skip, cling, the bullets came howling past our heads, spattering the poor innocent trees unmercifully. Then suddenly came a quick flush in the face, a feeling at the small of the back as if a charge of electricity was passing through it, then a desperate attempt to keep cool, and whang went the carbines one after another all along the line. 'Stand firm! Don't flinch! Hold your ground, men!' "[11]

Grierson's attack order sent one battalion of the Sixth single file over the bridge while the other two battalions were fording the river in flanking movements. When the first platoon hit the bridge, Lieutenant-Colonel Blackburn raised himself up and waved them forward. Although he had regained consciousness, he was still trapped with one leg under his dead horse.*

The charging platoon swept on past him, firing at the enemy retreating through the trees.

Shaken by the unexpected shelling from the two-pounders, Major De Baun's Confederates were unable to make a stand against the onrushing Yankees. They broke into retreat, leaving the road strewn with blankets, coats, hats, and occasional firearms. De Baun explained it as follows: "My command being small, . . . and fearing to be surrounded, I ordered a retreat in the direction of Osyka."[12]

While the Sixth Regiment continued in pursuit of the fleeing rebels, a squad from the Seventh went forward to gather up the dead and wounded. G Company had lost eight men in the charge on the bridge, five captured and three wounded. Lieutenant-Colonel Blackburn had received head, chest, and thigh wounds, and had lost considerable blood.

Sergeant Surby, suffering from a deep flesh wound in one leg, was able to ride back to the rear of the column. His old comrades of Company A — called back from skirmishing on foot — helped

* When Colonel Grierson reached the bridge, Blackburn said to him: "Onward, Colonel, whip the rebels. Onward and save your command, don't mind me." — Grierson's manuscript autobiography, p. 430.

him from his horse. Even before attending his wound, they removed his Secesh disguise and dressed him in his regulation Union uniform. Realizing why they were doing this, the sergeant protested strongly. He did not want to be left behind.

But Surby was too weak to argue for long, and when an old friend, Cornelius Griffin, warned him that the Confederates would hang him for a spy if they found him in the Butternut Guerilla disguise, the sergeant submitted. He realized he could not sit in a saddle for a long march, and so he gave Griffin his side-arms and a diary which he had faithfully kept each day of the raid.*

Meanwhile the Seventh was assembling to move across Wall's Bridge after the Sixth. The brigade was intact, except for Lieutenant G. W. Newell's squadron of the Sixth, which Grierson had sent on a search for fresh horses early that morning. But Grierson could not wait for Lieutenant Newell. A wagon impressed from the adjoining plantation was converted into a blanket-lined ambulance, and the wounded were transported a mile beyond the river to Newman's Plantation.

"I remember being carried through the front into a back room, joining the kitchen," Surby wrote afterwards, "and laid upon a pile of unginned cotton, which Hughes, Roy and myself occupied, the Colonel remaining in the front room."†

Surgeon Erastus Yule, who had been detached from the Second Iowa Regiment when Colonel Hatch turned back north, volunteered to remain with the wounded. Augustus Leseure, Blackburn's French-speaking sergeant-major, and Private George Douglas of Blackburn's original Company A, also requested permission to stay with the colonel and assist in nursing the wounded men.

Grierson granted them permission to remain, and before giving the Seventh orders to resume march, he went into the plantation house with Colonel Prince to bid Blackburn and the men farewell. During this interview, Grierson kept to himself his feelings about the misadventure at Wall's Bridge, but he said later that Blackburn was "not as discreet and wary as he was brave.

---

* From the diary, later recovered, Surby wrote his account of the raid. Cornelius Griffin had come to Illinois with him from the east, and they had joined up the same day in Lieutenant-Colonel Blackburn's original cavalry company at Paris, Illinois.

† Private Rees M. Hughes and Bugler William Roy, of Company G. Hughes died of his wounds, but Roy later recovered.

. . . The passage of the Tickfaw might have been a complete surprise and accomplished without loss but for the accident of the firing and alarm. Unfortunately, Lieutenant-Colonel Blackburn, calling on the scouts to follow him, dashed forward to the bridge without waiting for the column to come into supporting distance."[13]

Colonel Prince was visibly moved by the serious condition of his lieutenant-colonel; he had depended heavily upon Blackburn's limitless energies in commanding the Seventh Regiment. Now Prince was left without a second in command; there was not even a major in rank below him in the regiment, and the realization of this seemed to shake his confidence in himself.

"Colonel Prince was exceedingly excited by his first serious loss," Grierson said, "and wanted to go into camp."[14]

But Blackburn, who was still conscious, did not agree with Prince. He urged Grierson to march on to Baton Rouge and save the command.

V

After leaving his mortally wounded lieutenant-colonel at Newman's Plantation, one of Grierson's first acts was to assign a new leader for the Butternut Guerillas. The scouts had lost both their sergeant and their officer in the fight at Wall's Bridge. Grierson chose Corporal Samuel Nelson, the stuttering young man from southern Illinois, who had saved the brigade from a surprise attack by his long night ride after encountering Captain R. C. Love's Confederate cavalry regiment in the Piney Woods country. "Samuel Nelson was a robust heavy-set muscular man, sandy complexion, reddish hair," said Grierson, "and looked as honest and harmless as a Presbyterian deacon."[15]

Sam Nelson took his scouts forward at a gallop and began patrolling the road ahead of the Sixth Regiment, which was continuing in advance of the Seventh. Within an hour the column had crossed into Louisiana. But the Union picket line outside Baton Rouge was still more than fifty miles away.

About two o'clock in the afternoon Nelson sent a messenger racing back to Grierson to inform him that a Confederate cavalry force was approaching on a side road. While the scouts delayed the rebels with carbine fire, Grierson ordered Captain Smith to bring up the first two-pounder. The artillery shells exploding suddenly from nowhere sent the surprised Confederates scattering back down the side road. Grierson ordered one battalion of the Sixth in pursuit, recalling them as soon as he was fairly certain the rebels would not attempt to delay him with a fight.

This Confederate force was Major W. H. Garland's Mississippi Battalion, and as soon as Garland could rally his men he sent a courier to General Franklin Gardner at Port Hudson, advising Gardner that Grierson was continuing on the road to Greensburg. "They will cross at Williams' Bridge, on the Amite River," Garland said. "If a force can be thrown there, they may yet be cut off. Williams' Bridge is about 16 miles from Greensburg and about 14 miles from Clinton. To stop them at Williams' Bridge is the last chance."

Colonel Grierson also knew that Williams' Bridge was his last chance to escape. "The enemy were now on our track in earnest," he said. "We were in the vicinity of their stronghold [Port Hudson] and, from couriers and dispatches which we captured, it was evident they were sending forces in all directions to intercept us. The Amite River, a wide and rapid stream, was to be crossed, and there was but one bridge by which it could be crossed, and this was in exceedingly close proximity to Port Hudson. This I determined upon securing before I halted."[16]

At four o'clock in the afternoon, the column was approaching Greensburg, with the strategic bridge over the Amite still sixteen miles away. Grierson ordered the scouts to move in rapidly and search for evidences of enemy troops. On Greensburg's outskirts Sam Nelson encountered a single mounted picket, and before capturing the man he questioned him long enough to discover there was no armed force in the town. The column once again had outrun the news of its approach.

During this brief halt Lieutenant G. W. Newell and his squadron from the Sixth Regiment overtook the column. Detached by Grierson during the morning with orders to search for horses, Newell had not learned of the Wall's Bridge fight until he reached the scene of action. He narrowly escaped capture, and only by swift riding had managed to bring the squadron through to rejoin the column.

With his command intact once again, Grierson marched through Greensburg, turning southwestward into the late sun on the road to Williams' Bridge. Every man knew there could be no halting for night camp, not even a brief stop for feeding or watering, until they reached the bridge. And what fate waited upon them there? Would they be forced to fight again, this time against greater numbers? Or had the rebels, anticipating their coming, already burned the bridge, trapping the raiders between Port Hudson and the pursuing Confederates along the New Orleans & Jackson Railroad?

Samuel Nelson and his alert scouts brought in two couriers carrying dispatches from General Franklin Gardner to the commanding officer at Osyka. Grierson read the intercepted messages with keen interest; they were orders urging Gardner's men to move with all haste to Williams' Bridge to block a crossing by the Yankee raiders.

Near midnight the advance heard the first rumblings of big guns somewhere to the west. Grierson guessed they might be Admiral David Farragut's mortarboats dueling with Port Hudson. He ordered Corporal Nelson and his men to visit some of the plantation houses, posing as Confederate guides, and obtain information about the defensive strength at Williams' Bridge. "Our scouts . . . learned that a company was stationed near the bridge about one mile away, while a detachment of ten men were kept at the bridge by day and all but two recalled at night."

The column moved on into the dark Amite bottoms. About a mile from the river the road slanted downward and became quite muddy. Grierson halted the column and sent Nelson ahead, on foot and alone, to determine if their information as to the size of the guard was correct. As he came down the shadowed road to the river, Nelson saw the bridge; it was almost 200 yards long, a solid structure wide enough for a column of twos to ride easily abreast. When he heard the river splashing he moved up so that he could see the strong full current running under the pale light.

Within a few minutes Nelson discovered the presence of the two Confederate guards. He reported back to Grierson, who described subsequent events as follows: "On went the scouts, the two guards were taken as usual. The scouts advanced with letter in hand as couriers on the way to Port Hudson. A cocked revolver quickly placed at the heads of the guards, no words were spoken above a whisper and both were readily captured."[17]

Captain Henry Forbes also wrote of this long night ride:

To our right as we marched into that last night, of May 1st, the occasional boom of a big gun pointed out the position of Port Hudson, then undergoing bombardment by the mortar-boats. Our scouts had already reported a picket at the bridge on the Amite, a stream which could not be forded. Would this picket, apprised of our approach, put the torch to the bridge, or would a force from Port Hudson present itself to contest passage? Either event would be equally fatal to us.

About midnight we were in the vicinity of the bridge. Our advance dashed down on the charge. A single horseman was turning southward from the bridge towards the lights moving about a house said to be the headquarters of the guard.

The way was ours, and the steady beat of our horses' feet on the bridge assured us of success.

The best of the story is yet to be told. We afterward learned that General Gardner commanding at Port Hudson, apprised of our approach, had correctly foreseen our destination and made his dispositions for our capture. He preferred not to burn the bridge, as he needed it for his own uses, but thought it better to meet and capture us at that point. Dispatching, therefore, an ample force of infantry and cavalry, accompanied by a battery of artillery, to command the bridge, he awaited our arrival. His detachments marched through Clinton (Louisiana) and bivouacked for refreshment in the outskirts of the town. The good citizens, rejoiced at the foreseen capture of Grierson and his raiders, tendered a complimentary dance to the officers of the rebel command.

The officers had carefully estimated the time of our possible arrival near the bridge, and accepted the compliment as an incident too pleasant to be needlessly rejected. While, therefore, we were stretching our legs for the bridge, these gentlemen were stretching theirs in the cotillion. After they had danced they marched. After we had marched we danced — when we learned they arrived at the bridge just two hours after we had crossed it.[18]

VI

Captain Forbes did not name the commander of the force dispatched by General Gardner from Port Hudson to defend Williams' Bridge, but from an examination of Confederate troop movements in that area on the evening of May 1, it may reasonably be assumed that he was referring to Colonel Alexander J. Brown of the Fifty-fifth Tennessee Infantry. Colonel Brown actually did not arrive at Williams' Bridge until several hours after the Yankees crossed it; at 9:30 o'clock the next morning he was still six miles from the bridge when he sent a report back to General Gardner: "A courier from Williams' Bridge . . . is just in, and informs me the enemy, 1,500 strong, crossed the bridge last night between 12 and 1 o'clock."

As for the other Confederate troops assigned to block Grierson's escape, Major James De Baun had reached Osyka at five o'clock on the afternoon of May 1, four hours after his fight at Wall's Bridge. "I reached Osyka, but found no re-enforcements," he said. "Not being in force (the enemy being at least 1,000 strong and four pieces of artillery), I was unable to pursue them. During the night cavalry re-enforcements, under Colonel Richardson, numbering 400 men, reached Osyka."

Richardson, marching south from Summit, learned of the Wall's Bridge fight when he rode into Magnolia. This news only whetted his eagerness to overtake the raiders, and he resumed march to Osyka, arriving there at 10 P.M. "The enemy had not approached Osyka nearer than Wall's Bridge," he said, "but had gone on the road to Greensburg. . . . I fed my horses, and rested my men three hours, when, with a force of about 470 men, I resumed the march to Greensburg."[19]

And so, for the fourth straight night, Richardson's weary troops, joined now by the three companies of Major De Baun, found themselves pressing forward after the elusive Yankees. Richardson was counting heavily on Captain Wren's having reached Williams' Bridge in time to burn it; he did not know that General Gardner had forbidden destruction of the bridge.

When Colonel Wirt Adams, following Richardson down the Jackson railroad, learned of the Wall's Bridge fight, he turned his column westward at Magnolia, hoping to get on Grierson's rear. Late in the afternoon Adams' regiment passed over Wall's Bridge and the colonel stopped long enough at Newman's Plantation to interview Lieutenant-Colonel Blackburn, who was still conscious. In his next message to General Pemberton, Colonel Adams was careful to record that the wounded Yankee officer had assured him that the raiders' plans to march on to the Mississippi River and join Grant had been thwarted by Adams' strong defense at Union Church. Upon leaving Newman's Plantation, Adams began a night march in pursuit of Grierson over the same route the raiders were traveling.

A few hours after Adams departed, Colonel W. R. Miles moving east from Clinton toward Osyka also arrived at Wall's Bridge. Miles visited the wounded Yankees at Newman's Plantation, a meeting that was recorded by Sergeant Surby. "I could plainly see the column [Miles's Legion] from my window as it moved along," he said. "It consisted of about three hundred cavalry, two thousand infantry, and one battery of artillery — four and six pound rifled guns. They felt confident of capturing the 'Yanks' and did not appear to be in any hurry, stating that a force had been sent out from Port Hudson, and that they would intercept our forces when they attempted to cross the Amite River. . . . We were visited by the Colonel [Miles] while his command was passing. He informed us that he had instructed the nurses that they should pay every attention to the wounded. He treated us with kindness, and I shall never forget his kind manner and venerable form."[20]

Less confident than these subordinates in the field, and overwhelmed by more ominous intelligences of Grant's successful river crossing at Bruinsburg, General Pemberton on this day abandoned all hope of capturing Grierson's raiders. Realizing at last that Grant's army was the real danger and that all available cavalry would be needed in the efforts to stop him, he dispatched an order to Colonel Robert V. Richardson: "Instead of pursuing Grierson farther, your command will return in direction of Port Gibson, to operate against enemy there. If you can communicate with Colonel Wirt Adams, tell him same thing."[21]

THE LAST LONG MARCH:
WILLIAMS' BRIDGE TO BATON ROUGE

From the time they crossed Williams' Bridge on the Amite River at midnight, through the twelve hours until noon of Saturday, May 2, Grierson's 900 fatigued and hungry raiders dared not risk their luck by halting to eat or rest.

Baton Rouge, their goal and sanctuary, still lay thirty miles away, and even a short delaying fight now might give the enemy time to bring up forces too formidable to outrun or defeat, might undo all their clever feints and long hard marches. And so they rode on through the night under the ghostly moss-hung trees, past shadows of plantation houses and sugar mills. Sleep was now the enemy. Fifteen days and nights of riding — with nerves and muscles always taut, with rest measured out by minutes — began to react now that the excitement and danger of the bridge was past. They knew that all streams remaining between them and Baton Rouge were fordable; they believed they had outrun the larger forces of the enemy. They could endure the pangs of hunger, but sleep and weariness were irresistible numbing foes.

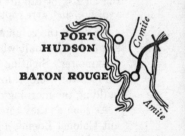

Some of the men pulled off the road, tying each others legs beneath the saddles, resuming march slumped forward with heads resting in their horses' manes.

Captain Henry Forbes and the troopers of Company B were assigned to rear guard duty on the long night ride southwestward across the bayou country, charged not only with keeping alert themselves but also with preventing the men in the column from straggling.

Men by the score were riding sound asleep in the saddles. The horses, excessively tired and hungry, would stray out of the road and thrust their noses to the earth in hopes of finding something to eat. The men, when addressed, would remain silent and motionless until a blow across the thigh or shoulders should awaken them, when it would be found that each supposed himself still riding with his company, which might perhaps be a mile ahead.

We found several men who had either fallen from their horses or dismounted and dropped on the ground, dead with sleep. Nothing short of a beating with the flat of a saber would awaken some of them. In several instances they begged to be allowed to sleep, saying they would run all risk of capture on the morrow. Two or three did escape our vigilance, and were captured the next afternoon.[1]

At dawn the column was approaching Sandy Creek, and Grierson ordered a halt while the scouts crossed the narrow bridge to reconnoiter. Sighting an enemy camp 200 yards beyond the bridge, they crept forward until they discovered two Negroes building the morning cooking fires. No sentinels were in evidence.

As soon as they reported back to Grierson, he ordered Lieutenant-Colonel Loomis to send two companies of the Sixth forward to make the attack, the remainder of the regiment to bring up the rear. Captain Samuel Marshall of H Company dismounted his men, and they crossed the bridge silently with carbines at ready. When H Company was within a hundred yards of the camp, Captain John Lynch led E Company, mounted, in a thundering charge across the bridge. Both companies swept through the long rows of tents, yelling and firing off carbines and pistols.

But most of the tents were empty. Captain Marshall and Captain Lynch flushed out less than forty men, mostly convalescents, those left behind of Lieutenant-Colonel C. C. Wilbourn's regiment of Mississippi state troops. Grierson was much amused to learn that the regiment had departed only twenty-four hours earlier on orders from General Franklin Gardner to march to Osyka and assist in the interception of the raiders. "Having destroyed the camp," said Grierson, "consisting of about one hundred and fifty tents, a large quantity of ammunition, guns, public and private stores, books, papers, and public documents, I immediately took the road to Baton Rouge."[2]

While the Sixth was engaged in destroying the Sandy Creek camp, the Seventh Regiment moved on to take the advance. The sun was already hot in another cloudless morning sky; the road running across level land occasionally twisted to avoid slashes and bayous filled with sluggish, chocolate-brown water. When they passed through woodlands, the road became a tunnel with streamers of gray-green Spanish moss above their heads, and on either side impenetrable twisting masses of blackberry briers, brambles, and vines. In the more open country they saw scattered fan-leaved palmettos moving under the warm breeze like playing fountains.

The sugar plantations were all of a pattern, fields greening rapidly in the May heat, white, two-storied plantation houses with fluted columns and broad galleries, slave quarters of unpainted frame or logs with mud chimneys, surrounded by tiny vegetable patches — and the sugar mills beyond with their rows of huge blackened kettles.

They saw few white men this morning, but the Negroes were everywhere, waiting and watching for them along the fences, standing and waving from the slave quarters. That mysterious communication system of the slaves, running from plantation to plantation, had brought the news of Grierson's raiders long before their white masters even suspected the enemy's presence in the countryside.

Several Negroes ran forward with little gifts or bouquets of pink carnations to press upon "the Yanks come to free the black folks." Some of them wanted to join the column, greeting their liberators in a strange mixture of English and Cajun French, bowing and grinning as they lifted their wide-brimmed palmetto hats.

Throughout the raid, a few slaves from time to time had attached themselves to the column, but most of them had been unable to keep up with the swift pace of the cavalrymen. This morning as the raiders neared Baton Rouge, more and more Negroes deserted their quarters on the sugar plantations and began to form a procession in the drifting yellow dust at the rear

211

of the column. They rode in crude wagons, some stuffed with feather beds, wagons drawn by mules, horses, oxen, sometimes a horse and a mule, or an ox and a mule, the animals hitched to the shafts with ropes, chains, or rawhide.

Not all the slaves, however, trusted the Yankees; some had run away into the woods to hide until the column passed. T. H. Bowman, one of Wirt Adams' cavalrymen, recorded the story of Uncle Billy, a slave who had become a Methodist circuit rider for his people: "Them poor white trash, dressed in blue, come here. I axed 'em in, and told 'em I was a minister of the gospel, but law, chile, that never done a bit of good. They stole Mary's chickens and some of my pigs, and was jist getting off de premises, when, fore God! old Selim whickered, and dem blasted rascals broke down de do' of de smokehouse and tuk my pony."[3]

II

Between eight and nine o'clock in the morning the first platoon of the Seventh Regiment's Company A, riding advance for the column, saw a mounted Confederate officer enter the road about 200 yards ahead of them. They shouted a halt command, but the rebel replied with a few quick shots from his long-barreled revolver and sped on down the road. In a few moments he overtook Corporal Sam Nelson and the scouts dressed in their butternut disguises. As he galloped up to them, he shouted: "Get out of here, boys! The road's full of Yankees in our rear!"

The scouts, revolvers already drawn, surrounded him quickly. "That's right, Mister, and you're right among them now."[4] They had captured Lieutenant Joseph Hinson of Miles's Legion. Lieutenant Hinson had heard the firing from Sandy Creek as he was approaching there at dawn, and admitted to his captors that he was on his way to warn the picket-post on the Comite River, the last defense post between Grierson's column and Baton Rouge. The raiders' luck, their advantage of surprise, still held.[*5]

Three miles farther on, Sam Nelson proved that he was an able replacement for Sergeant Richard Surby. Stopping at a farm-

---

* Lieutenant Hinson, sent to New Orleans as a prisoner, later distinguished himself by escaping from a steamer somewhere in Chesapeake Bay while in transit to a Delaware prison camp. — *Records of Louisiana Confederate Soldiers and Louisiana Confederate Commands,* compiled by Andrew B. Booth, New Orleans, 1920, vol. 3, p. 317.

house to obtain information concerning the size of the picket at the Comite River crossing, he discovered that another rebel lieutenant was inside enjoying a late breakfast. Nelson's "Presbyterian deacon" manner and his soft, hesitant speech soon won him an invitation to join the lieutenant and three ladies at the table. As he had eaten very little for twenty-four hours, the scout did not have to pretend hunger, and in a few moments he and the young Confederate officer were conversing like old friends. Nelson learned that only one rebel company was stationed on the Comite and that there was no bridge, but the water was low enough for cavalry to ford it.

When he finished eating, Nelson arose and without ceremony informed the lieutenant that he was a prisoner.

"I am an officer, sir!" replied the lieutenant with sudden indignity. "You have nothing to do with me, if you are a conscripting officer."[6]

Sam Nelson, stammering and hesitating over every word, was not able to convince the lieutenant that he had been captured by a "live Yankee" until Company A arrived and halted outside on the road.

After reporting his information on the Comite guard to Colonel Grierson, Nelson went forward again with orders to locate the exact position of the Confederate camp. The Butternut Guerillas met with no trouble whatsoever, as the camp was on the east side of the Comite and the pickets were kept on the west side, facing Baton Rouge where the enemy was supposed to be. The Comite bottoms were thickly wooded and the scouts were able to approach within three hundred yards of the camp without being seen.

Arthur Wood volunteered to go in alone for a closer inspection, but Wood had no sooner disappeared than a Confederate soldier, coming up from the stream, accidentally discovered the waiting scouts.

"How're you, boys," the rebel greeted them cordially. "Did you come to relieve us?"

Nelson nodded, hastily swallowing his word of surprise. "That's right. Our company'll be up in a few minutes."

"Well, it's about time you come. We been here four days now and are clean out of rations."[7]

As soon as Wood returned, Nelson invited their welcoming host to accompany them back down the road to meet the "relief company."

III

After listening to the reports of Corporal Nelson and Arthur Wood, Colonel Grierson decided to send the First Battalion of the Seventh on a charge into the Comite camp. Company A moved out on the flank through a cane field, while the Butternut Guerillas and Companies D, E, and I went in directly on the road. The attack was a complete surprise, the thundering hoofbeats and the first volleys from the raiders creating a panicky flight among the Confederates, who left their shotguns, camp kettles, rifles, old blankets, coats and hats scattered in every direction. Loose horses stampeded through the brush.

Captain William Ashmead of Company I dismounted his men and sent them in pursuit of stragglers. One private from this company discovered sixteen rebels hiding in a washed-out cavern under the river bank. Forty-two prisoners were captured, but several escaped, among them the commanding officer, Captain B. F. Bryan, who climbed a tree and concealed himself among the leaves and Spanish moss until the Yankees departed.

"I was surprised by a body of the enemy, under command of Colonel Grierson, numbering upward of 1,000 men," Captain Bryan reported later. "They made a dash and surrounded me on all sides before I was aware that they were other than our own troops, their advanced guard being dressed in citizens' garb. Indeed, I could not think it possible that an enemy could approach my camp without my being notified in ample time to be prepared to meet them. . . . Most of my men being on picket, and having only about 30 of them immediately in camp, there was no possible chance of my making a stand."[8]

While the Seventh Regiment was completing destruction of Captain Bryan's camp and rounding up the prisoners, Grierson ordered the Sixth to ford the Comite and take the advance. The column was now only nine miles from Baton Rouge; they had broken through the last outpost station of the enemy.

They marched three miles west of the Comite and halted near the first large plantation house, turning off the road on high ground dotted with palmettos and patches of sedgegrass. The hot sun, the continuous marching, the lack of food, were all telling heavily upon the horses. And the men, believing that their enemies now lay far behind them, were nodding in their saddles again. The regiments were ordered to fall out, feed, and rest.

"So tired they were," observed Grierson, "they scarcely waited for food, before every man save two or three was in a profound slumber." To keep himself awake Grierson entered the plantation house, wandered into the parlor and began playing upon a piano which he found there. "I astonished the occupants by sitting down and playing upon a piano which I found in the parlor and in that manner I managed to keep awake, while my soldiers were enjoying themselves by relaxation, sleep and quiet rest."

What music did Grierson play at his moment of triumph? Might it have been *Life Let Us Cherish*, the first piece of music he had learned — when he was twelve years old — worked out laboriously on a large yellow box-wood flute while he sat upright in the middle of his bed? Or was it, as one of his friends back in Jacksonville, Illinois, suggested later, *The Bold Soldier Boy?*

He did tell of his thoughts while he was there, playing the piano: "Only six miles then to Baton Rouge and four miles would bring us inside of the lines guarded by the soldiers of the Union. Think of the great relief to the overtaxed mind and nerves. I felt that we had nobly accomplished the work assigned to us and no wonder that I felt musical; who would not under like circumstances?"

He did not become so absorbed in his music and his thoughts that he forgot his cavalrymen; in his autobiography he told of how he interrupted his playing to order his adjutant, Lieutenant Woodward, to "wake up a couple of orderlies and place them on each flank of the command" as guards.

An hour or so after these pickets were sent out, one of them came riding up to the plantation house where Grierson was still playing on the piano. A Confederate force, the trooper reported excitedly, was approaching from the west! With skirmish lines out.

Grierson took one look at the dust cloud of the oncoming cavalry column, smiled, and shook his head. His Illinois boys had been looking for rebels so long they could not recognize Union cavalry when they saw it! "Feeling confident that no enemy could come against us from that direction," he wrote, "I rode out alone to meet the troops without waking up my command."[9]

IV

When Colonel Grierson had ordered his brigade to halt beside the plantation six miles outside Baton Rouge, neither he nor anyone else had observed that one of the colonel's orderlies had continued riding on down the road toward the Union-held city. Nor had the orderly been aware of his digression, being sound asleep in his saddle. And if he did occasionally slip sideways or slump forward and come awake over the next two or three miles, he must have adjusted himself to the horse's movements without bothering to open his eyes and so discover that he was riding alone.*

His first moment of wakefulness came on a rough challenge from either a Massachusetts or a New York infantry private, on picket duty along the Baton Rouge outer defense line.

Both the picket and the orderly stared at each other for a moment with mutual distrust. The orderly, still only half awake, then identified himself as a soldier of the Sixth Illinois Cavalry Regiment, Colonel Grierson's brigade. The picket, his carbine at ready, insisted he had never heard of such a command; there were no Illinois boys in Baton Rouge; they were New York and Massachusetts boys. But the orderly insisted he had come from La Grange, Tennessee; he said there were two regiments of Illinois cavalry a short piece back down the road, certainly no more than a few miles; he guessed he'd fallen asleep and gone ahead of the column. Still skeptical, the picket hustled him back to a lieutenant, but the lieutenant did not believe the story either. He suspected it was a rebel trick to draw the Union troops out to ambush, and passed the man on to General Augur.

General Christopher C. Augur, commanding land forces in Baton Rouge for General Nathaniel P. Banks's Department of the Gulf, had heard nothing of any Illinois cavalry regiments in that vicinity. Banks's headquarters was in continual communication with General Grant's headquarters, and as far as Augur knew there had been no advice from the Department of the Tennessee concerning such cavalry. (As a matter of fact, neither

---

* "One of my orderlies who happened to be asleep and therefore did not hear the order, went moping on nodding to the motion of his horse and the tired steed realizing that a town was near and a better resting place, walked on to the Federal picket line . . ." — Grierson's manuscript autobiography, p. 438.

Grant nor General Hurlbut, Grierson's corps commander, had informed the Department of the Gulf that a cavalry raid was in progress across the state of Mississippi. Both Grant and Hurlbut had assumed that Grierson would return to his Tennessee base through Mississippi or Alabama.)

General Augur, however, may have recalled hearing rumors of a cavalry raid on the Vicksburg railroad some days ago; at any rate he decided to send out two companies of cavalry under Captain J. Franklin Godfrey to "proceed cautiously" and "ascertain the truth."[10]

Colonel Grierson described the meeting as follows: "I rode out to meet them, and found it difficult to approach, so cautious were they, with their skirmishers creeping along behind the fences." By this time, Godfrey had all his men dismounted and "apparently was not at all satisfied with the looks of things." Grierson also dismounted and walked forward, waving his handkerchief and shouting out his name. "The Captain then climbed on the fence while I kept on towards him, and soon thereafter he jumped off to the ground and when we met and shook hands, his soldiers sprang up and clambered onto the fence and gave a shout. The Captain ordered his men to mount and we walked on to where I left my horse, and upon his being brought to him we rode to our camp."

No doubt the taunts of Grierson's captured Confederate prisoners helped convince Captain Godfrey's skirmishers of the true identity of the raiders. "The prisoners were rather jubilant," Grierson commented. "They twitted the Baton Rouge soldiers that *they* couldn't take them, only ten miles off, and that the Union Army had to send a force all the way from Tennessee to take them in the rear."[11]

As soon as he was positive that Grierson and his men were genuine Yankees, Captain Godfrey dispatched a courier back to Baton Rouge. "About noon," said a correspondent for the St. Louis (Missouri) *Republican*, "the inhabitants of Baton Rouge were startled by the arrival of a courier, who announced that a brigade of cavalry from General Grant's army had cut their way through the heart of the rebel country, and were then only five miles outside the city. The information seemed too astounding for belief."[12]

General Augur responded immediately by sending Colonel

Nathan Dudley and a staff in full regalia to escort Colonel Grierson into the city.* Grierson's first request of General Augur was permission to bring his brigade into Baton Rouge for such time as would be required to recuperate his men and horses and to receive further orders. The Department of the Gulf was honored, General Augur assured him, to receive the Illinois cavalry regiments from the Department of the Tennessee. But first, was not a welcoming parade in order?

Grierson demurred politely. His horses were blown and laming; his men looked more like freebooters than soldiers; their uniforms were barely recognizable as such.

But General Augur insisted on a parade, and early in the afternoon the column formed on the road outside Baton Rouge in the following order: the Sixth Regiment, the four two-pounder guns, the Confederate prisoners, the Seventh Cavalry, the led horses and mules, and then the Negroes. According to one newspaper account there were 300 former slaves at the end of the procession, celebrating their new-found freedom, "their white teeth and the whites of their eyes shining, all grinning, singing, playing and shouting, they presented the most wonderful appearance imaginable." Some of them probably joined the march in Baton Rouge; Grierson gave no estimate of the original number, but said there were "about thirty vehicles of every description, from the finest carriage to lumber wagons."

This parade, two miles long and probably the most tatterdemalion procession ever officially sponsored by the United States Army, moved into the streets of Baton Rouge about three o'clock in the afternoon. Under their common coloration of yellow road dust, Grierson's cavalrymen and their Confederate prisoners could scarcely be distinguished. A number of the raiders had exchanged their woolen blouses for captured linen dusters; many were hatless, trousers were ripped and torn, boots were cracked and crusted with mud.

"For half a mile before entering the city," said Grierson, "the road was lined with wondering spectators, old and young, male and female, rich and poor, white and black, citizens and soldiers. Amidst shouts and cheers, and waving of banners, heralded by

---

* Colonel Nathan A. M. Dudley achieved national fame some years later when he became embroiled with Billy the Kid in New Mexico's Lincoln County War.

music, the tired troops marched through the city, around the public square, down to the river to water their horses, and then to Magnolia Grove, two miles south of the city."[13]

It was a long, slow parade, and the sun was setting when the last company filed into Magnolia Grove, halted, and dismounted. "Magnolia Grove, a most delightful spot, shaded by the magnolia, whose long green leaves encircle a beautiful white flower, which fills the air with its rich perfume."

For the first time in sixteen days, Grierson's raiders could sleep without fear. No guards were assigned. As soon as saddles could be stripped off and the horses fed, the men rolled in their blankets. And only a few of them could be aroused when squads from the Forty-eighth Massachusetts and the 116th New York Infantry Regiments brought over cooking stoves and attempted to serve coffee and refreshments. "A noble and kind act," said one of the raiders, but food could wait until tomorrow.[14]

Colonel Grierson summed up the raid as follows:

During the expedition we killed and wounded about one hundred of the enemy, captured and paroled over 500 prisoners, many of them officers, destroyed between fifty and sixty miles of railroad and tele-graph, captured and destroyed over 3,000 stand of arms, and other army stores and Government property to an immense amount; we also captured 1,000 horses and mules.

"Our loss during the entire journey was 3 killed, 7 wounded, 5 left on the route sick; the sergeant-major and surgeon of the Seventh Illinois left with Lieutenant-Colonel Blackburn, and 9 men missing, supposed to have straggled. We marched over 600 miles in less than sixteen days. The last twenty-eight hours we marched 76 miles, had four engagements with the enemy, and forded the Comite River, which was deep enough to swim many of the horses. During this time the men and horses were without food or rest.[15]

V

At noon on this day in Memphis, General Stephen Hurlbut — Grierson's corps commander and the man who had given the orders setting the raid in motion — received his first news of the brigade's activities south of Jackson. Sensing that Grierson might be accomplishing the first dramatic cavalry raid for the Union Army in the war, Hurlbut decided the news was worth more than a routine report to General Grant or to General-in-Chief Halleck in Washington. With his usual disregard for military channels, he addressed himself to:

His Excellency ABRAHAM LINCOLN,
President of the United States:

I learn from two independent sources that Colonel Grierson has passed below Jackson, Miss.; cut the railroad at Hazlehurst, and destroyed 50,000 pounds of bacon and an ammunition train, and is on his way down to Baton Rouge to join General Banks. I believe it to be true, as my orders were to push south if safer than to come north.

S. A. HURLBUT.[16]

VI

And where were Grierson's pursuers, the brave men who had failed, on this last day of the raid?

Major James De Baun, the tall Creole from New Orleans, who had given Grierson's cavalrymen their only real fight, reported as follows:

At 2 a. m., May 2, we started in pursuit of the enemy toward Greensburg. On arriving at that place, we received positive information that the enemy had traveled all night, crossed Williams' Bridge, and were beyond our reach, in Baton Rouge. My men and horses being almost exhausted for want of food and rest, I proceeded to Camp Moore, it being the nearest commissary depot. . . . My loss is 1 captain, 1 lieutenant, and 6 privates. The lieutenant and men belonged to the rear guard; all captured. Too much praise cannot be awarded the officers and men composing the detachment for the bravery and coolness displayed, the officers fighting with their revolvers, and all showing a disposition to punish the daring of our enemies.[17]

As for Grierson's old enemy, Colonel Robert Richardson, who had hoped to even old scores, he also regretfully abandoned the futile chase:

I reached Greensburg at 9 o'clock in the morning of the 2d of May, where I learned that the enemy at great speed had passed the previous evening at about sunset, and had crossed the Amite River at Williams' Bridge, which had not been destroyed. I sent a scout on his track, from whom I learned that the enemy had crossed at Williams' Bridge about midnight . . . of the 1st May, and had stopped about day to feed and rest at Sandy Creek, 15 miles beyond the Amite, and had gone on the road to Baton Rouge.

From the best information I could get, the enemy's strength consisted of the Sixth and Seventh Illinois Regiments of Cavalry, the pride and boast of the United States Army, numbering in all about 1,100 picked men, well armed and mounted. It was not his desire to fight. He wanted to make observations, destroy railroads and telegraphic communications. It is said he pressed horses, the best he could find, to mount his men when a horse was jaded. He also captured mules and horses, negroes, forage, subsistence, and stole money and jewelry from the people in his course. He has made a most successful raid through the length of the State of Mississippi and a part of Louisiana, one which will exhilarate for a short time the fainting spirits of the Northern war party.

We may expect a repetition of this raid on a smaller and a similar scale. We had forces enough to have captured and destroyed him, but his movements were so rapid and uncertain of aim that we could not concentrate our scattered forces or put them in concert of action. You had assigned to me men enough to have whipped him, but they were so scattered that I could not find half of them until the enemy had entered his own lines. While I had to pursue him, I could not do more than send out couriers to find the commands ordered to report to me. I followed him two days and nights with only 170 men, one day and two nights with 270 men, and one day and night with 470 men.[18]

HEROES TO THE UNION

**Seventeenth Day
Sunday, May 3**

"Grierson has knocked the heart out of the State [of Mississippi]," an unnamed informant told General Grant a few days after the raiders reached Baton Rouge. Grant was quick to acknowledge the military value of the Illinois cavalry leader's achievements. On May 3, he said in a report to General-in-Chief H. W. Halleck: "Colonel Grierson's raid from La Grange through Mississippi has been the most successful thing of the kind since the breaking out of the rebellion. . . . The Southern papers and Southern people regard it as one of the most daring exploits of the war. I am told the whole State is filled with men paroled by Grierson."

In his final report to Washington after the fall of Vicksburg, Grant was more explicit concerning the relationship of the raid to his campaign. Grierson, he said, made "a raid through the central portion of the State of Mississippi, to destroy railroads and other public property, for the purpose of creating a diversion in favor of the army moving to the attack on Vicksburg. On April 17, this expedition started, and arrived at Baton Rouge on May 2, having successfully traversed the whole State of Mississippi. This expedition was skillfully conducted, and reflects great credit on Colonel Grierson and all of his command. The notice given this raid by the Southern press confirms our estimate of its importance. It has been one of the most brilliant cavalry exploits of the war, and will be handed down in history as an example to be imitated."[1]

Grant also said later: "It was Grierson who first set the example of what might be done in the interior of the enemy's country without any base from which to draw supplies."[2]

Years afterwards, when he recounted Grierson's operations in his *Personal Memoirs,* Grant said that the raid "was of great importance, for Grierson had attracted the attention of the enemy from the main movement against Vicksburg."[3]

It is probable, however, that Grierson himself relished most of all the terse compliment of Grant's tough, red-bearded infantry commander, General William T. Sherman, who was always reluctant of praising anyone, particularly a cavalryman. "The most brilliant expedition of the war," said Sherman.[4]

Because of lack of telegraphic communication between the Department of the Gulf and the states of the Union, most citizens of the North did not learn of Colonel Grierson's cavalry raid until two weeks after the brigade's parade through Baton Rouge. But when the story finally reached New York on May 17, it swept across the country on the front pages of almost every newspaper, and Grierson's raiders suddenly became national heroes. After many grim weeks of winter stalemate, the dramatic story of their exploits was the first cheering news for the North, the first truly successful raid of the much maligned Union cavalry.

Leaving New Orleans on May 10 with correspondents' dispatches, the United States Mail Steamship *George Washington* docked in New York on Sunday, May 17. Next morning the New York *Times* devoted most of its front and back pages to Grierson's raid, under such headlines as the following:

IMPORTANT FROM NEW ORLEANS!

The Great Cavalry Raid Through Mississippi

Safe Arrival of Colonel Grierson's Command
at Baton Rouge

Wonderful Cavalry Exploit

The two national picture magazines, *Harper's Weekly* and *Frank Leslie's Illustrated Newspaper* vied with each other in their issues of June 6, presenting the Grierson raid in glowing words and highly imaginative illustrations. *Frank Leslie's* front cover was a full face-and-shoulder portrait copied by an artist from a photograph of Colonel Grierson made by Karl Jacobs of New Orleans. *Harper's Weekly* also devoted its cover to Colonel Grierson. The artist used the Jacobs photograph as a model but also dressed the Union's new hero properly in a neatly buttoned blouse, polished knee-boots, plumed hat, scarf, and spotless gloves — and mounted him upon a rearing white charger. Another drawing by J. R. Hamilton, "Triumphal Procession of Colonel Grierson, commanding Sixth and Seventh Illinois Cavalry, through Baton Rouge," filled one inside page. A third page carried a short account of the raid and a large map showing the route. All this was topped off by an editorial, "Symptoms of Caving-In," in which the writer concluded that the western Confederacy was weaker than the Union had formerly believed it to be, but he also extolled Grierson's raiders for their courage and audacity.

"The illustrated newspapers of New York," Grierson later wrote, "pictured us riding trimly and daintily in, as if carpet soldiers on dress parade; but the Baton Rouge correspondent who witnessed it, says: 'We were exceedingly surprised to-day, by the arrival of a brigade of Cavalry from the interior of the country, dust covered to an extent that made it nearly impossible to judge from appearance whether they were Federals or Confederates — their horses blown and loaded down with miscellaneous plunder.' "[5]

The first accounts in the New York *Times*, which were the sources of most of the Grierson stories which spread rapidly across the Union, contain several minor inaccuracies, but for the most part agree with diaries and letters of the participants.

One of the dispatches began quite leisurely:

The Department of the Gulf has, at last, aroused itself to action, and events of the most startling character are so rapidly succeeding each other down here, that it is not very easy to keep pace with them. You have been so long accustomed in the North, to keep your eyes constantly fixed on Richmond and the Rappahannock that I can readily imagine the surprise with which you must read the tidings which each successive mail brings you from this distant latitude. Be assured that you have only yet received the first instalment of events that will electrify the world.

After directing the reader to provide himself with a good map of the state of Mississippi, the *Times* correspondent finally got down to facts and gave a detailed description of the raid. He said in summation:

Let the reader think of the dangers these men had to encounter, the physical difficulties to overcome, their small numbers and the forces opposed to them, their hair-breadth escapes, the enormous amount of injury they have done to the enemy, and the terror they have inspired, — and then ask himself whether for rapidity of movement, strategic conception and daring execution, courage, patience, and heroic endurance, he ever heard or read of anything to surpass it in the whole annals of warfare, ancient or modern. To go over all that these men have accomplished, men, the majority of whom probably were, but a very short time ago, following the peaceful avocations of life, seems almost encroaching on the marvelous, and yet the record is clear enough. . . .

How can we measure the extent to which this new and unexpected manifestation of our military power will cripple the rebels, by compelling them to divide their forces everywhere, to keep ten or fifteen thousand men guarding their railways, not knowing when or where a *Grierson* may come down upon them like an avenging thunderbolt?

As a matter of course, the presence of these heroes among us has created the wildest excitement.

II

After their first night of unguarded sleep in more than two weeks, the men of the Sixth and Seventh Illinois Cavalry Regiments awoke to a pleasant Sunday dawn, their camping ground shadowed by magnolias and beeches intermingled with muscadine vines. Some went off to church in Baton Rouge; others lay on their blankets watching the six-mule teams bringing in provisions and forage. "The sun is shining with a lazy sultriness out of the smoky-looking sky, and the wind is wandering around in little cool puffs. . . . The horses stand dozing lazily in the heat, and the men are rolling around under the shade with open shirts and bare feet, telling idle stories and swearing at the weather."[6]

During this placid morning, Captain Henry Forbes of B Company suddenly broke into a raving delirium. "It was pathetically significant of the stress and strain of the long hard ride," said his young brother, Sergeant Stephen Forbes, "that he was taken with cautious violence to the post hospital, tearing the curtains from the ambulance on the way, and swearing that we might kill him if we would but we could never take him prisoner."[7] Stephen, better than anyone present, understood the meaning of those last words.

But the rugged Captain Forbes recovered rapidly, and in a few days was writing letters home:

I have risen refreshed this morning and have thrown open my windows and opened my paper to write you a letter. I would like you to look out of this back window of Madam Wilson's boarding house with me. There flows the ever glorious old river, broad and cloudbearing to the Gulf, and numerous odd little craft, belonging to this Frenchiest of places, cling along the shore. Across you see the huge buildings of sugar plantations as far as the eye can reach, and right here almost within reach of my arm are fig-trees full of growing fruit. The birds are particularly jubilant this morning, too, and what with the fresh breezes from the woods dripped with a little night rain, and suntempered with a light transparency of clouds, the morning is sufficiently delightful. . . .

I suppose there is no need of telling you of our dare-devil expedition — our neck-or-nothing ride through the heart of Dixie, as I believe among all the startling events of the immediate past, that has made its own noise and secured its own record. The facts of our having performed the greatest march in a given time on record, you understand, the thousand and one incidents of it can only be talked up. I have neither time nor strength to write them . . . we were the blind used to obscure the real movements by seeming to threaten the rebel sensitive points ourselves. . . . I was once forty-eight hours without tasting food, and we rode at one time fifty-two miles without feeding. This was thought to be doing pretty well for one little company, and indeed my officers speak of it in terms too kind to bear repetition from me. We tried to do the best we could, and there was One who covered our defenceless heads. We had one man killed and had one wounded, though he rode bravely through for fully four hundred miles bearing two severe wounds. With *such* men you can accomplish what you will.[8]

In another letter, written after he and Stephen had heard from their family in Illinois, Captain Forbes wrote:

I observe in your Grandma's and mamma's letter to Stephen a very considerable amount of the most delightful distress on my account because I don't make a fuss about myself in the papers. I hadn't thought of the matter before, but have since, and have concluded to have the daguerrotype of the seat of my unmentionables as viewed before and after the "great raid" sent to Leslie, that I may become immortal by this clever evidence of endurance and Enterprise. You see I put a capital E to that last word! Can't help it! Enterprise is my destiny, henceforth, and I am known throughout this corps as "the man who took Enterprise" and then skedaddled.[9]

Meanwhile, nineteen-year-old Sergeant Stephen Forbes had dismissed the raid from his thoughts — with the sensibility of youth — and did not even mention it in his letters home until three months afterwards when the Seventh Regiment was returned to Memphis by river boat. "Sleeping under a tent for the first time since April 17," he began. "Unspeakable luxury to have a change of clean clothes, soft bread, and milk to eat, if you buy it. Morning papers and monthlies to read."

It was not the dashing dangerous raid that had most impressed Stephen Forbes; it was the Southland.

We see the level, rich bottomlands, covered with swaying sugarcane; and the massive brick sugar houses, low and dark and full of ponderous machinery and with huge brick chimneys rising high into the air; fields surrounded with the wildest and gayest of hedges (just think of a fence of roses in the place of your rail abominations) groves of dark-leaved snowy-blossomed magnolias, sweet-scented enough to make one sick with delight, the most elaborate and beautiful of gardens, and oh! the acacias! so delicate and handsome, the most angelic of all the trees that God ever made I know; and the wild dark forests literally streaming with vines and draped with half-mourning veils of Spanish moss, cut by crooked, still bayous, in which "the alligator flaps his tail and the cat-fish jumps," (rather a sudden fall, isn't it? but I had to fall to something to get out of the sentence, and I haven't got out of it yet.)

And the wide, cool plantation-houses, where the opulent old planters bring up their fiery sons and delicate daughters in dignified idleness, stocked with splendid libraries and ringing with grand, rich music from heavy pianos from which dainty fingers will give you *Dixie*, the *Southern Marsellaise*, and the *Bonnie Blue Flag* with infinite spirit, and once in a while, away back in the dark woods, an old musty house, the residence of some gloomy tyrant or ruined speculator, where the stocks and handcuffs lying about hint at a small history which we won't interfere with if we are at all nervous. All this we see down here. . . .

Let me see, I have never written you a word of the "famous raid," have I? But I guess that is just as well; I suppose that you have heard of it in some way, and I am heartily sick of it.[10]

III

On May 5, after three days of rest in Baton Rouge, Colonel Grierson, Colonel Prince, Major Mathew Starr, Lieutenant Samuel Woodward, and two unidentified privates boarded a steamboat for New Orleans. Grierson's main object in going was "to have the battery of little 'Woodruff Guns' repaired, there being no means available at Baton Rouge. The wheels of the gun carriages had all been broken to pieces coming through from

Grierson and his staff in Baton Rouge. Presumably Colonel Edward Prince and Colonel Reuben Loomis are in this photograph. Some authorities have identified the officer with his chin in his hand as Grierson; others believe Grierson to be the man seated on the right.

La Grange." But he was also interested in a visit to the paymaster of the Department of the Gulf; the brigade was several months behind in pay and few of the officers or men had any money with which to celebrate the success of the raid. Grierson had small hope of persuading the Gulf to pay off Tennessee men, but he intended to make a try.

The boat trip was quiet and pleasant. Grierson enjoyed the May sun and the river breeze, sweet-smelling from masses of blossoms lining the fences of the river-front plantations. The New Orleans wharves were exciting — great stacks of grain in sacks, piles of cotton bales covered with canvas as protection

Grierson's raiders arriving in Baton Rouge, as depicted by a *Harper's Weekly* artist. "The illustrated newspapers of New York," said Colonel Grierson, "pictured us riding trimly and daintily in, as if carpet soldiers on dress parade." In reality the paraders' uniforms were tattered and dust-covered; the horses were lame, and loaded with miscellaneous plunder.

Camp of Grierson's raiders in Baton Rouge, described by one of them as "a most delightful spot, shaded by the magnolia, whose long green leaves encircle a beautiful white flower, which fills the air with its rich perfume."

against the sudden drizzling spring rains. Paddle-wheelers and ocean steamships were loading and unloading; six-mule teams and drags and carts rattled over the round cobblestones, the drivers cracking whips; and everywhere were the roustabouts, singing and shouting.

From the moment of arrival, all quiet and privacy ended. "Many persons were shouting: 'Hurrah for Illinois!' I innocently asked what all the fuss was about. I did not then have the least idea it was on account of our arrival or about myself and the officers who were with me." They rode in carriages to the St. Charles hotel. "I was 'captured' by citizens, gun-boats, school-children, photographists,* reporters, and everybody in general."[11]

Waiting in the hotel rotunda was the band of the Forty-seventh Massachusetts Infantry Regiment, and as soon as Grierson and his party arrived, a serenade began. "It is to be questioned," the New York *Times* correspondent reported, "if the rotunda of the St. Charles ever exhibited such a scene of uproarous loyalty as it presented on that occasion. . . . By 9 o'clock P.M., when the band woke up the echoes of the long corridor of the St. Charles with the 'Star Spangled Banner,' immense numbers had filled the spacious entrance portico."[12]

One of Grierson's enthusiastic admirers was George Hepworth, a chaplain from New England. "I rushed out to the St. Charles," wrote Hepworth. "I cried out 'Eureka!' and rushed hither and thither until I found the hero, whom I grasped by the hand as though he had been my brother."[13]

Captain John L. Swift of the New Orleans command was present to welcome Grierson and his party, and he climbed upon one of the St. Charles's marble tables to introduce the heroes to the crowd. Colonel Grierson also "diffidently got upon the table, amid deafening shouts of applause, that seemed as if they would never cease; the circular gallery up in the dome, being filled with ladies, waving scarfs and handkerchiefs, and joining in the loud chorus of praise and welcome."[14]

Grierson had expected no reception such as this. He was not prepared to speak, and according to the newspaper reports said

---

* "I have sat for my likeness here — have some photographs taken small and also large — one of the large photographs will be sent to you by the artist who took them. . . . I will enclose you one in this letter — of the small ones." Benjamin Grierson to Alice Grierson, May 9, 1863 (Grierson Papers).

only a few words, thanking the crowd and then giving all credit for the success of the raid to his officers and men.

Next day, Grierson visited the New Orleans paymaster's office and discovered that as a hero it was no trouble at all to collect several months' back pay which he had been unable to obtain from his own department before his last furlough home. He immediately wrote a jubilant letter to his wife, enclosing $500 and telling her of the New Orleans reception.*

Believing that all official ceremonies were over, he took a leisurely sight-seeing trip around the city, bought some presents to be sent to his family, and returned to the hotel. There a committee was waiting to inform him that the citizens of New Orleans would be honored that evening to present him with a gift — a horse. "A noble bay," said the New Orleans *Era* of May 7, "a very beauty of a horse, not too large, compactly built, sleek and with limbs and body displaying such perfect lines of beauty from the point of his nose to the tip of his tail, as would have rejoiced the heart of a sculptor to look upon."

Grierson accepted graciously, of course. His feelings about horses he kept to himself. Always the reluctant cavalryman, he trusted no horse, and from his first sight of the magnificent bay he suspected that no good would come of that spirited beast.

Colonel Prince in his usual secondary role (which he the more resented now that Grierson had become so suddenly a hero) was given a saddle and bridle, richly trimmed with gold lace.

This second reception drew a larger crowd than the first, long lines of people extending down Canal Street. After the usual introductory speech, the Forty-seventh Massachusetts Infantry band played *Hail to the Chief*, and then two little girls dressed in white, each carrying a flag in one hand and a bouquet of magnolias in the other, were lifted up to the speaker's stand beside Grierson to present their offerings. "The colonel stood bowing all the time," reported the New Orleans *Era*, "and we imagined he would much rather at that moment have been facing Stuart's Black Horse cavalry, or John Morgan's guerillas."

Forewarned, Grierson had written his speech this time, and it is still preserved, filled with the rousing patriotic phrases of 1863.

---

* "May 6, 1863. My dear Alice, I like Byron have had to wake up in morning and find myself famous. Since I have been here it has been one continuous ovation. I have received 4 months pay today and enclosed you will find draft on New York for $500." — (Grierson Papers, 1863)

Its most significant sentence is one in which he refers to his command as being from the West, rather than from the North.[15]

Grierson and his party stayed three more days in New Orleans, enjoying their fame and glory. Then, on May 9, he wrote his wife that he would be leaving for Baton Rouge at five o'clock P.M. on the steamer *Sally Robinson*. "Early in the week," he continued, "I presume we will endeavor to form a junction with the forces of General Grant, who are now said to occupy Port Gibson and Grand Gulf. We may go through Louisiana on the west side of the Mississippi, or may go north from Baton Rouge, passing near the line of the railroad from Port Hudson to Clinton. We will endeavor to select the best possible route, to inflict the most injury to the rebels. We have had a very pleasant visit here. I take my fine horse and equipments with me to Baton Rouge."

IV

"Grierson's cavalry," said General Grant in an urgent message to General Banks on May 10, "would be of immense service to me now, and if at all practicable for him to join me, I would like to have him do it at once."[16] With his main army across the Mississippi River, Grant was cutting loose from his base at Grand Gulf and starting his land drive for Vicksburg. He needed all the cavalry he could get.

Grierson was as eager to join Grant as Grant was to have him, but he was now under Banks's command, and Banks seemed reluctant to issue orders returning the Illinois regiments to their proper department. Three weeks after arriving in Baton Rouge, Grierson was still waiting. "I remained here another day to write my official report," he informed his wife on May 21. "It will be ten days or more before I can give it to General Grant, and should I march through the country to join him, as I expect, I will have another report to make by that time."

Two days later, Captain Henry Forbes, now fully recovered, said in one of his letters home: "Just how long we shall remain here before proceeding to rejoin the army of General Grant, I don't know. We have waited already for some time, but Colonel Grierson will do what is prudent. He is a great fellow."

On May 25 Grant again politely reminded Banks: "Colonel Grierson would be of immense value to me now. If he has not already started, will you be kind enough to order him here immediately? He should come up the Louisiana shore to avoid delay."

Banks's reply was to agree with Grant that Colonel Grierson's cavalry was of great importance. "He has rendered us great service," he said, "and his immediate departure will entirely cripple us."[17]

Thus did Grierson, who had escaped capture by the Confederates during his daring raid, now find himself a captive of a rival department of the Union Army.

His men, however, did not seem to mind their enforced stay in Baton Rouge. They had no money, but the restaurant and saloon keepers pampered them for the first few days with free food and drinks. "On finding themselves such privileged characters," Grierson commented, "it was not strange they should indulge in some skylarking." They engaged in such pranks as seizing the Provost Marshal's office and locking that worthy official outside. They took over a saloon, chasing the proprietor, and served each other drinks. The saloon-keeper protested to the Provost Marshal, but the harassed officer replied: "It's no use to try to do anything with those terrible raiders." And he recommended that the man shut up his shop. But when the rambunctious cavalrymen created a disturbance in an ice cream parlor, the marshal decided the mischief-making was getting out of hand. He made a stern-faced entrance into the place only to receive a charge of gas from one of the soda founts hidden behind a door.

The Illinois boys were fascinated by the Negro street criers of Baton Rouge who went about the city carrying advertising banners, ringing bells, and crying out announcements of sales, auctions, and entertainments. One afternoon a group from the Seventh Regiment prepared a sign advertising a free band concert in Magnolia Grove by Grierson's raiders, and sent a crier through the streets ringing bells and inviting the citizens to attend. That evening when a crowd gathered at the Grove, everyone flatly denied any knowledge of a concert. How could they present a concert with no musical instruments other than the trumpeters' bugles and the colonel's jew's-harp?

"All this disorder was but the effervescence of a few days," Grierson said. It was ended by an order from General Banks directing Colonel B. H. Grierson to take command of the First Cavalry Brigade attached to the Department of the Gulf's

Fourth Division, such brigade to consist of the Sixth and Seventh Illinois Cavalry, the Second Massachusetts Cavalry, the First Louisiana Cavalry, and the Fourth Wisconsin Mounted Infantry. Grierson's orders were to clear out and guard the approaches to Port Hudson, while Banks marched his infantry in to surround that formidable river fort.

And so was ended, temporarily, Grierson's hopes of rejoining General Grant and the Department of the Tennessee.

V

June, 1863, was the month of decision in the Civil War. In that month General Grant smashed the armies of General Pemberton and moved forward to squeeze Vicksburg into the surrender of July 4. Far away to the east, the armies of General Robert E. Lee were marching up the Allegheny valleys toward Gettysburg and destruction. And down at Port Hudson — the Confederacy's last blockade point on the Mississippi — General Banks was pressing a relentless siege against General Franklin Gardner's stubborn defenders.

Grierson's raiders played an important role in the Port Hudson siege. They marched and fought along some of the roads over which they had galloped to escape Pemberton's pursuing cavalry on the last days of the raid. They battled some of these same rebel forces — Miles's Legion and Wirt Adams' wild riders.

In their first few days of field service, the Sixth and Seventh Illinois Regiments were at a disadvantage, half of the men being armed with Union and Smith's carbines for which no ammunition was available in the Department of the Gulf. During Grierson's first engagement along the Comite River near Clinton, a battalion of the Seventh Regiment was forced into retreat because of lack of ammunition. Grierson sent a hurry call to New Orleans for 500 Sharp's carbines.[18]

The bitter rivalry between Colonel Grierson and Colonel Prince finally reached the breaking point during the Port Hudson campaign, a breach which was probably aggravated by Grierson's appointment as Brigadier-General on June 16. A few days after the regiments left Baton Rouge, Prince deliberately disobeyed orders, and personally led a battalion of the Seventh off to Thompson's Creek to capture a pair of Confederate steamboats.

Grierson overlooked this defection — after all, it was not too often that the cavalry was victorious over the navy.*

Three weeks later, however, when Prince disobeyed another order, Grierson immediately addressed an angry message to Banks's headquarters: "Colonel Prince has not reported with his command, in obedience to orders. I would respectfully recommend that he be placed under arrest for gross disobedience of orders."

As this message does not appear in the official records, it is probable that Grierson either changed his mind and did not send it, or that General Banks persuaded Grierson to withdraw his request. The original message, penciled on a scrap of paper, still remains in Grierson's military file.

A few days later, on July 4, Vicksburg surrendered to Grant; and personal enmities were temporarily forgotten in the high hope that Port Hudson would also immediately capitulate. But General Franklin Gardner refused to stop the fighting. ("Old Gardner says he will hold the place as long as there is any

---

* Forty years afterwards (April 28, 1904) Colonel Prince wrote an account of this incident for the *National Tribune*, a publication for veterans: "I found out that there would be a chance to capture two steamboats which were partially under the guns of Port Hudson, in a bayou called Alligator Bayou, into which Thompson's Creek emptied. I had made some efforts to get permission to try and capture these boats from Colonel Grierson, commanding the brigade, but he was averse to it and I got an order over his head from General Banks and I was careful not to tell Colonel Grierson anything about it until I could get well under way on the road . . . but having asked General Banks to send me a section of artillery (two pieces) when this section came through the camp Colonel Grierson found out that I had started off to capture the boats and sent a detail of his command with an order to me."

Grierson's order was in part as follows: "The Colonel commanding thinks that your expedition will be useless as he thinks it impossible to reach the boats. . . . The Colonel wishes you to save the command, and rest men and horses as much as possible."

"I placed this order in my pocket," Prince said, "sent the escort back to Colonel Grierson and marched away to capture the steamboats if possible." The steamboats were the *Starlight* and the *Red Chief*. Approaching under cover of an early morning fog which concealed him from the Port Hudson gunners, Prince set his artillery in position and ordered the *Starlight's* watchman to bring the boat into shore if he wished to save himself and the boats from being blown to bits. Prince captured both boats and thirty prisoners — the crew and engineers sleeping on board the vessels.

"In regard to my violation of the order of Colonel Grierson, my brigade commander, I did not think then, and do not think now that that amounted to anything because I was proceeding according to the order of Major-General Banks, then in command of the whole army, and because the splendid success of the enterprise was a complete vindication."

horses and mules left to eat," a Confederate captain had written to his wife a few days before Banks began the siege.)

Banks kept hammering away, moving his infantry trenches closer and closer until Confederate and Union lines in some places were only a few feet apart. Then, on July 7, copies of a newspaper announcing the fall of Vicksburg were tossed into the Confederate trenches. Two days later Franklin Gardner surrendered.

One of the first men Gardner asked to meet was General Grierson. "Grierson caused the surrender of Port Hudson," Gardner said, "by cutting off communications and supplies." The Confederate general asked several questions about the raid, and then showed Grierson a handful of conflicting telegrams. "Grierson was here; no, he was *there*, sixty miles away. He marched north, no, south, or again west." Gardner then claimed that the raiders would have been trapped if his orders had been fully obeyed. "The trouble was, my men ambushed you where you did not go; they waited for you till morning while you passed by night."[19]

VI

The western Confederacy was now severed; after two years of war and blockade the Mississippi was open again from Illinois to the Gulf of Mexico. In the east, the broken Confederate armies of Virginia were retreating from Gettysburg. A wave of optimism swept the Union states; surely the rebels were beaten at last.

The Confederates were beaten, all right, but they did not believe they were beaten, and most of the men in the Union Army knew that the Confederates did not and would not believe they were beaten.

Grant knew the Confederates would come back and fight him hard. One of his first concerns after he took Vicksburg was the shortage of cavalry, which he needed more than ever now to deal with the swooping attacks of such avengers as General Bedford Forrest — who was already back in the Mississippi valley after capturing the entire regiment of Colonel Abel Streight in Alabama.*

---

* See page 37. Streight's raid was coordinated with Grierson's and was planned partly as a cover for the latter. General Forrest, outnumbered three to one by Streight, made his capture by a clever ruse. He marched

General Banks also knew the Confederates had no intention of quitting the war. On orders from Washington he was planning an invasion of Texas, and one of his main deficiencies was experienced cavalry.

Grierson's cavalry, therefore, even after the collapse of Vicksburg and Port Hudson, was still considered a prize by these rival department commanders, as their exchange of correspondence plainly shows: "I ask that General Grierson be sent here as soon as possible," Grant wrote Banks on July 10. "I am very much in want of cavalry and of Grierson to command them." Banks replied that the enemy's cavalry would outnumber his mounted forces if he gave up Grierson. When Grant became more insistent, Banks suggested a trade: Grierson's cavalry for a full division. Sherman was also eager to obtain Grierson for the coming assault on Jackson, Mississippi, but Grant was not too hopeful. On July 13, he informed Sherman: "I have written to Banks to send Grierson up, but do not believe he will send him."[20]

During this time Colonel Prince wrote to General Banks directly, stating that he desired to have the Seventh Illinois Cavalry regiment remain with the Department of the Gulf for service in the Texas expedition. "On hearing of this," Grierson said, "I promptly told the officers of the 7th Ill. Cavalry that if they wished to remain they had only to say so; but they unanimously requested to stay in my command and go back with me to Tennessee. General Banks, much as he wanted Cavalry, would take it in no such way, and when he learned that the proposal was made without my knowledge, Colonel Prince was promptly informed that correspondence must pass through the Headquarters of his commanding officer."

Then at last, on July 18, the long-awaited orders came for Grierson's raiders: "Brigadier-General B. H. Grierson, commanding cavalry, will proceed with the Sixth and Seventh Regiments of Illinois Cavalry and the First Illinois Battery, under

---

his few pieces of horse-artillery around and around again through a cut-off in a mountain road until Streight became convinced he was out-manned and out-gunned, and so surrendered. "I ordered my men to come forward and take possession of the arms," Forrest said afterwards. "When Streight saw they were barely four hundred men, he did rear! Demanded to have his arms back and that we should fight it out. I just laughed at him and patted him on the shoulder, and said, 'Ah, Colonel, all is fair in love and war, you know.'" — Theo. F. Rodenbough, "Some Cavalry Leaders," *Photographic History of the Civil War,* vol. 4, pp. 280-82.

his command to Vicksburg, and will there report to Major-General Grant for duty in the Department of the Tennessee."[21]

General Banks, however, never completely gave up the idea of obtaining Grierson's cavalry for his department. As late as August 16 he was still begging Grant to let him have Grierson and some "Western men"* for the invasion of Texas.

VII

Grierson and his men traveled up the Mississippi River to Vicksburg aboard the steamers *Planet* and *Imperial*, accompanied by two hundred Confederate officers who had been captured and paroled when Port Hudson fell. "I was warmly received by General Grant," Grierson said, "and was invited by him to inspect the fortifications."[22]

Originally Grant had planned to send the Illinois cavalry into the field with General Sherman, but the day before Grierson arrived at Vicksburg, Sherman's army overran Jackson, Mississippi, burning the city, and sending the Confederates in full retreat eastward. Grant was agreeable, therefore, to Grierson's strongly expressed wish to return to duty with Hurlbut's Sixteenth Corps in Tennessee, and travel orders were issued on July 19: "General B. H. Grierson will proceed on the steamers on which his command is embarked to Memphis, Tennessee."[23]

In notifying Sherman that he was not to expect Grierson's regiments to join him, Grant said: "Grierson is very anxious to get back to Tennessee to get his troops together. By having him there, I can organize a large cavalry force under his command, to make a big raid through the eastern part of the State, or wherever required."[24] Five days later, Grierson was assigned to duty as Chief of Cavalry of the Sixteenth Army Corps.

Grant, however, did not then know of Grierson's serious accident, an accident which occurred as he was leaving Vicksburg and would bar him from field duty for several months. "As I returned to the boat," Grierson said, "passing down a very narrow way among the huge piles of stores at the landing, my own New Orleans gift horse kicked at the horse on which I was mounted." Grierson was struck painfully upon the knee. As a cavalryman he

---

* "Eastern troops do not fight like Western troops and Genl. Banks has very few Western troops in his department." — Benjamin Grierson to Alice Grierson, June 16, 1863 (Grierson Papers).

was chagrined; but he had known from childhood his incompatibility for horses, and probably was not surprised. "It proved afterward the most annoying injury received during the war; the effect remaining, and weakening the knee for many months."[25]

A short time later, after hobbling painfully about Memphis headquarters on crutches and attempting several times to return to field duty, he was ordered on leave to recuperate from the injury. His home town of Jacksonville, Illinois, took advantage of his enforced furlough to give him an ovation. His old concert band played *Home Again* for him, and his friends, who had always thought of Ben Grierson as a mild-mannered musician rather than a dashing cavalryman, delivered laudatory orations. ("There was far more in him than *bugle-blowing*.")

Grierson replied with a carefully prepared speech. ("Amid all this strife we are, as a nation, making rapid strides to greatness. We are living many years in one; elements of power are being developed and changes transpiring wonderful to behold.") And then six little girls dressed in white and wearing sashes of red, white, and blue advanced upon the stage singing a song and bearing a magnificent bouquet which they presented to the hero of Jacksonville.[26]

VIII

During the rapid sequence of events in that fateful summer of 1863, Sergeant Richard Surby of the Butternut Guerillas was also meeting with strange new adventures. Three days after he was wounded at Wall's Bridge and left behind at Newman's Plantation with Lieutenant-Colonel Blackburn, Surgeon Yule, and the four other men, a squad of Confederate cavalry from Osyka arrived with orders to remove all of them to that station. The rebels had brought along a rickety old ambulance, barely large enough to carry the wounded men.

Surgeon Yule protested strongly, declaring that it was impossible to move any of the wounded except Sergeant Surby. The Confederates finally agreed to leave Lieutenant-Colonel Blackburn, Private Hughes, and Bugler Roy at the plantation, but they insisted that the surgeon and the two volunteer nurses, Sergeant Leseure and Private Douglas, must go to Osyka with Surby.

As soon as he learned he would be leaving, Sergeant Surby dug down into the pile of unginned cotton which served as his bed and retrieved his pocket knife, a breast pin which bore a miniature picture of his wife, and twenty-five hundred dollars in Confederate money, all carefully concealed the day he was brought there. Trusting the wife of the plantation owner more than the rebel cavalrymen, Surby gave her his knife and pin and a large part of the money.*

He was then loaded into the ambulance. Surgeon Yule, Sergeant Leseure and Private Douglas were ordered to accompany the escort on foot, "which made them puff, on an eleven mile march, they not being used to infantry tactics." They arrived at Osyka about six o'clock that evening. "I was surprised," Surby said, "to hear and see the rebel Colonel Richardson, from Tennessee, who took particular delight in heaping abuse upon the Sixth and Seventh cavalry, by saying everything that was mean and unbecoming a gentleman."

Meanwhile Surgeon Yule had persuaded the Confederate authorities to permit him and Sergeant Leseure to return to Newman's Plantation to attend Lieutenant-Colonel Blackburn and the two wounded troopers. Private Douglas, however, was retained, to be sent with the next prisoner shipment to Richmond.

Surby was put aboard the first train north, his destination a convalescent hospital at Magnolia. En route, his boots were stolen from beneath his cot. But he found the Magnolia hospital a pleasant, leisurely place, the food scanty but well-cooked — "corn-bread, molasses, mush, sassafras tea, and almost invariably the leg of a goose for breakfast, baked, no dressing, sometimes tender as a spring chicken, then again tough enough to make a good whip-cracker; however my appetite was sufficient for all I could get."

One day while reading the Jackson (Mississippi) *Appeal*, he was startled to come across an account of his own death in a story recounting events of Grierson's raid. This did not worry Surby nearly as much as another news dispatch claiming that a Texas cavalry regiment had defeated Grierson's command, wounding the colonel and capturing him and nearly all of his men. He decided philosophically that the latter story might be as grossly exaggerated as the first.

---

* See page 110 for an explanation of how Sergeant Surby obtained this Confederate money. Mrs. Newman later arranged to return his personal belongings and a considerable amount of money left over after she paid the burial expenses of Blackburn and Hughes.

Unable to learn any news of Lieutenant-Colonel Blackburn and his comrades, he finally arranged to employ a man to journey to Newman's Plantation, which was only twenty miles from Magnolia. The messenger brought back bad news. Blackburn and Hughes had died of their wounds; Surgeon Yule and Sergeant Leseure were at Osyka awaiting transportation to a Confederate prison.

After recovering from his wound, Surby was taken on a ten-day journey across the Confederacy to Libby Prison in Richmond. He was exchanged almost immediately, returned to his home in Illinois a few weeks, and then rejoined his regiment in Tennessee, October 13th, 1863.[27]

Sergeant Surby and most of his comrades of Grierson's raid fought through two more years of war, a war which they had helped to decide in the spring of 1863, but which dragged on bitterly to surrender in April 1865 and then into long months of reconstruction duty in the vanquished and disrupted Southland. The Sixth and Seventh Illinois Cavalry Regiments were not mustered out of service until late in November, 1865, seven months after Lee surrendered to Grant at Appomattox.

During the last years of the war the raiders did not often see General Grierson; after his promotion they served directly under their old friend of the raid, Colonel Edward Hatch of Iowa. They engaged in several fights and battles, were twice badly beaten by the rebel cavalryman they most respected, Nathan Bedford Forrest. But when Sherman began his famous march to the sea in the spring of 1864, the Sixth and Seventh Illinois Regiments — back in the field with Grierson — successfully kept Forrest off Sherman's rear by a long diversionary drive deep into Mississippi.

In late summer of 1864, the volunteers' three-year enlistment periods ended and they were all free to go home. A majority, however, re-enlisted as veterans for the duration, many receiving long-deserved promotions. They also were issued better cavalry equipment and weapons, such as the highly prized Spencer carbines which fired seven shots and could be loaded with two motions of a lever.

Before the fighting ended, the Sixth Regiment lost two commanders, Lieutenant-Colonel Reuben Loomis, killed November 2, 1863, and his successor, Colonel Mathew Starr also killed, in October, 1864, when General Forrest made a sudden dawn attack on the regiment's camp near Memphis.

Colonel Prince of the Seventh Regiment chose to be mustered out at the end of his three-year enlistment in October, 1864. Embittered by events following the raid, Prince had lost much of his early popularity with his officers and men, some threatening not to re-enlist if he continued as commanding officer. Major John Graham succeeded Prince as colonel of the Seventh, and Captain Henry Forbes of the famed Company B became second in command with the rank of lieutenant-colonel.

Young Stephen Forbes followed his brother as Company B's captain, and in his journal, faithfully kept to the end of his service, he left a sensitive record of the death of a land he had come to love. Stephen Forbes was fascinated by the Gothic horrors of the events in which he was involved, by the sudden dissolution of a human civilization symbolized in the deserted old houses with the smell of a dead time already upon them:

"The old houses, so dark and solemn, where the windows were gone and doors rusted open and floors sunken and stairways tipped away and chimneys leaning away as if weary with standing erect so long, and with door-sills decayed and fireplaces scowling black, and roofs spotted with moss-tufts, and clapboards rattling loose, what scenes of horror or mystery or tales of love or agony could not the imagination call up from their death-haunted interiors."[28]

And when his regiment for the last time broke camp at La Grange — the once lovely village which after so many months seemed like home to him and his comrades — the young captain recorded their final leave-taking, an eloquent farewell to the old Southland in its last tragic weeks of dying:

When we left La Grange, we evacuated the place entirely. It looked miserably dreary. I rode through the streets after everything had left, and the long lines of dark, empty houses that looked through the open doors and windows as if they were opening their mouths to show the blackness and confusion of their interiors, with no living thing moving, save one solitary refugee woman, worn and dreary, who sat in the doorway of a large house without a window or a door, gazing down the street quietly and as if nothing under heaven could especially interest her, and three little black children playing slowly on the sidewalk, made me feel as if I was moving along the veins of some dead body looking in at the holes where were once the eyes, and into the great shell where seethed the brain, and this dark cavity where throbbed the heart, now all dry and pulseless and black.

So I put spurs to my horse and fled, the clatter of his hoofs echoing loudly back as I left the desolation behind me.[29]

Notes

Abbreviations used for most frequently cited sources

FFL: Forbes family letters, and journals of Stephen Alfred Forbes, collected and arranged chronologically by Ethel Forbes Scott. Manuscripts.

FORBES: Stephen A. Forbes, "Grierson's Cavalry Raid," Illinois State Historical Society, *Transactions*, 1907, pp. 99-130.

GRIERSON: Benjamin Henry Grierson, autobiography. Manuscript.

OR: *The War of the Rebellion: a Compilation of the Official Records of the Union and Confederate Armies*, Washington, 1880-1901.

RS: Benjamin Henry Grierson, *Record of Services Rendered the Government, 1863* [Ft. Concho, Texas], privately printed.

SURBY: Richard W. Surby, *Grierson Raids*, Chicago, 1865.

FIRST DAY — *Friday, April 17*

1. Surby, p. 21.
2. OR, ser. I, vol. 24, pt. 3, p. 197; Surby, p. 20.
3. FFL, Henry Forbes to Nettie Forbes, July 25, 1864.
4. Forbes, p. 125.
5. David D. Porter, *Incidents and Anecdotes of the Civil War*, New York, 1885.
6. OR, ser. I, vol. 24, pt. 3, p. 50.
7. Ibid., p. 95.
8. Ibid., p. 185.
9. Headquarters, Army, Memphis via Cairo, to Col. B. H. Grierson, April 13, 1863 (Grierson Papers).
10. OR, ser. I, vol. 24, pt. 3, p. 197.
11. Lloyd Lewis, "Taps for the Cavalry," *American Mercury*, August, 1930, pp. 409-16.
12. Francis Morris, "Cavalry Horses in America," *Report* of the U. S. Commissioner of Agriculture, 1863, pp. 159-75.
13. William F. Scott, *Story of a Cavalry Regiment*, New York, 1893, pp. 2-3.
14. FFL, Henry Forbes to Agnes Forbes, Sept. 21, 1861.
15. FFL, Stephen Forbes to Nettie Forbes, Oct. 6, 1861.
16. FFL, Stephen Forbes's journal, Nov. 20, 1861.
17. FFL, Henry Forbes to Agnes Forbes, Feb. 8, 1862.
18. *Photographic History of the Civil War*, New York, 1911, vol. 4, pp. 56-58.
19. FFL, Henry Forbes to Agnes Forbes and others, March 12, 1862.
20. Scott, p. 283.
21. Ibid., pp. 27-28.
22. Ibid., pp. 26-27.
23. Grierson's military papers, 1863 file; RS, p. 101.
24. Fred A. Shannon, *Organization and Administration of the Union Army, 1861-1865*, Cleveland, 1928, vol. 2, pp. 270-71.
25. FFL, Stephen Forbes to Flavilla Forbes, April 13, 1863.

SECOND DAY — *Saturday, April 18*

1. Surby, pp. 20-21, 23; Adjutant General of the State of Illinois, *Reports, 1861-1866*, Springfield, 1901, vol. 8, pp. 50, 103.
2. OR, ser. I, vol. 17, pt. 1, p. 502.
3. OR, ser. I, vol. 24, pt. 1, p. 529.
4. Ibid., p. 522.
5. Grierson, p. 101.
6. *Illinois State Register*, July 1, 1852.
7. Lyman B. Pierce, *History of the Second Iowa Cavalry*, Burlington, Iowa, 1865, pp. 9-13.
8. OR, ser. I, vol. 24, pt. 1, p. 484.
9. FFL, Henry Forbes to Nettie Forbes, May 23, 1863.

10. The excerpts that follow are from the journal of Stephen Forbes, the letters of both Forbes brothers, and from a book of reminiscences by Henry H. Eby entitled *Observations of an Illinois Boy in Battle, Camp, and Prisons*, Mendota, Ill., 1910, pp. 30-31.

11. OR, ser. I, vol. 24, pt. 1, pp. 529, 534-35; pt. 3, p. 777.

12. OR, ser. I, vol. 24, pt. 1, p. 522; Surby, p. 24.

13. Surby, p. 24.

14. RS, p. 102.

15. OR, ser. I, vol. 24, pt. 1, p. 522; Surby, pp. 24-25.

16. R. R. Hancock, *Hancock's Dairy: or a History of the Second Tennessee Confederate Cavalry*, Nashville, 1887, pp. 236-38.

17. OR, ser. I, vol. 24, pt. 3, pp. 654-55.

18. Ibid., p. 716.

19. John K. Bettersworth, *Confederate Mississippi*, Baton Rouge, 1943, pp. 60-89.

20. Bettersworth, pp. 194-95; John Clifford Pemberton, *Pemberton, Defender of Vicksburg*, Chapel Hill, 1942, pp. 41-58.

21. OR, ser. I, vol. 24, pt. 3, pp. 737-38; 740-41, 745-46.

22. OR, ser. I, vol. 24, pt. 1, p. 690.

THIRD DAY — *Sunday, April 19*

1. OR, ser. I, vol. 24, pt. 1, p. 557; pt. 3, pp. 196, 203, 206.

2. *Illinois State Journal*, May 8, 1863.

3. OR, ser. I, vol. 24, pt. 1, p. 522.

4. Elizabeth Jane Beach to Nathan and Smithy Renfroe, July 29, 1864, *Journal of Mississippi History*, vol. 2 (1940), pp. 42-48.

5. Ibid.

6. Eby, pp. 35-36, 60.

7. FFL, Stephen Forbes's journal, Oct. 13, 1864.

8. FFL, Stephen Forbes to Nettie Forbes, Jan. 5, 1862.

9. FFL, Henry Forbes described this method of scouting, including a diagram, in a letter to Nettie Forbes, May 19, 1862.

10. Surby, p. 25.

11. Hancock, pp. 578-81.

12. George F. Hager, "Second Tennessee Cavalry," *Military Annals of Tennessee*, ed. by John B. Lindsley, 1886, p. 623.

13. Hancock, pp. 238-39; OR, ser. I, vol. 24, pt. 1, p. 534.

14. OR, ser. I, vol. 24, pt. 1, p. 253.

FOURTH DAY — *Monday, April 20*

1. Hancock, p. 232.

2. FFL, Henry Forbes to "Friends at Home," July 30, 1862.

3. Cordelia Scales to Lulie Irby, Nov. 24, 1861, and Jan. 27, 1863, *Journal of Mississippi History*, vol. 1 (1939), pp. 171-79.

4. Grierson, p. 381.

5. RS, p. 102.

6. OR, ser. I, vol. 24, pt. 1, pp. 521-22.
7. Surby, pp. 26-27.
8. OR, ser. I, vol. 24, pt. 3, p. 215.
9. Ibid., p. 770.
10. Ibid., pp. 550-51.
11. Ibid., p. 551.

FIFTH DAY — *Tuesday, April 21*

1. Pierce, pp. 191-94.
2. Surby, p. 194.
3. Grierson, p. 384.
4. OR, ser. I, vol. 24, pt. 1, p. 523.
5. RS, p. 103.
6. OR, ser. I, vol. 24, pt. 1, p. 530.
7. Pierce, p. 49.
8. Robert W. Banks to Lucretia Banks, Sept. 18, 1862, *Journal of Mississippi History,* vol. 5 (1943), p. 145.
9. OR, ser. I, vol. 24, pt. 1, pp. 534-35.
10. Ibid., p. 535.
11. Hager, p. 613.
12. OR, ser. I, vol. 24, pt. 1, p. 552.
13. Richmond *Examiner* as reprinted in *The Rebellion Record,* edited by Frank Moore, New York, 1864, vol. 7, pp. 24-25.
14. Pierce, p. 50.
15. OR, ser. I, vol. 24, pt. 1, p. 530.
16. Ibid.
17. Grierson, pp. 366-67.
18. OR, ser. I, vol. 24, pt. 1, p. 422.
19. Surby, pp. 29-30.
20. Based on Surby, p. 30.
21. Columbus (Mississippi) *Republic,* as cited in Forbes. Date of newspaper not given.

SIXTH DAY — *Wednesday, April 22*

1. FFL, Henry Forbes to Frances Snow, Feb. 15, 1862.
2. OR, ser. I, vol. 24, pt. 1, p. 523; Surby, p. 31.
3. FFL, Henry Forbes's account of Grierson Raid, p. 207; Forbes, pp. 110-11.
4. FFL, Henry Forbes's letters, Aug. 25 and Oct. 18, 1862, and Stephen Forbes to Agnes Forbes, Dec. 11, 1862.
5. FFL, Stephen Forbes's prison journal, June, 1862.
6. Ibid., July, 1862.
7. FFL, Henry Forbes's account of Grierson Raid, p. 207.
8. OR, ser. I, vol. 24, pt. 1, p. 524.
9. Surby, pp. 33-34.

10. *National Tribune*, July 12, 1883, p. 1.
11. Grierson quotation based on OR, ser. I, vol. 24, pt. 1, p. 524.
12. Ibid., p. 528.
13. New York *Times*, May 18, 1863.
14. Pierce, pp. 51-52.
15. Hancock, pp. 240-41; OR, ser. I, vol. 24, pt. 1, p. 535.
16. OR, ser. I, vol. 24, pt. 1, p. 552.
17. OR, ser. I, vol. 24, pt. 3, p. 776.
18. Ibid.
19. Ibid.

SEVENTH DAY — *Thursday, April 23*

1. This section is based on the first edition of Surby's account (pp. 36-38) and also the revision which appeared in the *National Tribune* for July 12, 1883.
2. Surby, pp. 38-39.
3. Grierson, p. 397.
4. Surby, p. 39.
5. OR, ser. I, vol. 24, pt. 1, p. 528; Forbes, pp. 105-106.
6. Surby, pp. 39-40.
7. FFL, Henry Forbes's account of Grierson Raid, p. 208.
8. FFL, Stephen Forbes to Nettie Forbes, April 8, 1862.
9. Surby, pp. 40-45.
10. FFL, Stephen Forbes's journal, Oct. 1, 1864.
11. OR, ser. I, vol. 24, pt. 1, p. 552.
12. Pierce, p. 52.
13. OR, ser. I, vol. 24, pt. 3, pp. 778, 779.

EIGHTH DAY — *Friday, April 24*

1. OR, ser. I, vol. 24, pt. 1, pp. 79-80; pt. 3, pp. 225-32.
2. OR, ser. I, vol. 24, pt. 3, p. 231.
3. Ibid., pp. 214-15.
4. Surby, p. 45.
5. Surby, pp. 45-46.
6. Based on Surby, p. 46.
8. *National Tribune*, July 19, 1883, p. 1.
9. Surby, p. 48.
10. OR, ser. I, vol. 24, pt. 1, p. 524.
11. OR, ser. I, vol. 24, pt. 3, p. 781.
12. OR, ser. I, vol. 24, pt. 1, p. 525.
13. Paulding (Mississippi) *Clarion*, May 1, 1863, as cited in Forbes, p. 127.
14. Grierson, p. 402.
15. Surby, pp. 50-51.
16. Forbes, p. 110.

17. FFL, Henry Forbes's account of Grierson Raid, p. 208.
18. Forbes, p. 110.
19. Ibid.
20. OR, ser. I, vol. 24, pt. 1, p. 552.

NINTH DAY — *Saturday, April 25*

1. B. H. Grierson to T. W. Lippincott, March 13, 1886 (Grierson Papers).
2. OR, ser. I, vol. 24, pt. 1, p. 525.
3. Paulding (Mississippi) *Clarion*, May 1, 1863, as cited in Forbes, p. 127.
4. Bettersworth, pp. 202-204, 225-28.
5. Surby, pp. 53-55.
6. Based on Surby, pp. 57-58.
7. Based on Paulding (Mississippi) *Clarion*, May 1, 1863, as cited in Forbes, p. 127.
8. Surby, p. 59.
9. Grierson, pp. 403-404.
10. Ibid.
11. OR, ser. I, vol. 24, pt. 3, p. 791.
12. OR, ser. I, vol. 24, pt. 1, p. 525; Surby, pp. 60-61.
13. OR, ser. I, vol. 24, pt. 1, p. 532.
14. OR, ser. I, vol. 24, pt. 3, p. 785.
15. OR, ser. I, vol. 24, pt. 1, p. 544.
16. FFL, Henry Forbes's account of Grierson Raid, p. 208.
17. FFL, Stephen Forbes's prison journal, June, 1862.
18. FFL, Henry Forbes's account of Grierson Raid, pp. 208-209. Quoted dialogue as recalled by Captain Forbes.
19. Ibid.
20. Ibid.
21. Jackson (Mississippi) *Appeal*, April 28, 1863, as cited in Forbes, p. 129.
22. Cordelia Scales to Lulie Irby, Jan. 27, 1863, *Journal of Mississippi History*, vol. 1 (1939), pp. 175-76, 179.

TENTH DAY — *Sunday, April 26*

1. OR, ser. I, vol. 24, pt. 1, p. 525.
2. Surby, pp. 28-29.
3. Scott, p. 381.
4. Surby, p. 61.
5. Surby, p. 63.
6. OR, ser. I, vol. 24, pt. 1, p. 526.
7. Forbes, pp. 112-13; FFL, Henry Forbes's account of Grierson Raid, p. 210.

8. Forbes, p. 113.
9. Forbes, pp. 113-14.
10. Pierce, p. 55.
11. OR, ser. I, vol. 24, pt. 1, p. 531.
12. OR, ser. I, vol. 24, pt. 3, p. 789.
13. Ibid., p. 790.

ELEVENTH DAY — *Monday, April 27*

1. Grierson, pp. 505-506; RS, p. 119.
2. Surby, pp. 64-65; New York *Times*, May 18, 1863.
3. OR, ser. I, vol. 24, pt. 1, p. 526.
4. Grierson, pp. 409-10; RS, p. 104.
5. Grierson, p. 410; RS, p. 104.
6. Forbes, p. 114.
7. FFL, Henry Forbes's account of Grierson Raid, p. 212.
8. OR, ser. I, vol. 24, pt. 1, p. 528.
9. RS, p. 105.
10. Surby, pp. 66-69.
11. OR, ser. I, vol. 24, pt. 3, pp. 791-94.
12. Surby, pp. 75-76.
13. OR, ser. I, vol. 24, pt. 1, p. 31.

TWELFTH DAY — *Tuesday, April 28*

1. RS, pp. 105-106; OR, ser. I, vol. 24, pt. 1, p. 526.
2. Surby, p. 78.
3. Grierson, p. 415; OR, ser. I, vol. 24, pt. 1, p. 526.
4. FFL, Stephen Forbes's journal, August 28, 1864. Forbes left no account of the Union Church attack. These descriptions of a similar surprise attack on the Seventh Illinois Regiment are inserted here for dramatic effect.
5. Ibid.
6. RS, p. 106.
7. Grierson, p. 415; OR, ser. I, vol. 24, pt. 1, p. 526.
8. OR, ser. I, vol. 24, pt. 3, p. 792.
9. OR, ser. I, vol. 24, pt. 1, p. 538.
10. FFL, Stephen Forbes's prison journal, June, 1862.
11. Clement A. Evans, *Confederate Military History*, 1899, vol. 7, p. 235.
12. Surby, pp. 90-91. Conversations as recorded by Sergeant Surby, with some omissions and rearrangement for clarity.
13. Jackson (Mississippi) *Appeal*, April 28, 1863, as cited in Forbes, pp. 127-28.
14. OR, ser. I, vol. 24, pt. 3, pp. 256, 547, 797-99.

THIRTEENTH DAY — *Wednesday, April 29*

1. OR, ser. I, vol. 24, pt. 3, p. 111.
2. Ibid., pp. 798-99.
3. OR, ser. I, vol. 24, pt. 1, p. 547.
4. B. H. Grierson to T. W. Lippincott, March 13, 1886 (Grierson Papers).
5. Grierson, p. 419.
6. Forbes, p. 115.
7. OR, ser. I, vol. 24, pt. 1, p. 527.
8. RS, p. 106.
9. Forbes, p. 116.
10. Surby, p. 99.
11. New York *Times,* May 18, 1863.
12. OR, ser. I, vol. 24, pt. 1, p. 547-48.
13. Ibid., p. 533.
14. Ibid., p. 32.

FOURTEENTH DAY — *Thursday, April 30*

1. Ulysses S. Grant, *Personal Memoirs,* New York, 1885, vol. 1, pp. 480-82; OR, ser. I, vol. 24, pt. 1, pp. 48, 83, 128, 142.
2. Moore, vol. 7, p. 24.
3. OR, ser. I, vol. 24, pt. 1, p. 548.
4. Ibid., 527.
5. Grierson, pp. 423-24; RS, p. 106.
6. Grierson, p. 422.
7. OR, ser. I, vol. 24, pt. 1, p. 549.
8. Grierson, p. 422.
9. RS, p. 106.
10. OR, ser. I, vol. 24, pt. 1, p. 527.
11. Grierson, pp. 424-26; RS, pp. 106-107.
12. OR, ser. I, vol. 24, pt. 1, p. 548.
13. Ibid., p. 553.

FIFTEENTH DAY — *Friday, May 1*

1. OR, ser. I, vol. 24, pt. 1, pp. 548-49.
2. Forbes, p. 102.
3. RS, p. 107.
4. Surby, p. 104.
5. Andrew B. Booth, comp., *Records of Louisiana Confederate Soldiers and Louisiana Confederate Commands,* New Orleans, 1920, vol. 2, p. 672.
6. OR, ser. I, vol. 24, pt. 1, p. 539.
7. Surby, p. 105; *National Tribune,* Aug. 16, 1883, p. 2.
8. Surby, p. 106.

9. OR, ser. I, vol. 24, pt. 1, pp. 539-40; Surby, pp. 107-109. Dialogue as indicated in Surby's narrative.
10. Based on Surby, pp. 109-10. *National Tribune*, Aug. 16, 1883, p. 2.
11. FFL, Stephen Forbes to Nettie Forbes, May 11, 1862. A description of a similar encounter.
12. OR, ser. I, vol. 24, pt. 1, p. 540.
13. Grierson, pp. 428-29.
14. RS, p. 107.
15. Grierson, p. 432.
16. OR, ser. I, vol. 24, pt. 1, pp. 527, 543.
17. Grierson, p. 432.
18. FFL, Henry Forbes's account of Grierson Raid, pp. 213-14.
19. OR, ser. I, vol. 24, pt. 1, pp. 537, 540, 549.
20. Surby, p. 153.
21. OR, ser. I, vol. 24, pt. 3, p. 814.

SIXTEENTH DAY — *Saturday, May 2*

1. FFL, Henry Forbes's account of Grierson Raid, p. 214.
2. OR, ser. I, vol. 24, pt. 1, p. 528.
3. T. H. Bowman, *Reminiscences of an ex-Confederate Soldier; or Forty Years on Crutches*, Austin, Texas, 1904, p. 21.
4. Based on RS, p. 108.
5. OR, ser. I, vol. 24, pt. 1, p. 538.
6. Surby, pp. 120-21. Surby learned of this incident, probably from Samuel Nelson, after he rejoined the Seventh Regiment.
7. Grierson, p. 436.
8. OR, ser. I, vol. 24, pt. 1, pp. 537-38.
9. Grierson, pp. 437, 439.
10. RS, p. 108.
11. Grierson, pp. 439-40.
12. St. Louis (Missouri) *Republican*, as cited in Springfield, *Illinois State Journal*, May 21, 1863.
13. RS, p. 108.
14. Based on Surby, pp. 126-27. As a friend later described it to Surby, who on that day still lay wounded at Newman's Plantation, Miss.
15. OR, ser. I, vol. 24, pt. 1, pp. 528-29.
16. OR, ser. I, vol. 24, pt. 3, p. 264.
17. OR, ser. I, vol. 24, pt. 1, p. 540.
18. Ibid., pp. 549-50.

SEVENTEENTH DAY — *Sunday, May 3*

1. OR, ser. I, vol. 24, pt. 1, pp. 33-34, 58.
2. Francis Grierson, *The Valley of Shadows*, New York, 1913, p. 297 (1948 ed., p. 262).
3. Grant, *Memoirs*, vol. 1, p. 489.

4. Grierson, p. 483.
5. RS, p. 109.
6. FFL, Stephen Forbes to Nettie Forbes, May 11, 1862. Description of a similar camp scene.
7. Forbes, p. 120.
8. FFL, Henry Forbes to Nettie Forbes, May 23, 1863; Henry Forbes to Flavilla Forbes, May 23, 1863.
9. FFL, Henry Forbes to Frances Snow, June 24, 1863.
10. FFL, Stephen Forbes to Nettie Forbes, Aug. 2, 1863.
11. Grierson, pp. 450-51; RS, pp. 109-10.
12. New York *Times*, May 18, 1863.
13. George H. Hepworth, *The Whip, Hoe, and Sword; or the Gulf-Department in '63*, Boston, 1864, p. 285.
14. New York *Times*, May 18, 1863.
15. RS, p. 111.
16. OR, ser. I, vol. 24, pt. 3, p. 289.
17. OR, ser. I, vol. 24, pt. 3, pp. 347, 360.
18. Grierson, p. 493.
19. Based on RS, p. 118.
20. OR, ser. I, vol. 24, pt. 3, pp. 493, 508.
21. RS, p. 119.
22. RS, p. 119.
23. OR, ser. I, vol. 24, pt. 3, p. 530.
24. Ibid., p. 528.
25. RS, p. 119; Benjamin Grierson to Alice Grierson, July 28, 1863 (Grierson Papers).
26. RS, pp. 125, 127.
27. Surby, pp. 156-81.
28. FFL, Stephen Forbes's journal, Oct. 18, 1864.
29. Ibid., Sept. 2, 1864.

Index

Adams, Gen. John, 113, 127, 144
Adams, Col. Wirt, 82, 157, 159, 161, 163, 164, 165, 166, 171, 172, 176, 177, 179, 183, 186, 188, 190, 207, 208, 234
Agnew, Surgeon Archibald, 136
Alligator Bayou, 235n
Amite River, 190, 191, 204, 208, 209, 220
Appomattox, Va., 241
Arkansas River, 7
Artesia Depot, Miss., 82, 83
Ashmead, Capt. William, 214
Augur, Gen. Christopher C., 216

Augusta (Ga.) *Chronicle*, 155
Augustus Plantation, 84

Bahala, Miss., 161
Baldwyn, Miss., 82
Banks, Gen. Nathaniel P., 114, 216, 233, 234, 235, 237, 238
Barteau, Lt.-Col. Clark R., 50, 51, 54, 60, 91, 99, 103, 117, 118, 156; military record, 33-35; early life, and military activities, 45-47; pursuit of the Second Iowa Cavalry, 66-71, 89, 90

253

Baton Rouge, La., 128, 167, 168, 177, 181, 185, 186, 188, 189, 190, 203, 209, 211, 212, 213, 214, 215, 216, 217, 220, 222, 223, 225, 232, 233

Battery K, First Ill. Artillery, 6 and passim

Bayou Pierre, 181

Beach, Dr. Asahel, 39

Beach, Elizabeth Jane, 39

Beauregard, Miss., 161n

Beauregard, Gen. Pierre G. T., 82, 86

Bender Plantation, 116, 119

Benton Barracks (St. Louis, Mo.), 26

Big Black Bridge, 156, 157

Big Black River, 156

Bird's Point, Mo., 14, 26

Birmingham, Miss., 117, 118, 143n

Blackburn, Lt.-Col. William, 62, 86, 94, 98, 99, 100, 101, 122, 138, 139, 175, 192, 196, 201, 202, 203, 207, 219, 239, 240; in charge of scouting, 64; described, 72; in action at Newton Station, 107-113; in action at Wall's Bridge, 197-99; wounded, 199; death of, 241

Blackland, Miss., 82

Bogue Chitto, Miss., 183, 187

Bogue Chitto Creek, 179

Bogue Falema River, 114

Bowen, Gen. John S., 106, 157, 163

Bowman, T. H., 212

Bragg, Gen. Braxton, 82

Brandon, Miss., 125

Brookhaven, Miss., 168, 173, 175, 179, 182, 184, 187

Brown, Col. Alexander J., 206

Brown, Lt.-Col. W. N., 170

Bruinsburg, Miss., 181, 208

Bryan, Capt. B. F., 214

Bryson, John, 84

Buckner, Gen. Simon, 127, 144

Buena Vista, Miss., 90

Buffington, Sgt. William, 74, 80, 85, 116, 191

Buford, Gen. Abraham, 91, 92

Bullard, Cpl. Jonathan, 97

Bull Run, battle of, 134

Butler, Gen. Benjamin, 174n

Butternut Guerillas, the, 80, 85-87, 135, 136, 138, 148, 151-55, 172, 175, 185, 194-99, 203, 213, 214; organized, 74; first raid, 74-75; capture of Pearl River Bridge, 94-95; advance on Newton Station, 99-102; action at Newton Station, 107-113

Cairo, Ill., 14, 25

Cameron, Simon (Secretary of War), 14

Camp Butler, Ill., 11, 26, 73, 79, 145

Camp Creek, Miss., 118

Camp McClellan, Iowa, 11, 26

Camp Moore, La., 220

Cavalry, Confederate, superiority of, 10

Cavalry, equipment of, 14-15, 17-18

Cavalry, Union, development of, 9-18

Cavalry, Union, table of organization of, 19

Cavalryman, life and routine of, 27-30

Cedarville, Ill., 79

Chalmers, Maj. Alexander, 33, 43

Chalmers, Gen. James R., 35, 37, 38, 39, 114, 144

Charleston, Mo., 26

Charleston (Mo.) *Independent*, 26

Chesterville, Miss., 31, 36, 39, 43, 45, 47, 59

Chiwapa Creek (below Pontotoc), 45, 54

Chunkey River, 58, 111

Clark, Maj. M. R., 168, 174

Clear Springs, Miss., 57, 62, 65, 67n, 72n

Cleveland, Ohio, 46

Cleveland, Capt. S. B., 163, 164, 165, 172

Clinton, La., 177, 205, 207, 232, 234

Coldwater, Miss., 37

Columbus, Miss., 5, 6, 33, 59, 62, 63, 65, 67n, 72, 177

Columbus (Miss.) *Republic*, 75

Comite River, 212, 213, 214, 219, 234

Confederate army units
  Eighteenth Mississippi Cavalry, 33
  Fifty-Fifth Tennessee Infantry, 206
  First Alabama Cavalry, 147, 148
  First Mississippi Cavalry, 47, 163, 165
  First Mississippi Infantry, 188
  First Tennessee Cavalry, 47
  Louisiana Legion, 177, 178, 207, 234
  Mississippi state troops, 30, 39, 43, 44, 47, 66, 69, 71, 118, 210
  Partisan Rangers, Mississippi, 8, 20, 22, 26, 35, 169, 178
  Second Alabama Cavalry, 59, 69, 90, 103
  Second Tennessee Cavalry, 33, 46, 47, 50, 59, 66, 67-71, 90, 118, 156
  Seventh Tennessee Cavalry, 46, 47
  Thirty-Fifth Alabama Infantry, 128
  Twentieth Mississippi Mounted Infantry, 168, 169, 171
  Twenty-Seventh Alabama Infantry, 156

Corinth, Miss., 26, 33, 37, 38, 46, 164

Crystal Springs, Miss., 155

Cunningham, Lt.-Col. James, 59, 69, 90, 103

Daggett Plantation, 45

Davenport, Iowa, 11

Davis, Jefferson, 34, 164, 168, 174n

De Baun, Maj. James, 178, 188, 192-93, 195, 196, 200, 201, 207, 220

Decatur, Miss., 81, 97, 101, 102, 108, 117

De Shroon Plantation, 179, 180

Dinsmore (citizen of Macon, Miss.), 84-85

Dockery, Col. Thomas, 156

Douer, Pvt. William, 147

Douglas, Pvt. George, 202, 240

Dudley, Col. Nathan, 218

Duke, Basil, 177

Eby, Pvt. Henry, 42, 78, 136n

Edgar County, Ill., 73

Edwards Depot, Miss., 156

Eighteenth Mississippi Cavalry, 33

Ellis Plantation, 20

Ellsthorp, Charles, 143

Enterprise, Miss., 97, 128, 131-32, 142, 144, 150, 155

Estes Plantation, 89, 93

Falkner, Col. William C., 20, 165, 166

Falkner Plantation, 20

Farragut, Adm. David, 52, 205

Faulkner, William, 20

Fayette, Miss., 160, 163, 164, 165, 172, 177

Fifty-Fifth Tennessee Infantry, 206

First Alabama Cavalry, 147, 148

First Louisiana Cavalry, 234

First Mississippi Cavalry, 47, 163, 165

First Mississippi Infantry, 188

First Tennessee Cavalry, 47

Forbes, Capt. Henry C., 6, 52, 79, 92, 97, 132, 138, 149, 150, 210, 232; comment on uniform, 11, 14-15; background and military record, 79-80; in diversion toward Macon, 79-85, 98-99; skirmish at Philadelphia, Miss., 116-17; wrong

255

turn at Newton Station, 128-29; flight from Enterprise, 130-32; overtaking regiment, 142; crossing Williams' Bridge, 205; battle fatigue, 225-26; comment on raid, 226; appointed lieutenant-colonel, 242

Forbes, Sgt. Stephen A., 81, 102, 117, 130, 132, 143, 149, 150, 175, 225; comment on uniform, 14; comment on soldiering, 20; comment on looting, 42; capture in 1862, 82-84; overtaking regiment, 140, 142; comment on Colonel Wirt Adams, 164; describes Southland, 227; comment on leaving La Grange, Tenn., 242; appointed captain, 242

Forest Station, Miss., 124, 126, 136, 144, 156

Forrest, Gen. Nathan Bedford, 9, 38, 48, 164, 236, 241

Fort Donelson, 46

Fort Sumter, 46

Fourth Wisconsin Mounted Infantry, 234

Fowler, Uriah, 74, 196, 197, 198

Frank Leslie's Illustrated Newspaper, 224

Fulton, Miss., 46

Gallatin, Miss., 158, 160

Gallatin County, Ill., 125

"Galvanized Confederate," definition of, 35n

Gardner, Gen. Franklin, 114, 156, 163, 177, 188, 192, 204, 205, 206, 207, 210, 234, 235, 236

Garland, Maj. W. H., 204

Garlandville, Miss., 114-15, 121, 126, 128, 132, 138

Garlandville Avengers, the, 132

Garman's Mills, Miss., 50

Gaston, Lt. James, 195

Gholson, Miss., 99

Gholson, Maj.-Gen. Samuel, 34, 35, 99, 103, 118

Gill Plantation, 179, 181, 186

Godfrey, Capt. J. Franklin, 217

Goodwin, Col. Edwin, 131, 150

Gorgas, Josiah, 52

Graham, Maj. John M., 23, 31, 33, 45, 77, 88, 242

Grand Gulf, Miss., 105, 106, 107, 113, 120, 124, 127, 139, 154, 157, 158, 159, 160, 161, 163, 172, 177, 178-79, 180, 185, 232

Grant, Gen. Ulysses S., 8, 37, 38, 51, 58, 105, 159, 161, 172, 175, 177 and passim; views on looting, 41; moving on Vicksburg, 168; attack at Grand Gulf, 181; acknowledges value of raid, 222, 223; asks for Grierson's cavalry, 232-33, 237; overcomes Vicksburg, 234

Graupner, Herr, 26

Greensburg, La., 204, 207, 220

Grenada, Miss., 60, 91

Grierson, Col. Benjamin H., extent of command, 6; background and early years, 23-25; military record, 25; at Sloan Plantation, 32-33; conversation with Mrs. Beach, 40; detaches Hatch for diversionary raid, 62-64; in action at Newton Station, 111-13; decision to make for Baton Rouge, 185; meeting with Union troops in Louisiana, 217; march into Baton Rouge, 218-19; summarizes success of raid, 219; commended by Grant, 223; speech in New Orleans, 231; commands First Cavalry Brigade, 233; appointed brigadier-general, 234; credited with surrender of Port Hudson, 236; ordered to Vicksburg, 237; appointed chief of cavalry, 238; injured, 238; mentioned, passim

Griffin, Cornelius, 202

Hager, Sgt. George, 69

Halleck, Maj.-Gen. Henry W., 25, 58, 159, 179, 219, 222

Ham, Capt. T. W., 47, 48, 68, 69, 90

Hamilton, J. R., 224

Hancock, Sgt. Richard, 50-51

Hard Times Landing, La., 106, 113, 168

Hargraves, Miss., 159

Harlan, Senator James, 11

Harper's Weekly, 224

Hartsville, Tenn., 46

Hartsville (Tenn.) *Plaindealer*, 46

Hatch, Col. Edward, 9, 22, 31, 39, 43, 47, 90, 99, 103, 117, 118, 143, 241; background, military record, 61-62; detached from brigade with Second Iowa Cavalry, 62-65; encounter with Barteau, 66-71; raid on Okolona, 89

Hazlehurst, Miss., 150, 152-55, 156, 157, 158, 163, 167, 171, 176, 182, 184

Hemmenway (cavalryman), 28

Hepworth, George, 230

Herring, Capt. Joseph, 111, 182

Hill, James, 40

Hinson, Lt. Joseph, 212

Hodge, Dr., 140

Hodge Plantation, 133, 140

Holly Springs, battle of, 134

Horses, cavalry, regional characteristics, 10; requisitioning of, 38; return of disabled mounts to La Grange, 55; procurement by Surby's scouts, 86; crossing swamp near Okolona, 89; gift to Grierson, 231; mentioned, passim

Houlka River, 71

Houston, Miss., 53, 56, 57, 59, 60, 72n

Hughes, Pvt. Rees M., 202, 239, 241

Hurlbut, Gen. Stephen A., 8, 9, 52, 58-59, 107, 169-70, 178, 217, 219, 220

Ingate, Capt. F., 60

Inge, Maj. W. M., 47, 48, 68, 90

Island Number Ten, 14, 26

Iuka, Miss., 26, 164

Jackson, Miss., 8, 38, 59, 88, 90, 104, 106, 113, 120, 125, 144, 149, 152, 155, 156, 168, 169, 170, 171, 178, 238

Jackson, Col. James, 156

Jackson (Miss.) *Appeal*, 167

Jacksonville, Ill., 24, 25, 32, 186, 215, 239

Jacobs, Karl, 224

Jasper County, Miss., 115

Johnston, Gen. Joseph E., 34, 48, 92, 103, 127, 143, 168, 169, 170

Jonican, Vernon, 18

Kelly, Lt.-Col., 52

Kelly, Lycurgus, 74, 152, 153, 198

Kilgore, Dr. Benjamin, 57, 62

Kilgore Plantation, 57, 62, 66

King's Bridge (New Albany, Miss.), 33, 39, 43

Kirk, Alice, 24

La Grange, Tenn., 5, 6, 26, 34, 37, 48, 58, 61, 63, 71, 72, 143, 178, 216, 242

Lake Providence, La., 8

Lake Station, Miss., 113, 127, 144

Leaf River, 124, 138

Lee, Gen. Robert E., 234

Leighsburg, battle of, 134

Leseure, Sgt.-Maj. Augustus, 87, 202, 240, 241

Libby Prison, Richmond, Va., 241

Liberty, Miss., 183, 186, 187, 192

Lincoln, Abraham, 7, 24, 49, 106, 220

Lippincott, Lt. Thomas W., 144n

Loomis, Col. Reuben, 21, 62, 210, 241

Looting, 41-42

Loring, Gen. William W., 91, 92, 104, 113, 127, 128

Louisiana Legion, 177, 178, 207, 234

Louisville, Miss., 87, 89, 97

Love, Maj. Hiram, 55, 56, 64, 67

Love, Capt. R. C., 125, 140, 167, 182, 183, 187, 188, 203

Lynch, Capt. John, 88, 97, 98, 210

Mackadore, Dr., 135, 136

Mackadore Plantation, 124, 126, 135, 137, 138

Macon, Miss., 78, 79, 80, 81, 82, 84, 85, 88, 92, 97, 98, 103, 129, 142, 150

Macon (Miss.) *Beacon*, 85

Magee, Warren, 45

Magnolia, Miss., 186, 189, 190, 191, 240

Magnolia Grove, La., 219, 233

Manassas, battle of, 134

Marshall, Capt. Samuel, 210

Martin, Charles, 116

McCausland, Lt. William, 11, 28, 81, 129, 131

McClellan, Gen. George B., 11

McClernand, Gen. John, 106, 180

McKnight, Capt. Moses, 47

Memphis, Tenn., 37, 38, 61, 107, 178, 227, and passim

Memphis & Charleston Railroad, 6

Meredosia, Ill., 24, 25

Meridian, Miss., 9, 85, 91, 92, 104, 106, 113, 127, 128

Miles, Col. W. R., 177, 178, 207, 208

Milliken's Bend, La., 58, 107

Mississippi Central Railroad, 55, 58, 71

Mobile, Ala., 83, 127, 132

Mobile & Ohio Railroad, *see under* Railroads

Molino, Miss., 22, 30, 31

Montpelier, Miss., 71, 72n

Montrose, Miss., 116

Morgan, John Hunt, 10, 73, 149

Morgan County, Ill., 24

Morton, Maj. George, 68

Morton, Miss., 113

Mosby, John, 9

Muscatine, Iowa, 61, 62

Natchez, Miss., 158, 160, 161, 163, 164, 165, 167, 168, 172, 176, 177

Nelson, Cpl. Samuel, 74, 124-26, 135-36, 140, 167, 198, 203, 204, 205, 212-13, 214

New Albany, Miss., 22, 23, 30, 31, 32, 36, 37, 39, 43, 55, 60

New Carthage, La., 106

Newell, Lt. G. W., 191, 202, 204

Newman Plantation, 202, 203, 207, 240

New Orleans, La., 34, 227, 228, 230-32, 234

New Orleans & Jackson Railroad, *see under* Railroads

New Orleans (La.) *Era*, 231

Newton County, Miss., 81

Newton Station, Miss., 98, 99, 101, 102, 105, 107-13, 114, 117, 118, 119, 127, 128, 129, 143n, 155, 156, 161, 167, 178

New York *Times*, 79, 88, 145, 223, 224, 225, 230

Nichols, Elias, 122, 123

Nichols Plantation, 123

Noxubee River, 81, 85, 98

Oakland Plantation, 52, 133

Ohio Wesleyan University, 46

Okolona, Miss., 33, 50, 53, 54, 60, 63, 89, 90, 114, 143n, 144, 178

Orizaba, Miss., 22

Osyka, Miss., 185, 186, 188, 189, 190, 191, 192, 201, 207, 210, 239, 241

Oxford, Miss., 54, 55, 58, 60, 114, 144

Palo Alto, Miss., 67, 69, 89, 91, 143

Panola, Miss., 37, 114

Paris, Ill., 73
Parker, Pvt., 79n
Partisan Rangers, Mississippi, 8, 20, 22, 26, 35, 169, 178
Paulding, Miss., 129
Paulding (Miss.) *Clarion*, 115, 121
Pearl River, 94, 95, 139, 140, 141, 143, 145, 149, 150, 151
Pemberton, Gen. John C., 34-35, 38, 48, 52, 59, 60, 63, 91-92, 103, 105-106, 107, 113, 120, 123, 125, 127, 128, 143, 144, 149, 155-56, 159, 163, 167, 168, 169, 170, 174, 182, 188, 207, 208
Pensacola, Fla., 132
Pettus, Governor John, 34, 35
Philadelphia, Miss., 95, 96, 98, 99, 116-17, 128, 140
Pierce, Sgt. Lyman B., 62, 65, 70, 71n, 89, 103, 143
Pineville, Miss., 121
Piney Woods, 119-25, and passim
Pittsburgh, Pa., 24
Plantations
  Augustus, 84
  Bender, 116, 119
  Daggett, 45
  De Shroon, 179, 180
  Ellis, 20
  Estes, 89, 93
  Falkner, 20
  Gill, 179, 181, 186
  Hodge, 133, 140
  Kilgore, 57, 62, 66
  Makadore, 124, 126, 135, 137, 138
  Newman, 202, 203, 207, 240
  Nichols, 123
  Oakland, 52, 133
  Sloan, 32, 43
  Smith, 106, 107, 139
  Snyder, 162, 163
  Spurlark, 186, 188
  Thompson, 159, 160
  Weatherall, 45
  Williams, 139, 148, 153

Pollard, William, 137
Ponchatoula, La., 188
Ponder, William, 110n
Pontotoc, Miss., 32, 43, 44, 45, 50, 53, 54, 55, 56n, 59, 60, 91, 103
Pontotoc Ridge, 20
Poplar Springs, Miss., 45
Porter, Adm. David D., 7, 8, 105, 106, 178, 179, 180, 181
Port Gibson, Miss., 154, 157, 158, 172, 208, 232, 234
Port Hudson, La., 78, 114, 156, 163, 173, 177, 204, 205, 206, 208, 232, 234, 235
Post, Pvt., 79n
Prentiss, Gen. Benjamin, 25
Prince, Col. Edward, 19, 21, 23, 31, 43, 44, 45, 62, 79, 80, 96-97, 121, 139, 140, 143, 145-46, 149, 150, 152, 154, 155, 200, 202, 203, 227, 234-35, 237, 242
Prisoners of war, parole of, 51, 159, 174-75

Quincy, Ill., 145
Quitman, Miss., 129

Railroads
  Memphis & Charleston, 6
  Mississippi Central, 55, 58, 71
  Mobile & Ohio, 22, 30, 33, 43, 48, 58, 62, 67, 71, 78, 80, 82, 85, 88, 92, 97, 98, 103, 126, 128, 129, 167
  New Orleans & Jackson, 139, 148, 149, 150, 156, 157, 161, 165, 167, 169, 172, 181, 182n, 205, 207
  Vicksburg, 58, 60, 62, 63, 80, 89, 92, 94, 98, 99, 102, 103, 107, 112, 114, 117, 118, 125, 129, 161
Raleigh, Miss., 124, 125, 138, 140
Rappahannock River, 224
Red Chief (steamboat), 235n
Red River, 7
Reynolds, Col. A. E., 156
Rhodes, Capt. Thomas C., 185

Richardson, Col. Robert V., 26, 169-71, 174n, 176-77, 179, 182, 187, 188, 189-90, 207, 208, 220, 240
Richmond, Va., 48, 103, 224
Richmond (Va.) *Examiner*, 69
Ripley, Miss., 20, 21, 22, 23
Robinson, Isaac, 74, 80, 85, 116
Root, Lt. George, 111, 171, 174
Roy, Bugler William, 202, 239
Ruggles, Gen. Daniel, 6, 33, 34, 35, 59, 60, 62, 90, 91, 92, 103, 117, 118

St. Charles Hotel (New Orleans), 230
St. Louis, Mo., 24
Sakatouchee Creek, 57, 90
Salem, Miss., 73
Sandy Creek, 210, 211, 220
Scales, Cordelia, 52, 133
Scott, Capt. E. A., 193, 197
Scott, Gen. Winfield, 10-11
Second Alabama Cavalry, 59, 69, 90, 103
Second Iowa Cavalry, 6, 26, and passim
Second Massachusetts Cavalry, 234
Second Tennessee Cavalry, 33, 46, 47, 50, 59, 66, 67-71, 90, 118, 156
Selma, Miss., 9
Seventh Illinois Cavalry, 6, 26, and passim
Seventh Tennessee Cavalry, 46, 47
Shawneetown, Ill., 25, 184
Sherman, Gen. William T., 8n, 25, 51, 106-107, 223, 237, 238
Shiloh, Miss., 33, 46, 184
Simonton, Col. John M., 188
Sixth Illinois Cavalry, 6, 26, and passim
Sloan Plantation, 32, 43
Smith, Col. J. F., 30, 31, 35, 47, 48, 90, 118
Smith, Capt. Jason B., 21, 56, 68, 69, 87, 93, 200, 203

Smith, Gen. William Sooy, 7, 9, 37, 38, 55, 56, 72, 178
Smith Plantation, 106, 107, 139
Snyder Plantation, 162, 163
Sparta, Miss., 9
Springfield, Ill., 11, 24
Spurlark Plantation, 186, 188
Starkville, Miss., 54, 64, 66, 71, 72, 73, 75, 76, 77, 78, 84, 90
Starlight (steamboat), 235n
Starr, First-Maj. Mathew H., 62, 87-88, 111, 144n, 227, 241
State troops, Mississippi, 18, 30, 39, 43, 44, 47, 66, 69, 71, 210
Steadman, George, 74, 100, 101, 124n, 152, 153, 161, 196, 197
Stevenson, Maj.-Gen. Carter L., 156, 163
Streight, Col. Abel, 37, 38, 236
Strong River, 139, 142, 143, 150
Stuart, Jeb, 9
Styles, Lt. William H., 195, 199
Summit, Miss., 182, 183, 184, 185, 186, 187, 188, 189, 190, 207
Surby, Sgt. Richard, 5, 19, 44, 85-87, 97, 116, 122, 124n, 136, 138, 148, 151-55, 158, 161, 165, 172, 173, 175-76, 181, 183, 184, 186, 191, 192, 199, 239-41; named to lead scouts, 64; raiding along Starkville road, 73-75; capture of Pearl River Bridge, 94-95; advance on Newton Station, 99-102; action at Newton Station, 107-110; action at Wall's Bridge, 194-99; wounded, 199; left at Wall's Bridge, 202; visited by Col. Miles; 207
Swift, Capt. John L., 230

Talking Warrior Creek, 76
Tallahatchie Bridge (New Albany, Miss.), 30, 31, 33
Tallahatchie River, 23, 31, 37, 39, 43, 48, 55
Tangipahoa, La., 156
Tennessee River, 37

Thirty-Fifth Alabama Infantry, 128

Thompson Plantation, 159, 160

Thompson's Creek, 234, 235

Tickfaw River, 191, 192, 203

Trafton, Capt. George W., 39, 43, 161, 162, 165, 171, 179, 195

Tupelo, Miss., 58, 103

Tuscumbia, Ala., 37

Twentieth Mississippi Mounted Infantry, 168, 169, 171

Twenty-Seventh Alabama Infantry, 156

Uncle Tom's Cabin, 30

Union army units
　Battery K, First Illinois Artillery, 6, and passim
　First Louisiana Cavalry, 234
　Fourth Wisconsin Mounted Infantry, 234
　Second Iowa Cavalry, 6, 26, and passim
　Second Massachusetts Cavalry, 234
　Seventh Illinois Cavalry, 6, 26, and passim
　Sixth Illinois Cavalry, 6, 26, and passim

Union Church, Miss., 161, 162, 164, 165, 166, 171, 172, 176, 207

Van Dorn, Gen. Earl, 34, 86

Verona, Miss., 33

Vicksburg, Miss., 7-8, 20, 22, 34, 37, 38, 48, 49, 52, 78, 80, 91, 104, 105, 109, 120, 122, 127, 132, 156, 161, 163, 168, 222, and passim

Vicksburg Railroad, *see under* Railroads

Wallihan, John, 24

Wall's Bridge, 191-203, 204, 207

Washington, D. C., 62

Washington (D. C.) *National Tribune,* 110n, 235

Water Valley, Miss., 55

Weapons, cavalry, 14-15, 17

Weatherall, Capt., 33, 35, 43, 44

Weatherall Plantation, 45

Weedon, Charles, 74

Westgate (cavalryman), 28

West Point, Miss., 69, 77, 90

Westville, Miss, 139

Whitefield, Miss., 85, 87

White River, 7

Willbourn, Lt.-Col. C. C., 210

Williams' Bridge, 190, 204, 205, 206, 207, 209, 220

Williams Plantation, 139, 148, 153

Wilt, Lt. Daniel, 56

Winnesheaks, the, 79, 80

Wolf, Miss., 73

Wolf River, 7

Wood, Arthur, 74, 80, 85, 196, 198, 213, 214

Woodville, Miss., 188

Woodward, Lt. Samuel, 62, 115, 174, 215, 227

Wren, Lt. William S., 185, 190, 207

Yockeney River, 55

Youngstown, Ohio, 24

Yule, Surgeon Erastus D., 64, 65, 202, 239, 240, 241

DATE DUE

NO 5 '7?			
GAYLORD			PRINTED IN U.S.A.